EARLY MUSIC SERIES 13

THE BAROQUE CLARINET

EARLY MUSIC SERIES

THE BAROQUE CLARINET

CLARINET

ALBERT R. RICE

CLARENDON PRESS · OXFORD
1992

Oxford University Press, Walton Street, Oxford OX2 6DP
Oxford New York Toronto
Delhi Bombay Calcutta Madras Karachi
Petaling Jaya Singapore Hong Kong Tokyo
Nairobi Dar es Salaam Cape Town
Melbourne Auckland
and associated companies in
Berlin Ibadan

Oxford is a trade mark of Oxford University Press

Published in the United States
by Oxford University Press, New York

British Library Cataloguing in Publication Data
Rice, Albert R. (Albert Richard)
The baroque clarinet. – (Early music series, 13).
1. Clarinets & Clarinet music, history
I. Title   II. Series
788.6209
ISBN 0-19-816188-3

Library of Congress Cataloging in Publication Data
Rice, Albert R.
The baroque clarinet/Albert R. Rice.
—(Early music series; 13)
Includes bibliographical references and index.
1. Clarinet—History.   2. Music—18th century—History and
criticism.   I. Title.   II. Series: Early music series (London,
England: 1976); 13.
ML945.R5   1991
788.6'2'09032—dc20
ISBN 0-19-816188-3

Typeset by Rowland Phototypesetting Ltd
Bury St Edmunds, Suffolk
Printed in Great Britain by
St Edmundsbury Press Ltd, Bury St Edmunds, Suffolk

DEDICATION

This book is dedicated to my wife, Eleanor, whose insight and embracing intellect never fail to impress me. It is also dedicated to my dear friend and teacher, Rosario Mazzeo, whose unbounded musical knowledge and tremendous enthusiasm for the history of the clarinet have been a constant inspiration. His thoughtful and perceptive discussions have always stimulated me to further investigations.

PREFACE

The clarinet has been a subject of discussion in journal articles ever since a lively description of its possibilities appeared in the *Musikalische Korrespondenz der Teutschen Filarmonischen Gesellschaft für das Jahr 1791* ('Berichtigungen' 1791). In 1887 Riccardo Gandolfi published for students at the Royal Musical Institute of Florence what was the earliest book devoted entirely to the clarinet. This thirteen-page account contained a short history of the clarinet family and mentioned some well-known compositions and performers. The first scholarly investigation, by Wilhelm Altenburg, appeared in 1904. Many statements from his book, which were later shown to be erroneous, continue to reappear in some of the most recent studies. Altenburg also wrote several specialized articles concerning the clarinet in the *Zeitschrift für Instrumentenbau* which are still valuable in their content.

Two general books on wind instruments appeared in 1939, by Adam Carse, and in 1957, by Anthony Baines (3rd edn., 1967). They both deal separately with mechanical and practical aspects of playing the modern woodwinds and provide brief historical sections. The most important books after these two general studies are the two posthumously published books by Oskar Kroll (1965, rev. Eng. edn., 1968) and by F. Geoffrey Rendall (1954, 3rd edn., 1971). The former deals mainly with the historical and musical development of the clarinet, while the latter is divided equally between practical and historical considerations. A highly scholarly three-part article on the clarinet by Wilhelm Stauder, Hans Hickmann, and Heinz Becker appeared in 1958 in the German encyclopaedia *Die Musik in Geschichte und Gegenwart* (*MGG* 'Klarinette'). It includes sections on acoustics, ethnic and ancient clarinet instruments, and the European clarinet. Much of the information presented in this encyclopaedia corrected earlier errors and misconceptions. Another important study, by Ekkehart Nickel, appeared in 1971 on the subject of woodwind instrument-building in the city of Nuremberg. This author relied on archival documents and examined some of the earliest extant clarinets by eighteenth-century makers from Nuremberg.

Some of the most useful studies are dissertations which appeared during the 1960s and 1970s. They are concerned with the solo clarinet music of the eighteenth century (Titus 1962); instructional material (Rousseau 1962); and chamber music of the eighteenth century (Rau 1977). Valuable books concerning clarinet virtuosi and orchestral players have been written by Pamela Weston (1971, 1977). Two studies concerning the chalumeau and its music, by Heinz Becker (1970) and Colin Lawson (1981a), have also added to our knowledge of

the early clarinet. Recent studies by Phillip T. Young (1980, and 1982b) and
Nicholas Shackleton (in his articles 'Bass clarinet', 'Basset horn', and 'Clarinet'
for the *New Grove Dictionary of Musical Instruments*, 1984) include valuable data on
many eighteenth-century clarinets. The most useful and detailed study concerning the construction of baroque clarinets is David Ross' recent DMA thesis, 'A
Comprehensive Performance Project in Clarinet Literature with an Organological Study of the Development of the Clarinet in the Eighteenth Century' (1985).

Most of these previous studies lack detailed treatment of such areas as
construction, playing techniques, music, and use of the early clarinet by pro-
fessionals and amateurs. Also, many do not quote the original text of sources,
which are often important to the understanding of these areas. Their common use
of a few secondary sources has tended to perpetuate previous errors and
misconceptions. My approach in this book is mainly historical; Chapter 1 provides
a general view of the precursors of the clarinet in the single-reed instruments of
antiquity, the Middle Ages, and up to the end of the eighteenth century. The
following four chapters discuss the baroque clarinet: its design and construction,
playing techniques, the music written for it, and its use by both amateur and
professional players. I also investigate aspects of performance practice at various
points in the instrument's development which have received little or no attention.
The Appendix provides a check-list and short descriptions of several extant
baroque clarinets. Acoustics and non-European clarinets are not discussed.
Much of the theoretical, musical, and iconographical evidence presented here has
never appeared in any previous study, to my knowledge.

One of the most rewarding aspects of the research for this book included the
citation and discussion of newly discovered information from early dictionaries,
tutors, treatises, and encyclopaedias. These findings draw together a large amount
of data to trace the development of the baroque clarinet, its playing techniques,
music, and significant performers. I hope that the book will kindle more interest in
the eighteenth-century clarinet as an instrument worthy of study and use in
performance of the music from that century.

When I refer to a clarinet at a specific museum, it is identified with the number
assigned by that museum. A list of abbreviations for the names of museums
referred to in the text is found on pp. xix–xx. This book is a revision of part of my
Ph.D. dissertation, which was completed in 1987 at the Claremont Graduate
School. Sections of Chapter 5 appeared in an article in *Early Music* in 1988.

The following system of musical notation is used throughout:

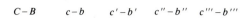

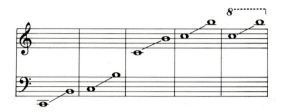

ACKNOWLEDGEMENTS

I would like to thank the many scholars and players who have given me advice and suggestions. Drs David Ross and Nicholas Shackleton have shared a great deal of their knowledge and information concerning the early clarinet. Several excellent players of the early clarinet who offered valuable suggestions and have inspired me by their playing are the following: Hans Rudolph Stalder, Eric Hoeprich, Keith Puddy, Dr Colin Lawson, Alan Hacker, Anthony Pay, Lawrence McDonald, Andrew Lyle, and Nina Stern. Others who have also been very helpful include Rosario Mazzeo, Jeremy Montagu, Dr Kurt Birsak, Dr Frank Traficante, William Waterhouse, Dr Herbert Heyde, Andreas Masel, Michael Nagy, Martin Kirnbauer, Erich Urbanek, Filadelfio Puglisi, Mrs Deutsch of the Musikinstrumenten-Museum, Staatliches Institut für Musikforschung, Berlin, Dr Jürgen Eppelsheim, Dr John Henry Van der Meer, William Maynard, Pamela Weston, Dr Phillip Young, Dr André Larson, Dr Benjamin Vogel, Brian Ackerman, Nora Post, Dr A. Peter Brown, Michael Finkelman, and Janet Page. If I have neglected to mention others who have contributed to this book, I hope that they will forgive the omission of their names. Research assistance was provided by a grant from the National Endowment for the Humanities in 1990.

I am particularly grateful to my wife Eleanor Montague for her expert work in editing and for much stimulating discussion concerning the early clarinet.

CONTENTS

LIST OF ILLUSTRATIONS

LIST OF MUSIC EXAMPLES

ABBREVIATIONS

DICTIONARIES AND ENCYCLOPAEDIAS

ADB	*Allgemeine Deutsche Biographie*
EB	*Encyclopaedia Britannica*[11]
GLE	*Grand Larousse encyclopédique*
GLM	*Das große Lexikon der Musik*
Grove 6	*The New Grove Dictionary of Music and Musicians*
MGG	*Die Musik in Geschichte und Gegenwart*
NGDMI	*The New Grove Dictionary of Musical Instruments*
NNBW	*Nieuw Nederlandsch Biografisch Woordenboek*
NOCM	*The New Oxford Companion to Music*
WBE	*The World Book Encyclopedia*

MUSEUMS

Antwerp, MV: Museum Vleeshuis

Berkeley, UC: University of California, Department of Music

Berlin, SI: Musikinstrumentenmuseum, Staatliches Institut für Musikforschung

Bochum, SM: Städtlisches Musikinstrumentensammlung Grumbt bei der Städtbucherei

Bonn, BH: Beethovenhaus

Brussels, MI: Musée Instrumentale du Conservatoire

Eisenach, BH: Bachhaus

Florence, MSM: Museo degli Strumenti Musicali di Conservatorio 'L. Cherubini'

The Hague, GM: Gemeentemuseum

Leipzig, KMU: Musikinstrumentenmuseum, Karl-Marx-Universität

Leningrad, ITMC: Institute of Theatre, Music and Cinematography

Linz, OLM: Oberösterreichisches Landesmuseum

London, RCM: Royal College of Music Museum of Instruments

Meiningen, SM: Musikgeschichtliche Abteilung der Staatliche Museen

Munich, SM: Musikinstrumentenmuseum im Stadtmuseum

Nuremberg, GN: Germanisches Nationalmuseum

Oxford, BC: University of Oxford, Bate Collection
Paris, MI: Musée Instrumentale du Conservatoire
Poznan, MN: Museum Nardowe w Poznaniu-Museum Instrumentow
Prague, HO: Hudební Oddělení Národního Muzea
Salzburg, MCA: Museum Carolino Augusteum
Stockholm, MM: Statens musiksamlingar Musikmuseet

I

Origins

THE word 'clarinet' was classified by Hornbostel and Sachs (1914) as a generic term for all pipes, usually made of cane, in which the sound is produced through the vibration of a single reed which is either cut from the pipe itself (idioglot) or produced separately and attached to a mouthpiece (heteroglot) (*NGDMI* 'Reed instruments'; Sachs 1930: 338). This book includes the further stipulation that the clarinet is an instrument which overblows, functionally, at the interval of a twelfth above the fundamental notes (*NGDMI* 'Overblowing').[1] These two characteristics—the production of sound by means of a mouthpiece with a single, vibrating reed and a cylindrically bored body providing the capability of being overblown at the twelfth—are what distinguish the present-day clarinet from all other woodwind instruments. To examine the clarinet's 'prehistory', however, we will use Hornbostel's and Sachs' generic definition. The more specific definition will become useful when we discuss the earliest manifestations of the eighteenth-century clarinet and distinguish these from the closest relative of the clarinet—the chalumeau with a heteroglot reed.

Antiquity

Predecessors of the eighteenth-century clarinet can be traced to instruments from as long ago as the third dynasty of the Old Kingdom in Egypt (2778–2723 BC). Double pipes called 'memet' were depicted on the reliefs of seven tombs at Saqqarra, six tombs at Giza, and the pyramids of Queen Khentkaus (Hickmann 1956: 155, 1961: 158; Manniche 1975: 19–20). The pipes of the memet were attached to each other by pieces of cloth and resin, each pipe having from four to six finger-holes and a separate tube with an idioglot reed (Manniche 1975: 18; Kroll 1968: 12–13).[2] This single reed is the link connecting the ancient memet to the instrument we know as the clarinet. The idioglot reed is an important

---

[1] Overblowing is the process by which the player causes the air column of his instrument to break up into several parts, each of which vibrates at a frequency in direct proportion to the fundamental frequency. On the clarinet it involves increased wind pressure, the adjustment of the pressure and position of the lips on the reed, and the use of a small 'speaker' hole in the body tube to assist the process.

[2] 2 examples of the memet are found in the Egyptian Museum, Cairo and one in the Ägyptische Museum, Berlin; see Manniche 1975: 19.

characteristic of the modern Egyptian double pipe, the arghūl, and may be cut so that the end where the tubes are inserted points either away from the player (downwards) or towards the player (upwards). Fig. 1.1 illustrates these types of idioglot reeds as used in two types of arghūl, the zummāra and mashūra (Kroll 1968:13; Hickmann 1961: 120, Abb. 87; Becker 1966: 77–9). The end of the double pipes (where a tube of cane with its idioglot reed is inserted) is placed entirely within the player's mouth, and the sound is produced by continuous or circular breathing (i.e., one stores air in the cheeks, blowing continuously while inhaling through the nose at the same time) (*NGDMI* 'Arghūl'). Pipes with idioglot reeds have been identified in sources from later civilizations, such as the aulos from Greece (*NGDMI* 'Aulos'; Barker 1984: 14–15, 186–9; Becker 1966: 79–80), the launeddas from Sardinia (*c*.900–500 BC and still in use; Bentzon 1969: i. 28–9, Pl. VIIa), and perhaps the halil from Palestine (fifth or fourth century BC) (*Grove 6* 'Jewish music'; cf. *NGDMI* 'Halil').

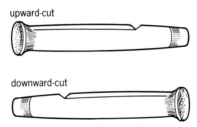

FIG. 1.1. Upward- and downward-cut idioglot reeds used in the mouthpieces of the mashūra and zummāra (Becker 1966: 79)

From the tenth century to the end of the sixteenth century there are some iconographical examples of reed pipes which may have made use of idioglot reeds. Single and double pipes are depicted with what resemble idioglot reeds, as used on present-day folk instruments, in a manuscript of the Bibliothèque Nationale, Paris (Fonds Latin 1118), dating from between the end of the tenth century and the middle of the eleventh century. An instrument with three pipes, similar to the present-day launeddas, is depicted in an illustration from the thirteenth-century *Cantigas de Santa Maria* (see Marcuse 1975: 660 and Seebass 1973: i. 9; ii. Pls. 4, 8, 11, 12, 16).[3] A variety of instruments are recorded in the French literature of the twelfth century by very similar names. These include 'chalumeau', 'chalemeau', 'chaleumeau', 'chaleumiau', 'chalemel', 'canameau', 'cannebaux', 'canimeaus', 'chalemiaus', 'chalemelle', 'chalemele', 'chalemie', 'chalemye', 'chalemise', 'chalemine', 'canamelle', 'kalemele', 'qualemele', and 'schalmaye' (La Curne de Sainte-Palaye 1875–82: i. 335; cf. Brücker 1926: 17–79). (A

---

[3] Seebass (1973: i. 18–19, 20–1, 42–4) identifies the instruments in the Paris MS as shawms.

common root of these words appears to be the Latin word *calamellus*, the diminutive of *calamus* (Brachet 1878: 79), or the Latin *calamum*, from the Greek *kalamon* (Clédat 1931: 123, s.v. 'Chaume') or *kalamos* (*EB* 'Clarinet'), all of which mean 'reed-pipe'.)[4] The instruments so named are interesting for us because they clearly presage the late-seventeenth-century chalumeau, an instrument that shares with the clarinet the fundamental characteristics of a single idioglot or heteroglot vibrating reed and cylindrical bore. There will be more about the chalumeau in the remainder of this chapter.

The Sixteenth Century

Several French dictionaries from the sixteenth century use the same term, 'chalumeau' (or the Latin *calamus*), to identify a variety of instruments. For example, Estienne (1552) described the *calamus* as a 'pype or whistle', and Luke Harrison (1570) defined the chalumeau as 'a reed, a pipe'. According to Sainliens (1593) the chalumeau is 'a reede, a pipe, stemmes of hearbs'. In Italy, an equivalent word for chalumeau was *zampogna*, defined by Florio (1598) as 'an oaten-pipe, a sheapheards-pipe, a bagge-pipe'; in a later edition of his dictionary (1611) he substituted a 'Reede-pipe' for the latter instrument. None of these definitions suggest that these instruments made use of a single reed; references to single-reed instruments begin to appear only in descriptions from the seventeenth and eighteenth centuries.

Nevertheless, three illustrations from the sixteenth century have been interpreted as depicting European single-reed instruments. Two of these are identified as chalumeaux in a valuable article concerning the clarinet by Kathleen Schlesinger, (*EB* 'Clarinet'); the third is described by Herbert Heyde (1970) as an ancestor of the clarinet.

The first is found in Plate 79 of the woodcut impressions made for the *Kaiser Maximilian I. Triumph* (Triumph of Maximilian I), a series compiled in 1518 for the Emperor Maximilian I and published in 1526 (Burgkmair 1964: 9 n. 38; see Fig. 1.2).[5] The plate illustrates ten men on horseback, playing wind instruments which are cylindrical in outward appearance. The leading group of five horsemen play instruments which are shorter than those played by the second group. According to Schlesinger, those of the leading group are chalumeaux; yet these instruments are identified in the anonymous compiler's descriptive text which accompanies the illustrations as double-reed shawms (ancestors of the oboe with a

---

[4] In the French poetic literature of the 12th cent. the shawm and pan-pipes were identified by similar names meaning 'reed-pipe'. See Brücker 1926: 43–7; Larousse 1865–76: iii. 864.

[5] This plate was attributed to the engraver Albrecht Altdorfer on stylistic grounds; see Meder 1932: 223.

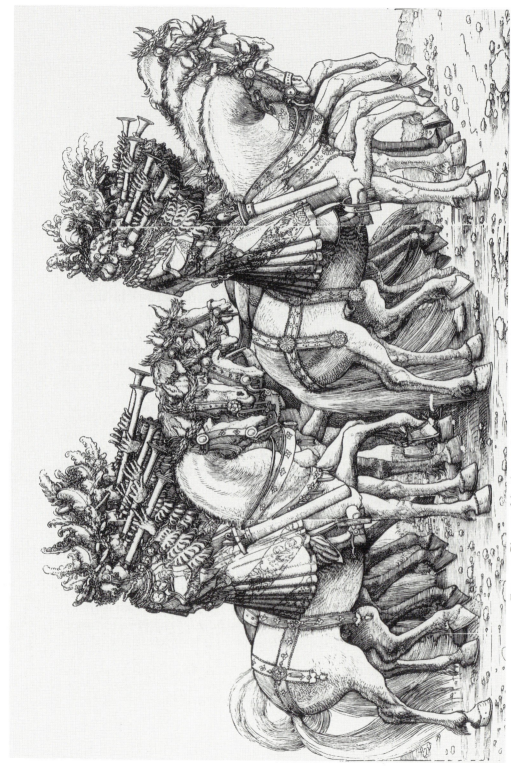

FIG. 1.2. Players of the shawm (left) and *Schreyerpfeife* (right) (Burgkmair, 1964, Pl. 79)

FIG. 1.3. A woman playing an organ (Amman 1589: 111)

FIG. 1.5. A section of a painting on an altar in the Stadtkirche, Bitterfeld, Germany (c.1525; see Fig. 1.4) (Heyde 1970, *Abb. 2*)

FIG. 1.4. A painting on an altar in the Stadtkirche, Bitterfeld, Germany (c.1525) (Heyde 1970, *Abb. 1*)

double reed), those of the second group as *Rauschpfeifen* (wind instruments with a cap covering a double reed).[6] It is not clear why Schlesinger did not take note of this descriptive text or, if she did, why her conclusion is in conflict with it.

Schlesinger's second example, from an engraving entitled 'Musica' in Jost Amman's *Wapen und Stammbuch* of 1589 (p. 111), is described as being similar to a small single-reed instrument exhibited at the Royal Military Exhibition in London during 1890. Amman's plate (Fig. 1.3), however, illustrates clearly that the instrument in question is a recorder (a vertical flute) having a beak-shaped whistle mouthpiece rather than a mouthpiece and reed.

The German organologist Herbert Heyde (1970: 121) has proposed an ancestor for the clarinet in a third pictorial representation from the sixteenth century. He describes and reproduces a painting (*c*.1525) which is found on the southern altar wing of a chapel in the Stadtkirche in Bitterfeld, Germany (Figs. 1.4, 1.5). In this painting, Job is depicted in a leprous state sitting on a dung heap, while a woman (his wife?) is cleansing him by pouring water over his head. Three musicians are taking part in this ceremony by playing instruments which appear to be made of metal, are held vertically, and terminate with a wide trumpet-like bell. Heyde suggests that what is partially inserted in each player's mouth is a single-reed mouthpiece with a metal reed attached to the upper side by a wire or cord. Indeed, there is ample evidence for the use of metal reeds in the Brandenburg inventory of 1582 (cited in Sachs 1910: 207) and in the phagotus (a bellows-blown organ) made by Afranio degli Albonesi (1480–*c*.1565; Heyde 1970: 122).[7] However, Heyde did not concede the possibility that the painting in fact may illustrate the use of a reed cap (covering a double reed) rather than a single-reed mouthpiece (see Baines 1974: 151). Thus, of the three illustrations, the first two clearly do not show single-reed instruments and the remaining one is not clear in this respect.

The Seventeenth and Eighteenth Centuries

Dictionary definitions of the chalumeau from the beginning of the seventeenth century are similar to those of previous dictionaries. For instance, the Englishman Cotgrave (1611) defined 'chalumeau' as 'a small reed, or cane; also, the stemme of

---

[6] A trans. of the Latin text is provided by Boydell (1982: 369–70 n. 364): 'And after these the Burgundian pipers should ride wearing the Burgundian colours with . . . shawms, and Rauschpfeifen, and they all [should] be wearing laurel wreaths'. This identification of the instruments in Fig. 1.2 is accepted by David Munrow (1976: 51), who points out that the pirouette of the shawm and the reed cap of the *Rauschpfeife* are visible in the engraving. Recently, however, the latter instruments have convincingly been identified (by Boydell 1982: 316) as *Schreyerpfeifen* (wind instruments with a reed cap covering a double reed; see *NGDMI* 'Rauschpfeife').

[7] See also Langwill 1975: 7–9; *NGDMI* 'Phagotus'.

an hearbe; also, a wheaten or oaten straw, or a pipe made thereof'. He also provided a definition of 'chalemelle' as 'a little pipe made of reed, or of a wheaten or oaten straw'.[8] Nicot (1606) defined the chalumeau as a 'tuyau de froment' (reed or wheat-stalk), an instrument which may have included an idioglot reed as described in what follows.

In his massive musical treatise *Harmonie Universelle* (1636), Marin Mersenne described several different reed-pipes as chalumeaux (iii. 228–9). In Proposition IX of the fifth book of wind instruments, four different types of chalumeau are illustrated (see Fig. 1.6). The first (viewing from left to right) is a pipe of willow open at both ends; the second is a simple recorder-like instrument without any finger-holes. The fourth is a wind-capped instrument called a 'mirliton' or 'kazoo', whose reed is a thin piece of onionskin wrapped around the inside of the capsule. It was set into vibration by speaking or singing into the only hole (B) near the top of the instrument. The third and fifth instruments have idioglot reeds and are made from wheat-stalk or 'tuyau de blé' (blade of grass). The third is cut in the middle and the fifth on the upper part to form a beating tongue which vibrates when it is taken into the mouth and air is blown across it. The first of these chalumeaux has two finger-holes, one placed at each end; the second has three finger-holes placed at the lower end of the pipe. Mersenne stated that 'one can make ten or twelve different pitches through the means of these three holes' (1957 trans.: 298).[9] These two instruments foreshadow the more sophisticated chalumeau with a heteroglot reed utilized by composers of the eighteenth century.

Mersenne mentions in the first book of wind instruments (Proposition XXVI, iii. 376–80) the various parts and reeds of the 'bagpipe of the country people', the *chalemie* or *cornemuse*. He illustrates two single idioglot reeds (marked L and H in Fig. 1.7) and one double reed (E) next to the tubes in which they were inserted. The first reed (L) is simply a tube of cane with its idioglot reed inserted at the end of the pipe marked N–L, protected by the section L–M and placed inside the bag. The pipe N–L is part of the great bourdon or drone-pipe (the part of the bagpipe which creates a drone), which is made in three pieces (P–O, O–N, and N–L). The second reed (H) is made from straw or wheat and is similar to that on the third and fifth chalumeaux of Proposition IX (Fig. 1.6 above). It is inserted at the end of the small bourdon or drone-pipe (H–K), placed in the bag, and protected by a sheath (D). The double reed (E), made from thin pieces of cane, is fitted to the same double joint as the pipe, called the 'chanter' or 'chalumeau' (E–FG), and protected by the sheath (D). Mersenne also notes that the chalumeau of this type of bagpipe (E–FG) is played in two ways: first, by using it as part of the bagpipe

---

[8] Pulver (1929: 208) interpreted this definition and others similar to it as signifying a primitive shawm.
[9] 1636: iii. 229: 'l'on puisse faire dix ou douze tons differens par le moyen de ces trois trous'.

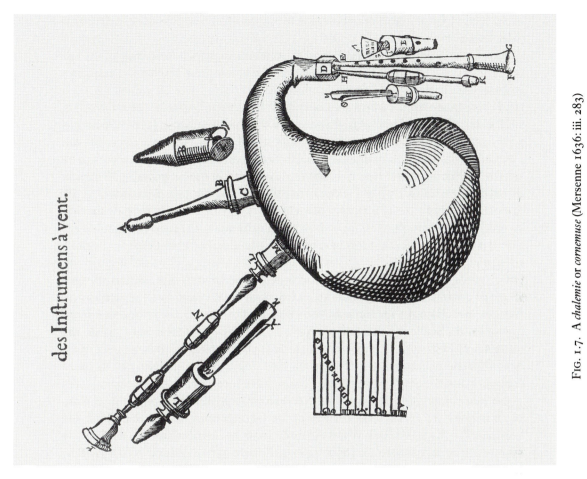

des Instrumens à vent.

Fig. 1.7. A *chalemie* or *cornemuse* (Mersenne 1636: iii. 283)

Fig. 1.6. Chalumeau instruments as shown by Mersenne (1636: iii. 229)

itself; second, by pulling it out of the skin to play as a small double-reed instrument (Mersenne 1636: iii. 376–80).

Another contemporary definition of the chalumeau which describes an instrument practically identical to those of Mersenne is found in Trichet's manuscript treatise 'Traité des instruments de musique' (*c*.1640): 'The chalumeau is (1) a rustic pipe made from a wheat stalk with a cut in its upper surface, half a foot long, such as are still played by children and young shepherds; it is also (2) the chanter of a cornemuse played as a separate instrument' (Marcuse 1975: 719; see Trichet 1957 edn.: 92–4). A contemporary illustration of an instrument that seems to be similar to Trichet's first type of chalumeau is found in the oil-painting 'Réunion de paysans' by Louis Le Nain (1593–1648) (*GLE* 'Classique: art classique': ii. Pl. 3; *WBE* 'Painting': xvi. 45). Here, a peasant boy is playing a small cane pipe that has an unidentifiable number of finger-holes. Unfortunately, the reed cannot be seen; thus it is debatable whether this instrument is a single-reed chalumeau or a simple reed pipe.

In France, the word 'chalumeau' continued to designate a pipe which utilized a single or double reed throughout the seventeenth century and into the eighteenth. For instance, both the chalumeau (sometimes called the 'chanter') and the drone of Borjon de Scellery's musette (a bagpipe; 1672) use a double reed, as do the musettes of Hotteterre (1737) and Garsault (1761: 648–9). Crousaz (1715: 239) describes the chalumeau as a 'tuyau de bled', also do the dictionaries of Duez (1694), Pomai (1709), Boyer (1719), and Furètiere (1727), the *Nouveau Dictionaire du Voyageur* (1732), and the *Dictionnaire Universel* (1734), implying the use of an idioglot reed. A distant relative of the French musette was the pibgorn (a hornpipe) of England and Wales, in use from the fifteenth to the end of the nineteenth century (Balfour 1890: 144–7; Peate 1947: 21–2; cf. *NGDMI* 'Pibgorn'). Two sections of an old double-pipe instrument, which seems to have been made for use with single reeds, is preserved at the Museo Civico in Bologna (Altenburg 1904: 3).[10] Indeed, folk instruments with idioglot or heteroglot single reeds are now in use in Czechoslovakia and several provinces of the USSR (Baines 1966: 112; Vertkov *et al.* 1975).[11] Additional evidence for the use of a single-reed wind instrument in European music before the end of the seventeenth century seems to be lacking. No single-reed instrument, with the exception of the regal organ (a small bellows-blown organ with metal idioglot reeds), is mentioned in the instrumental treatises of Virdung, Agricola, Luscinius, and Praetorius.

---

[10] In a letter to the author Filadelfio Puglisi described these 'objects' (Nos. 1725, 1820) as being covered with black leather, like cornetts. No. 1820 has the mark 'DV' embossed on the surface.

[11] See also the extensive listing of folk clarinets given by Nicholas Shackleton in *NGDMI* 'Clarinet'.

The Mock Trumpet

By the last decade of the seventeenth century a keyless wind instrument called the 'mock trumpet'[12] had become popular in England. It may be considered a type of chalumeau because of its resemblance to the recorder and its probable use of an idioglot reed. A unique extant tutor for this instrument is found in the Euing collection of the University of Glasgow.[13] Its title-page reads:

The Fourth / Compleat Book for the / MOCK TRUMPET / Containing Plain and Easy Directions to Sound yᵉ MOCK TRUMPET / Together with Variety of new TRUMPET TUNES AIRES MARCHES & MINUETS / fitted to that INSTRUMENT, and Very Proper for yᵉ BRAZEN TRUMPET, also / severall FIRST and SECOND TREBLES for two TRUMPETS / the whole Fairly Engraven / price 6ᵈ / Note yᵉ first Second and Third Books may be had where these are Sold / — / London Printed for I. Walsh at yᵉ Harp in Katherine Street, I. Hare at yᵉ Viol & Flute in Cornhill, and / P. Randall at yᵉ Violin and Lute with out Temple Barr in the Strand.

The imprint 'I. Walsh . . . I. Hare . . . and P. Randall' shows that this volume was published between November 1706 and October 1708 (Smith 1948: xxvi). The earliest three datable books for the mock trumpet, all published by John Walsh, appeared between 1698 and 1703. Their titles have been traced through newspaper advertisements:

A Collection of Ayers fitted for the new instrument call'd the Mock Trumpet, & also first and Second Trebles for two Trumpets: Graven price Iˢ (*Post Boy*, 13–15 Sept. 1698).[14]

A Second Book for the new instrument called, the Mock Trumpet; containing variety of Trumpet-tunes, Ayrs, Marches, Minuets, made purposely for that Instrument: with Instruction for Learners. Also several first and second Trebles for two Trumpets. Engraven. Price Iˢ (*Flying Post*, 4 May 1699).[15]

The 3d Book of the Mock Trumpet. Containing variety of new Trumpet Tunes, Airs and Minuets fitted to that Instrument, and very proper for the Brazen Trumpet, as also for Learners on the Violin, Flute or Hoboy, being both easy and pleasant. Likewise 1st and 2d Trebles for Trumpets, with directions for Learners, price Iˢ (*Post Man*, 23–6 Oct. 1703).[16]

The mock trumpet, clearly meant for the dilettante performer, was described as new in the first two books. Evidence of its early popularity in London is found in an advertisement from *The Diverting Post* of 25 November 1704:

---

[12] Not to be confused with the *tromba marina*.

[13] Class-mark B.e. 19. The contents of this tutor and nature of the mock trumpet were first investigated by Dart (1953).

[14] Smith 1948: 6, No. 17.

[15] Smith 1948: 8–9, No. 21. See also Tilmouth 1961: 28.

[16] Smith 1948: 41, No. 137. Walsh's catalogue of *c*.1721 advertises all 4 books; see Smith 1948, Pl. 28.

Wilder's Mock Trumpets, which have been so well approv'd of by the greatest Musick Masters in England, and allow'd to imitate the Real Trumpet almost to perfection, are sold at most Musick-Shops in London. The said Wilder does every Day, from 9 till 11 of the Clock in the morning, teach (several Gentlemen to sound first and second Trebles by Book so exact, that it is difficult to distinguish them from real Trumpets) privately at his own Lodgings at the Golden Horse-shoe in Blew Ball Court, in Salisbury Square, Fleet street, where any Musick-shop in England may be furnished with Mock-Trumpets Wholesale very reasonably.[17]

One or more mock trumpet tutors were a part of the large collection of music and instruments owned by Thomas Britton (1644–1714) and sold at auction on 6–8 December 1714.[18] From 1678, weekly music meetings were held at Britton's home in London, where the mock trumpet may have been played (*Grove 6* 'Britton, Thomas'). On 27 October 1718 the following advertisement appeared in *The St. Ives Post Boy or The Loyal Packet*: 'George Barton . . . Sells the following Things at his Shops in Peterborough, at St. Ives and at St. Neot's every Market Day, viz. . . . Violins, Hoit-boys, Flutes, Mock-Trumpets, Flagelets . . .' (Tilmouth 1961: 103).

By the 1720s the mock trumpet found its way to the New World. Increase Gatchell (d. 1729) owned a 'mock Trumpett' and was active in Boston as a schoolmaster, dancing teacher, music teacher, and music dealer from 1722. This instrument is listed with a 'Fidle' and a 'Harpsicord' in the household inventory of Gatchell's belongings taken on 4 March 1729 (Lambert 1985: 487–90, 987–8).[19] Two mock trumpet tutors were also part of the extensive music collection in The Hague of the collector Nicolas Selhof (1680–1758).[20]

The structural nature of the mock trumpet is uncertain, since it has not been described in any contemporary dictionary (see Dart 1953: 37). This makes the information contained in *The Fourth Compleat Book* especially important. After its title-page (transcribed above) there are a fingering-chart, one page of directions for playing, and a page devoted to the rudiments of music. These are followed by eighteen pages of music, paginated from 1 to 18. The fingering-chart, entitled 'The GAMUT or Scale for the Mock Trumpet', shows a scale of one octave from *g′* to *g″*, with seven tone-holes numbered from 1 to 7 (see Fig. 1.8). The second page

---

[17] Tilmouth 1961: 57.

[18] A printed catalogue of the collection included '[No.] 130. 9 books of instruction for the Psalmody, Flute and Mock-trumpet'; quoted in Hawkins 1853 edn.: ii. 792–3.

[19] The inventory (Suffolk County Probate Records, XXVII, 277–8) is reproduced (but dated incorrectly) in Lambert 1985, Fig. 263, p. 488. Lambert (p. 490) incorrectly identifies Gatchell's mock trumpet as a soprano chalumeau by Stuehnwal.

[20] 'No. 2801—The Compleat Book for the Mock Trumpet, for one or two Trumpets, no. 2802—idem, ut supra, the fourth Book' (Selhof 1973 edn.: 240).

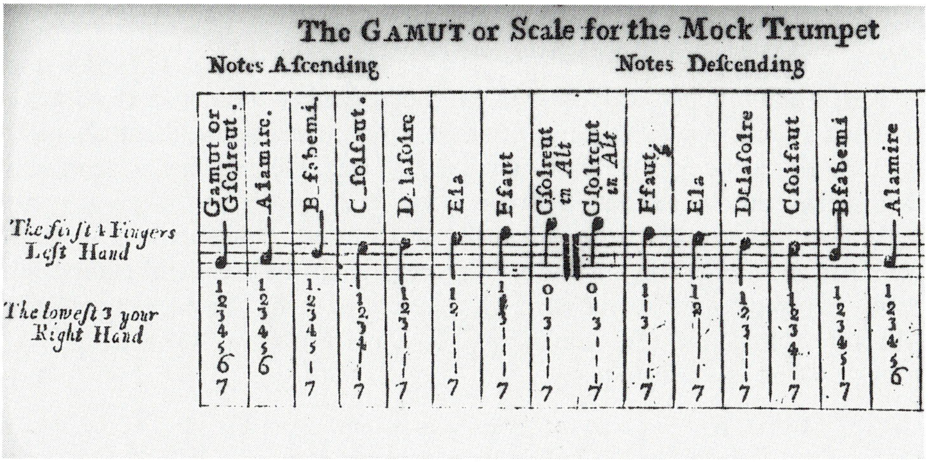

FIG. 1.8. A fingering-chart for the mock trumpet (*Fourth Compleat Book c.*1706–8: [iii])

of the tutor is worth quoting here at length since it provides important directions for playing:

Directions for the Mock-Trumpet, The Gamut must be learned backwards, and forwards, by heart, then you must observe how to hold your Trumpet, which is thus, your Left hand being uppermost, place the middle finger of your left hand, on yᵉ 3ᵈ Hole, and the fourth Finger of your Right Hand, on the lowest Hole, with you Right Hand Thumb beneath to Support, yᵉ trumpet, then the rest of your Fingers, will stop the other holes in Course. The Figures under the Gamut, Directs you how to place your Fingers upon the Holes, then put the Trumpet in your Mouth, as far as the Gilded Leather, and blow pretty strong, which will produce the Notes, in the Gamut whose Names, are set over them, which teaches the Names of the Lines and Spaces. Your Left Hand Thumb is called, your first Finger, which stops the Hole, underneath your fore Finger, the 2ᵈ your middle Finger, the 3ᵈ your next, the fourth The fore Finger, of your Right Hand, the 5ᵗʰ the middle Finger, the 6ᵗʰ your Fourth Finger, the 7ᵗʰ which stops the lowest Hole. The Marks and Rules for Graces are these viz. A close shake thus = an open Shake Beat or Sweeting thus + To Grace Gsolreut in Alt, you must put down the middle Finger, of your Left Hand, and the middle Finger of your Right Hand, upon their proper Holes, then close beat, the fore Finger of your Right Hand, and it produces a tingling Gsolreut in Alt. To make a ratling between 2 Notes, first put down the Thumb and fore Finger of your Left hand, and beat strong with your middle and 4ᵗʰ Fingers, of the same Hand, remaining on. A close Shake must be play'd from yᵉ Note above, Example, If you would Shake Ffaut in Alt, first sound Gsolreut in Alt, then Shake your thumb in the same breath, on its proper Hole, concluding with it on. An open Shake or Sweetning is by Shaking your Finger over the half Hole, next below the Note to be sweetned ending with it off. Thus you must sweeten Delasol sound your Delasol, Shaking the third Finger of your Left Hand, over the half Hole, next below, keeping your finger up. In short after a close Shake keep your Finger down, After an open Shake keep your Finger up.[21]

The mock trumpet was covered in gilded leather and otherwise closely resembled a recorder with the first finger-hole positioned for the thumb, beneath the hole for the index finger of the left hand. Indeed, the fingering is identical to that used for the alto recorder (Lawson 1981a: 31).

An instrument owned by the Flemish collector C. C. Snoeck which seems to have matched the description above was preserved into the twentieth century, only to be destroyed during World War II. It is described in the catalogue of the Royal Military Exhibition of 1890 edited by C. R. Day (1891: 110, No. 221, Pl. IVA), who identified it as a chalumeau:

CHALUMEAU, in g′, French pitch. This instrument consists of a tube of cane open at the lower end, the upper being closed by the natural joint of the cane. The tube is covered with red leather; and the reed consists of a small tongue detached from the cane itself, and shaved down to the required thickness. It is worthy of note that in this instrument the reed is placed upon the upper side, unlike the arrangement in the clarinets of the present day, and, therefore, the lips could have exercised but little control over the vibrations of the tongue. There are six finger-holes upon the upper side, with a seventh or thumb-hole below. The bell note is g′. The tone of the chalumeau is not unlike that of its successor the modern clarinet. Length 8¼ inches, diameter 6/10 inch.

In a catalogue of 1894, Snoeck described this instrument as a 'chalumeau à anche battante' (chalumeau with a beating reed), 21 cm. in length, but did not add new details to Day's earlier description (p. 174, No. 916). Eight years later, most of his collection was bought for the Staatliche Hochschule für Musik in Berlin, in whose catalogue this instrument is described as an 'Idioglot Klarinette' (Sachs 1922: pp. iii, 344, No. 2916). It appears that this instrument may be identified with the mock trumpet on the basis of its length and leather covering (cf. Lawson 1981a: 32).[22]

The early arrival of the chalumeau in the Netherlands is shown by the publication of two volumes of duets by J. P. Dreux during 1703–4 (Lesure 1969: 66). Originally published by Estienne Roger in Amsterdam, the extant volumes in the Herzog-August Library in Wolfenbüttel were pirated by Pierre Mortier about 1709 (*Grove 6* 'Roger, Estienne'). Their titles read: 'FANFARES / Pour les Chalumeaux & Trompettes / Propres aussi à joüer sur les Flûtes, Violins & Haubois / Composèes Par / JAQUES PHILIPPE DREUX / Livre Premier [Second] / A AMSTERDAM / Chez PIERRE MORTIER sur le Vygendam / qui vend les Livres Nouveaux en Musique'.

---

[21] This page is reproduced in Rice 1974: 12.

[22] A private letter confirming the loss of this instrument was received in June 1983 from Dr Dieter Krickeberg, formerly of the Staatliches Institut für Musikforschung, Berlin.

In his catalogue of 1706 Roger listed these *Fanfares* and offered chalumeaux for sale at three florins apiece.[23] The music is confined to the notes *g'*, and *c'* to *g''* and would therefore be playable on a keyless chalumeau. Like the contents of *The Fourth Compleat Book for the Mock Trumpet*, they illustrate further the early association of the chalumeau and trumpet in terms of musical idiom (Lawson 1974: 126–7).

Baines (1967: 296) suggests that a description of a keyless wind instrument in Buonanni's book of 1722 on musical instruments is, in fact, a description of the English mock trumpet. This is one of several which appear in section No. XXIII entitled 'Oboè':

Before ending this narrative, it remains to be pointed out that among the instruments which are played with breath there is one (at best not much employed) which is commonly called *scialumò* [chalumeau]. Usually this is made of cane in the manner of a *zampogna*, as long as the recorder; it has seven holes, that is six above and one below.[24]

Buonanni's *zampogna* was a wheat-stalk chalumeau similar to Mersenne's 'tuyau de blé' (cf. Harrison and Rimmer 1964b, Pl. 27). Gastone Vio (1980: 105–6) has shown from archival documents located at the Pietà in Venice that the German Lodovico Erdtman (Ludwig Erdtmann) was made 'Maestro Professore di Sala-muri' at the beginning of 1706.[25] The instrument in question was also known as the 'salmoni', 'salmo' and 'saltaron', and may have been identical to Buonanni's *scialumò* (cf. Talbot 1980: 158–62).

The 'Chalimo' or 'Chalimou'

In his catalogue of the wind instruments at the Bachhaus in Eisenach, Heyde (1976: 193, No. LI) quotes part of an invoice list of instruments dated 1687, show-ing 'Ein Chor Chalimo von 4. stücken' purchased from Nuremberg for the Duke of Römhild-Sachsen.[26] Heyde implied that these instruments were built by the

[23] *Catalogue de Musique*, appended to Felibien 1706.

[24] p. 68: 'Prima di terminare questa narrativa, non è da lasciarsi l'accennare, che trà gl'Istromenti, li quali si suonano col fiato uno ve n'è, (se bene non molto adoperato) il quali volgarmente se chiama Scialumò, suole esser questo fatto di canna a modo di Zampogna, e lungo come il Flauto, e hà buchi sette, cioè sei di sopra, ed uno di sotto.' (This and all other trans. not otherwise attributed are the author's.) Some of Buonanni's definitions are slightly changed in an Italian–French edn. by G. Ceruti (Buonanni 1776: 82–3). A similar definition is given in Gianelli 1801: i. 92. Lichtenthal (1826: i. 103) describes a *Bombardo Soprano* or *scialumò* with 1 key and a range from *f'* to *a''*, and another with 2 keys and a range from *f'* to *c'''*.

[25] According to the account book of the Pietà, 7 ducats and 16 grossi were paid to Ortoman (Erdtmann) on 17 March 1706 'per doi salamoni per choro', while on 30 July he received 40 ducats 'per saldo d'instrumenti salmo per coro'. See Talbot 1980: 159.

[26] Römhilder Kammerrechnungen, now in the Staatsarchiv, Meiningen, according to a private letter from Dr Heyde.

Nuremberg maker Johann Christoph Denner (1655–1707), whose stamp appears
on a 'Basset-Blockflöte' in the Bachhaus collection. During the eighteenth
century, 'chalimou' instruments were ordered from Denner's son Jacob (1681–
1735), and are recorded in archival documents from Nuremberg (1710) and
Göttweig (*c.*1720), discussed below. The origin of this instrument is suggested by
its French name, 'chalumeau' (as well as the cognates in English, 'shalamo';
Italian, *scialumò*; and German, *Schalamaux*), found in several books and musical
sources. Furthermore, during the late seventeenth century, French makers such
as the Hotteterre family, became widely celebrated for their superior craftsmanship in making recorders, flutes, oboes, and bassoons (Baines 1967: 276). In
1696 J. C. Denner and the woodwind-maker Johann Schell petitioned the
Nuremberg city council to be recognized as master craftsmen and to be granted
permission to make for sale the '. . . French musical instruments . . . which were
invented about twelve years ago [i.e., in 1684] in France'.[27] Only the recorder and
oboe are mentioned in this document, but the single-reed chalumeau was
probably one of the new instruments.[28] Their petition was granted in apparent
recogniton of these.[29]

It should be kept in mind that from the late seventeenth century the German
nobility slavishly copied their French contemporaries, adopting their language,
clothes, food, furniture, dances, and music (Fauchier-Magnan 1980: 26–9). The
use of the chalumeau and several other instruments originating in France[30]
reflects this tendency. The earliest evidence of the use of the chalumeau in
Germany is found in an anonymous collection inscribed 'Hannover 1690' and
entitled 'XIIe Concert Charivari ou nopce de village a 4 Violin, 2 Chalumeaux 3
Pollissons et un Tambour les Viollons en Vielle'.[31] Mattheson, in his biographical
sketch of G. P. Telemann (1740: 357), stated that during his stay at Hildesheim,
the composer became acquainted 'mit dem Hoboe, der Traverse, dem Schalümo,
der Gambe' as well as other instruments. This comment refers to Telemann's stay

---

[27] '. . . französischen Musicalischen Instrumenta . . . die ohngefahr vor 12 Jahren in Franckreich erfunden
worden . . .' Staatsarchiv, Nuremberg, Stadtrechnungsbeleg in Repertorium E 5 I, Drechsler 53, Produkt 26;
quoted in Nickel 1971: 203–5.

[28] Nora Post brought to my attention a Gobelin tapestry, *Argus et Mercure* (*c.*1718, Louvre, Paris), depicting an
instrument which appears to be a chalumeau or a baroque clarinet. See Fenaille 1904: iii. 122–3, 127, 129, and
Rice 1988a, Fig. 1. A keyless chalumeau was described as late as 1753 by Diderot and d'Alembert (1751–65: iii.
40).

[29] Several extant recorders by J. C. Denner and Schell were made at 'French pitch', between $a' = 392$ and
about $a' = 415$; see Haynes 1985: 100. Cf. *NGDMI* 'Denner'.

[30] Other French names used for instruments in the Staatsarchiv, Nuremberg, Stadtrechnungsbeleg in
Repertorium 54 a II, No. 1282, include *Haútbois*, *Flaúten*, and *Taillie*.

[31] In '12 Grands Concerts en Partition', Darmstadt, Hessische Landes- und Hochschulbibliothek, 1226/12
(see Koch 1980: 223). The beginning of this work is transcribed by Koch (p. 92), who believes that the
chalumeaux mentioned were 'Deutschen Schalmey' (p. 91).

at Hildesheim (some time between 1697 and 1701), where he established contact with French musicians of the court of Brunswick. Reinhard Keiser's subsequent use of the chalumeau in Hamburg may also indicate his exposure to it when he was the Kapellmeister at Brunswick before 1695 (Becker 1969: 69). In Dresden, the 'Privat-Chatoulle' of August the Strong probably made use of the chalumeau. An invoice dated 1709 from the Dresden musician Johann Christian Müller mentions bassoon and oboe reeds and '4 cadalichen Röhr', which Heyde believes were reeds for the chalumeau or shawm.[32] Heyde's suggestion is corroborated by Cotgrave's definition (1611) of the word 'Cadaliec' as a bedstead, clearly alluding to the flat shape of the chalumeau reed (see La Curne de Saint-Palaye 1875-82: i. 174). Numerous musical sources also indicate that the greatest use of the chalumeau during the eighteenth century occurred in German and Austrian centres such as Frankfurt, Dresden, Darmstadt, and Vienna (Becker 1969: 357).[33]

In 1730 a biography of Johann Christoph Denner (1655–1707) appeared in J. G. Doppelmayr's *Historische Nachricht von den Nürnbergischen Mathematicis und Künstlern*, crediting this maker with the improvement of the chalumeau as well as the invention of the clarinet. In 1678 Denner, the son of Heinrich Denner, a Nuremberg turner of game whistles and hunting-horns ('Wildruff- und Horn-Dreher'), had established a well-known business by building many fine woodwind instruments, including recorders, pommers, oboes, dulcians, bassoons, racketts, and chalumeaux. He trained two sons, Jacob (1681–1735) and Johann David (1691–1764), in the art of instrument-building; but while some of Jacob's instruments have survived, there are no known examples of the work of Johann David. Today, at least sixty-eight instruments by J. C. Denner and forty by Jacob are extant in museums and private collections (Young 1982a: 84–5, 1982b: 20–6).[34]

A significant passage concerning the chalumeau and clarinet in Doppelmayr's biographical account of J. C. Denner is cited here:

Finally his artistic passion compelled him to seek ways of improving his invention of the aforesaid instruments [recorders], and this praiseworthy intention had the desired effect. At the beginning of the current century, he invented a new kind of pipe-work, the so-called clarinet, to the great delight of all music-lovers, discovered again from ancient times the

---

[32] Staatsarchiv Dresden, Rechnungen der Privat-Chatoulle Augusts des Starken, 1709, fo. 70, quoted in Heyde 1987a: 62–3.

[33] For a list of works composed *c.*1703–72 see Becker 1970: 40–6, Lawson 1981a: 172–82, and Selfridge-Field 1987: 138.

[34] Three instruments were recently acquired by Nuremberg, GN: a rackett by J. C. Denner, a bassoon by Jacob Denner, and an ivory flute by Jacob Denner. See Rice 1988b.

already well-known stick or rackett bassoon, and at length presented an improved chalumeau.[35]

This is the earliest written evidence crediting Denner with the 'invention' of the clarinet. It is the original source for virtually every eighteenth-century account which mentions the clarinet's inventor as Denner or a 'Nürnberger'; but in the light of recent research this source should not be accepted without careful scrutiny. Nickel observed that this text appeared almost twenty-five years after Denner's death and includes inaccuracies such as Denner's age at the time he left Leipzig to live in Nuremberg. Doppelmayr also tends to exaggerate the achievements of other Nuremberg craftsmen, such as Sigmund Schnitzer and Georg Grün (Nickel 1971: 214). Furthermore, he does not examine the contributions of other contemporary makers to the development of the chalumeau and clarinet, nor does he explain the exact nature of Denner's improvements to the chalumeau. However, the 'chalimo' purchased from Nuremberg for the Duke of Römhild-Sachsen in 1687 raises the possibility that Denner was making these instruments at that early date. In a book of 1698, Christoph Weigel mentioned numerous instruments made in Nuremberg by 'Zwey berühmte Meister' (two well-known masters—Denner and Schell?), but cited neither the chalumeau nor the clarinet (pp. 237–8; cf. *NGDMI* 'Denner'). Until further evidence is uncovered, a reasonable working hypothesis would seem to be that Denner became associated with the clarinet some time after 1698. Several eighteenth-century descriptions of the chalumeau provide us with a clearer idea of the structural nature of this instrument in different locations and at different times.

In addition to the type of *scialumò* described under the heading 'Oboè', Buonanni described a second type called the *calandrone*:

Another type of *scialumò*, according to performers, is the *calandrone*, which has holes like the recorders. Near the beginning of the mouthpiece are two keys that cover two diametrically opposite holes. The lips are pressed as in the *zampogna*, and it renders a raucous sound that is not pleasant. It is played in the same manner as the recorder.[36]

The only apparent difference between Buonanni's *calandrone* and his *scialumò* is

---

[35] 1730: 305: 'Zuletzt triebe ihn sein Kunst-Blieben annoch dahin an, wie er noch ein mehrers durch seine Erfindung und Verbesserung bey bemeldten Instrumenten dargeban mögte / dieses gute Vorhaben erreichte auch würcklich einen erwünschten Effect, indeme er zu Anfang diese lauffenden Seculi, eine neue Arth von Pfeiffen-wercken, die so genannte *Clarinette*, zu der *Music*-Liebenden grosen Vergnügen, ausfande, ferner wiederum die vor alten Zeiten schon bekandte Stock-Fagotte, endlich auch die Chalumeaux verbesserter darstellte.' Cf. the Eng. trans. in Kroll 1968: 13–14.

[36] 1722: 68: 'Un altra specie di Scialumò dicesi dalli Suonatori Calandrone, il quale hà li buchi, come li Flauti, e nel principio dell' imboccatura hà due molle, le quali premute, danno il fiato per due buchi opposti in diametro, dove si pone la bocca e inferita un Zampogna, rende questo un suono rauco, e poco grato, e si suona colle medesime regole delli Flauti.' Similar definitions are found in Gianelli 1801: i. 70 and Lichtenthal 1826: i. 110.

that it has two diametrically opposite keys near the mouthpiece. A more comprehensive definition of the word 'chalumeau' is found in J. G. Walther's *Musikalisches Lexicon* of 1732. Of the four types that he described, the last two instruments are the most important in this discussion:

Chalumeau, plural, Chalumeaux (French) *Fistula pastoritia* [Latin]. A shawm, shepherd's pipe made from some parts of cane called *calamus*. Besides this meaning, it is also found as the chanter in a bagpipe. Furthermore, it is a small woodwind instrument that has seven holes and a range from f′ to a″. Also the name for a little wind instrument made from boxwood that has seven holes, two brass keys up near the mouthpiece, and an additional *à partes* hole near the bottom. It has a range of from f′ to a″ and bb″, possibly also to b″ and c‴.[37]

Not surprisingly, the first two definitions correspond to Trichet's definition of a century earlier as well as to Mersenne's descriptions (1636, 1648; see Gutmann 1982: 45–59). The third instrument is identical to the mock trumpet and Buonanni's *scialumò*, with the additional a″ of its range presumably played in the overblown register. This higher register may have been achieved by fingering the lowest note, increasing the wind pressure, and tightening the lips on the reed, thus forcing the air column into a higher frequency (cf. *NGDMI* 'Overblowing'). Walther's fourth chalumeau with two keys corresponds to Buonanni's *calandrone* except for its *à partes*, or double hole, as the lowest finger-hole; this was provided to aid in the playing of the two lowest semitones of the range.

Walther's entire definition was repeated practically verbatim in Majer's instrumental treatise, *Museum Musicum* (1732: 32), between descriptions of the recorder and the transverse flute.[38] Heinz Becker (1970: 27–8) has pointed out that eighteenth-century writers such as Majer classified wind instruments on the basis of the number of finger-holes instead of the nature of the vibrating bodies as in present-day systems (cf. *NGDMI* 'Aerophone'). In addition to this description, Majer provided a section devoted to members of the chalumeau family:

It is usual to have soprano, alto or quart, and even tenor and bass chalumeaux, at either French or German pitch, and because of their difficult embouchure they are very hard to blow. The fingerings of these correspond most closely with the recorder, but their range does not extend much beyond an octave. For that reason, it is deemed unnecessary to

---

[37] p. 153: 'Chalumeau, pl Chalumeaux (*gall.*) *Fistula pastoritia* [*lat.*] eine Schallmey, Schäfer-Peiffe; weil sie mehrentheils aus Rohr [so *calamus* heisset] gemacht ist. Nebst dieser Bedeutung wird auch die an einem Dudel-Sacke befindliche Pfeiffe; ferner ein kleines Blaß-Instrument, so sieben Löcher hat, und von ein gestrichene f biß ins zwey gestrichene a gehet, also genennet. Ferner ein kleines aus Buchsbaum verfertigtes Blas-Instrument, so sieben Löcher oben beym Ansatze, zwo meszingene Klappen, auch bey der untern noch ein *à partes* Loch hat, und vom ein gestrichene *f* biss ins zwey gestrichene a und zwey gestrichene b, auch wohl biß ins zwey gestrichene h und drey gestrichene c gehet.' Words rather than symbols are used to indicate the position of the notes in this transcription, as in Majer 1732: 32. Cf. the trans. in Owen 1967: 7.

[38] Repeated in Majer 1741: 43–4.

report at further length on this matter, especially since if one can play the recorder, one can also perform easily [on the chalumeau].[39]

Chalumeaux were evidently made in a family to compensate for their small playing range. The 'quart' chalumeau was given this name because parts for it were transposed down a fourth to provide a convenient fingering for the player (see Becker 1970: 31). The instruments described as being at French pitch (*Cammerton*) and German pitch (*Chorton*) were a major second or a minor third apart from each other.[40] Those at *Chorton* may have been used in the few works composed for the chalumeau in sharp keys.[41] It should be noted that the lexicographer E. L. Gerber (1812–14: ii/1.871–2) credited J. C. Denner with the improvement of the chalumeau in both its tone and its tuning. Majer observed that the fingering of the chalumeau was very similar to that of the recorder, but that the embouchure (or position of the lips) required was more difficult to achieve. The modern player will agree that the slotted mouthpiece of the recorder offers less resistance than the reed-and-beak mouthpiece of the chalumeau. Buonanni, Majer, Walther, and Mattheson, however, do not mention the mouthpiece of the chalumeau in their writings.

In addition to Buonanni's rejection of the tone of the *calandrone*, there were previously two other unfavourable comments concerning the sound of the chalumeau. Walther noted in his manuscript 'Praecepta der Musicalischen Composition' (1708) that the 'Chalemau (French) is a short wind instrument which gives a sound similar to when a person sings through his teeth.'[42] Mattheson made a scornful remark about the sound of the chalumeau in his *Neu-Eröffnete Orchestre*: 'The so-called chalumeaux may be allowed to voice their somewhat howling symphony of an evening, perhaps in June or July and from a distance, but never in January at a serenade on the water' (Kroll 1968: 15).[43] His

---

[39] p. 32: 'Man hat sonst *Discant, Alt-* oder *Quart Chalumeaux,* wie auch *Tenor-* und *Bass-Chalumeaux,* theils mit dem Französischen / theils mit Teutschem Ton / und sind absonderlich *ratione* des schwehren Ansatzes / sehr hart zu blasen / die *Application* darauf *correspondi*ret meistens mit denen Flöthen; Allein deren *Ambitus* erstrecket sich nicht viel über eine *Octav.* Wird derhalben vor unnöthig erachet / weitläufiger hievon zu melden / zumalen / wann man eine Flöthen blasen kan / wird man auch hier *præstanda præsti*ren können.' Cf. the trans. in Kroll 1968: 14.

[40] For much 17th- and 18th-cent. documentation regarding these pitches see Mendel 1955: 337–8; Haynes 1985: 55–114, esp. 93–4.

[41] The majority of music written for the chalumeau demonstrates that the lowest pitch of these instruments was either *f, c,* or *F,* as in the recorder family. An instrument pitched at *Chorton* could have its lowest note sounding *d* and be playable in a work written in A major, such as the aria 'Meiner Seelen, Lust und Wonne' in Reinhard Keiser's opera *Croesus* (1730 version). See Lawson 1981a: 18, 36–7, 70–1. Eppelsheim (1983) and Nagy (1987: 98) believe that Lawson (1981a) misinterpreted the notation of several parts for chalumeaux, and suggest that they were to be played an octave lower than notated.

[42] p. 43: 'Chalemau (gall) ist ein kurtz blasend Instrument, giebt einem Klang von sich, als wenn ein Mensch durch die Zähne singet.'

[43] Mattheson 1713: 272: 'Den so genandten Chalumeaux mag vergönnet seyn / dass sie sich mit ihrer *etwas*

complaint may have reflected the mixing of different sizes or tunings of chalumeaux (see *MGG* 'Klarinette. C.'). It seems unlikely that an unpleasant instrument with a loud tone would have been used in combination with the particularly gentle instruments called for in such works as Graupner's Trio for bass chalumeau, viola d'amore, and basso continuo, and Telemann's *Ouverture* for two chalumeaux, two violettas, and basso continuo.

A few documents indicate that Jacob Denner constructed several sizes of both chalumeaux and clarinets. None of his chalumeaux, however, appear to be extant today. The earliest evidence dates from 1708, when Duke Dernath of Schleswig-Holstein, a friend of the composer Keiser, ordered four 'Chalimou-Partien' from Jacob Denner, though it is not clear whether instruments or pieces of music were being requested (Becker 1970: 34 n. 32a).[44] In 1710 a number of instruments were ordered for the Duke of Gronsfeld in Nuremberg from Jacob Denner. These are found in a document in the Nuremberg Staatsarchiv (Stadtrechnungs-beleg Repertorium 54a II, No. 1282) which includes the earliest reference to the 'clarinette', along with the 'chalimou' and other wind and stringed instruments:

4 Haútbois, von búxbaúm, à fl. 5	20 fl. [i.e. florins, or guilders]
1 Taillie	7 fl.
2 Fagott, à fl. 14	28 fl.
4 Flaúten, à fl. 3	12 fl.
1 Alt-Flaúden	5 fl.
2 Bass-Flaúden à fl. 8	16 fl.
4 Chalimoú, à fl. 3	12 fl.
1 Alt Chalimoú	5 fl.
2 Chalimoú-Basson, à fl. 14	28 fl.
2 Clarinettes	15 fl.
Die Kisten, Worrinen diese Instr: gepackt	1 fl.
4 Violinen, à fl. 7	28 fl.
1 Viola	7 fl.
1 Bass	15 fl.
Die Kisten, Worrinen die Violin: gepackt	1 fl.

Suma, 200
unterthäniger
Diener
Jacob Denner[45]

heulende Symphonie des Abends ctwann im Junio oder Julio, niemahls aber in Januario auff dem Wasser zum Ständchen / und zwar von weitem hören lassen.'

[44] The letter is in 'J. G. Dernaths Archiv, Reichsarchiv Kopenhagen', according to Hirschfeld 1959: 122 and n. *Pace* Hirschfeld, it is not cited by Krogh (1929).

[45] Nickel 1971: 251–2. A photocopy of this document, received from Martin Kirnbauer of Nuremberg, GN, shows a few minor differences in orthography from that given by Nickel.

Two documents written about 1720 at Göttweig, a Benedictine abbey about forty miles west of Vienna on the Danube, show that Jacob Denner's craftsmanship was admired in distant localities (Fitzpatrick 1968). The first (quoted in Fitzpatrick 1968: 83) is Denner's estimate of the cost of building three 'choirs' of woodwind instruments, including three sizes of oboes, chalumeaux, recorders, and two transverse flutes:

I Chor Hautbois mit 6 Stim̃en alle von buxbaum	
3 Primieur Hautbois à 5 fl	15 fl.
1 Taille	9 fl.
2 Basson, à 22	44 fl.
I Chor Chalimou mit 6 Stim̃en	
3 Primieur Chalimou, à 3 fl	9 fl.
1 Second Chalimou	7 fl.
2 Basson, à 18	36 fl.
I Chor Flauden mit 6 Stim̃en	
3 Primieur Flauden, à 3 fl	9 fl.
1 Second Flauden	6 fl.
2 Basson, à 15 fl	30 fl.
Zu diesen noch 2 Flaud d'Almanq	45 fl.

It is useful to compare this estimate with Denner's bill for the completed instruments (Fitzpatrick 1968, Pl. V(a)):

3 Haútbois	12 fl.
1 Taillie	8 fl.
1 Basson	20 fl.
1 Primieùr Chalimoù	2 fl. 30 X [Kreutzer]
1 Second Chalimoù	5 fl.
2 Basson	30 fl.
3 Primieùr Flaùd	6 fl.
1 Second Flaùd	5 fl.
2 Basson	24 fl.
2 Flaùd d'Almanqùes	12 fl.

This bill shows not only several price-reductions but also a decrease in the number of instruments from twenty to seventeen, with only one 'Primieùr Chalimoù' and one bassoon delivered. Every instrument in the Göttweig document is identical to those in the Nuremberg list with the exception that transverse flutes replaced the clarinets. A comparison of the prices of the three types of chalumeaux with the prices of the remaining instruments suggests that they are Majer's alto, tenor, and bass instruments (see Eppelsheim 1983: 87–90). The

Göttweig estimate for 'I Chor Chalimou mit 6 Stimen' further suggests that the combination made in 1687 for the Duke of Römhild-Sachsen and referred to as 'Ein Chor Chalimo von 4. stücken' was a similar group of instruments.

The woodwind-maker Christian Schlegel of Basle (1667–1746) appears to have made the chalumeau during the first decade of the eighteenth century. In a letter of 1708 he states that he can make a 'quantity of oboes, chalumeaux, flutes and other instruments in complete choirs'.[46] Since none of his chalumeaux are extant it is possible that Schlegel was referring to shawms, of which two signed 'CHRISTIAN S' are extant. However, it is also possible that his father, a maker who has not been traced in Basle's archives, could have made these two shawms (see Küng 1987: 63–5, 67, 74). Between 1714 and 1720 two works for the chalumeau were entered in a manuscript list of music at the court of Schwarzburg-Rudolstadt. They are noted as '1204. Pieces pour la Musique ex F-Dur con Calum.' and '1240. Sonatina à . . . 2 Chalume, ex F-Dur' (see Baselt 1963: 105–6, 127). By the 1730s the musical use of the chalumeau was well known among composers, as was implied by the important theorist Johann Mattheson in *Der vollkommene Capellmeister* (1739). In his characteristic sardonic tone, Mattheson cautioned his reader against the incorrect use of several instruments including the chalumeau: 'If, for example, someone had a viola da gamba contend with trumpets and timpani, had the oboe down to *g*, manipulated the chalumeau as a French horn, or used the flutes far more frequently than the violins, he would give rise to ridicule even if he otherwise played the clavier most beautifully.' (Harriss 1969: iii. 1403).[47]

During this time the sound of the chalumeau had attracted the attention of organ-builders in Germany. An eight-foot cylindrical reed stop called the chalumeau, first encountered in the organ of the Frauenkirche at Dresden, was built between 1732 and 1736 by the celebrated maker Gottfried Silbermann (Dähnert 1973: 122). On 3 January 1737 Sebald Pezold, the organist of Greiz, wrote to Hofrat Fickweiler that Silbermann was so pleased with his 'invention' on this organ that this stop would be included on Silbermann's new organ in Greiz. In fact, the imitation of the chalumeau was so exact that 'nothing more natural could be heard, in which there was no difference to notice, whether Mr Willhelmi, the virtuoso in Dresden on this instrument, was heard or whether it came from the

---

[46] Staatsarchiv Zürich, Proselyten 1701–1729 EL, 9.4, Supplication 1708, quoted by Küng 1987: 64: 'quantitet von Hautboys, Chalumeau, flutes undt dergleichen Instrumente angeförmbt sind, da von jeder gadtung gantze chor . . . machen kan . . .'

[47] Mattheson 1739: 470: 'Wenn izemand z.E. eine Viola da Gamba mit Trompeten und Paucken streiten lassen, oder den Oboe ins g herunter weisen; oder den *Chalumeau* als ein Waldhorn hantieren; oder die Flöten wiet häuffiger, als die violinen brauchen wollte, der würde, wenn er gleich sonst das schönste Clavier spielte, dennoch Gelegenheit zu lachen geben.'

organ' (Hülleman 1937: 20–1).[48] This 'chalumo' stop was described by Marpurg (1757: iii. 499) as a 'pleasant reed stop', and Adlung (1758: i. 78) reported that most of Silbermann's organs included it. Other names for it included 'chalemie' and 'Schallmey' (Adlung 1758: i. 78). Five further examples of this stop in eighteenth-century organs have been recorded: the 'Chalumeau' on the Ober-werk at Greiz (made by Silbermann, 1739); the 'Chalumeaux' on the Brustwerk at Zittau (Silbermann, 1741; James L. Wallmann, personal communication); the 'Chalümeau' on the Brustwerk in the Hofkirche, Dresden (made by Silbermann, 1750–4; Adlung 1758: i. 211; 'Miscellen'; see also Dähnert 1973: 122); the 'Chalimouii' (also called 'Schallmey') on the Oberwerk in the Church of St Maximi in Merseburg (1752; Adlung 1758: i. 78, 257–8); and the 'Shalumo' on the Pedal of the 'Kneiphofische' organ at the Domkirche in Königsberg (Marpurg 1757: iii. 515).

Descriptions from the Mid-eighteenth Century

Descriptions of the chalumeau from the mid-century are found in some countries where little or no music for the instrument survives. For example, on 27 July 1751 the chalumeau was being offered for sale by the book and music dealer J. Smit of Amsterdam[49] even though very little music for it is known from the beginning of the eighteenth century in Holland. In France, music for the eighteenth-century chalumeau has thus far not been found.[50] Nevertheless, a primitive chalumeau, quite similar to the mock trumpet and Buonanni's *scialumò*, was described in 1753 in Diderot and d'Alembert's *Encyclopédie* and illustrated in vol. v of the *Recueil de planches* (1767, Pl. 8; see Fig. 1.9). The description appears after a brief mention of

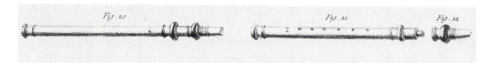

FIG. 1.9. A keyless chalumeau (Diderot and d'Alembert 1762–72, vol. v, Pl. 8, s.v. 'Lutherie, suite de instruments à vent')

---

[48] Stadtarchiv Weimar, Außenstelle Greiz: Akte Sign. a C II Ae 17e, fos. 30 f: '. . . nichts natürliches könne gehöret werden, indem kein Unterschied zu spüren, ob der Virtuos auf diesem Instrument in Dreßden Mons. Willhelmi sich hören läst, oder ob es aus der Orgel klingt.' Cited by Müller 1982: 267 n. 1655. I am grateful to James L. Wallmann for bringing these sources to my attention. I have been unable to trace the activities of Mr Willhelmi.

[49] See his advertisement in the *Amsterdamsche Courant*, reproduced in Smilke 1984: 117.

[50] A concert programme, however, reported in the *Mercure de France* (21 Feb. 1728), included a 'Concerto de chalumeau avec accompaniment de la symphonie'; see Pierre 1975: 234.

the use of wind instruments by the 'ancient' Phrygians, Lybians, Egyptians, Arcadians, and Sicilians:

> Our chalumeau is quite different from that of the ancients. It is a wind instrument with a reed like the oboe. It is composed of two parts; the head, on which is attached a reed resembling that of the organ, except that it is of cane, and the body made of wood; the body of the instrument, which has nine holes . . . It must be remarked that the eighth hole is double, that is the body of the instrument is pierced in this place with two small holes, placed one next to the other. Those that play this instrument hold and play it like the recorder, closing these two holes together or separately, when playing the lowest note or a semitone above it. Thus, they do what is practised on various other instruments.
> . . . It appears that the chalumeau, whose length is less than a foot, is able to play in unison with the tailles and the treble of the harpsichord. It is no longer in use in France.[51]

This instrument is quite short in comparison with other instruments shown in Plate 8 from volume v of the *Recueil de planches*.[52] Fig. 20 in the illustration shows the entire body of the instrument seen from the back and Fig. 21 from the front; Fig. 22 shows the beak mouthpiece separated from the instrument. The only differences between this chalumeau and the mock trumpet are that it has a doubled eighth hole for the little finger and a separate beak mouthpiece, like that of the clarinet, requiring a heteroglot reed tied on with string. Because of its short length it seems unlikely that the range of this chalumeau could be the same as that of the tenor oboe (taille) and the upper register of the harpsichord. Plate 21 of the *Recueil de planches* provides a comparison of many instruments' ranges by means of a table entitled 'Table du rapport de l'entendue des voix et des instrumens de musique comparés au clavecin.' Here the range of the chalumeau is printed on the same line as that of the musette. It is given as f' to c''', with d''' and e''' as additional

[51] iii. 40, 's.v. Chalumeau': 'Notre chalumeau est fort différent de celui des anciens: c'est un instrument à vent & à anche, comme le hautbois. Il est composé de deux parties; de la tête, dans laquelle est montée l'anche semblable à celle des orgues, exceptè que la languette est de roseau, & que le corps est de bouis; du corps de l'instrument, où sont les trous au nombre du neuf . . . Il faut remarquer que le huitième trou est double, c'est-à-dire que les corps de l'instrument est percé dans cet endroit de deux petits trous, placés à côté l'un de l'autre. Celui que joüe de cet instrument, qui se tient & s'embouche comme la flûte-à-bec, ferme à la fois ou séparément les deux trous, comme il convient, & tire un ton ou un semi-ton, ainsi qu'on le pratique sur divers autres instrumens . . . Il paroît que le chalumeau, dont la longuer est moindre que d'un pié, peut sonner l'unisson des tailles & des dessus du clavecin. Il n'est plus en usage en France.'

[52] For a reproduction of the entire plate see Lawson 1981a: 19, Pl. 4. A reconstruction of the chalumeau was made by Canon Francis W. Galpin and is preserved in the Museum of Fine Arts in Boston (No. 17.1870); see Bessaraboff 1941: 97, No. 107. It was erroneously attributed to Stuehnwal in Lambert and Quigley 1983: 29, No. 17. Two additional reconstructions have been recorded: a copy of Galpin's reconstruction made by T. Lea Southgate, now in the Miller collection in Washington, DC (see Gilliam and Lichtenwanger 1961: 21, No. 293), and one made by Galpin or V. C. Mahillon, now in the Metropolitan Museum of Art in New York (No. 89.4.1849; see *Catalogue* 1901–14: i. 133, No. 1849).

notes, indicating an upper register produced by overblowing (cf. Lawson 1981a: 20–2). Garsault (1761: 628) observed that the mouthpiece of the 'clarinet ou haut-bois de forêt' resembled that of the chalumeau, which has a long orifice (i.e., idioglot reed) cut on its upper section ('. . . s'embouche par le sifflet de chalumeau, c'est-à-dire, par une sente de long, coupée sur le haut de l'instrument'; see Rice 1979). La Borde in his *Essai sur la musique* repeated most of the information from the *Encyclopédie* article in his description of the chalumeau, adding that it was also called the 'zampogne' (1780: i. 248–9).

A short description of the chalumeau is found in the trilingual encyclopaedia (Czech, Latin, German) *Nomenclator Artifex, et Mechanicus* (Prague, 1768) by Jan Karel Rohn. A section entitled 'Pfeiffenmacher (Flötenbohrer)' (p. 233) provides descriptions of several woodwinds including 'The Human voice, a small pipe [which] has a mouthpiece like the small clarinet.'[53] The unusual use of 'Menschenstimm' (human voice) for the chalumeau may indicate a comparison of its tone with the voice, or as Lawson suggests (1981a: 170) an allusion to its range by analogy with the next instrument described by Rohn, the oboe da caccia. In Bohemia, the chalumeau was required in the opera *L'Origine di Jaromeritz in Moravia* (1730), and in two cantatas preserved in the Altmann Collection at the Mährische Museum, Brno (Lawson 1981a: 169, 195 n. 1).

A late tribute to the chalumeau was written between 1783 and 1785 by C. F. D. Schubart (1806: 326): 'The tone has so much interest, individuality, and un-ending agreeableness, that the entire scale of art will suffer a considerable deficiency if this instrument is lost.'[54] Although Schubart refers to the instrument as 'Die Schalmei' and states that it is probably the forerunner of our modern oboe, his range of sixteen tones and reference to works by Telemann and Gluck clearly identify the single-reed chalumeau (Lawson 1981a: 186 n. 70).

Several types of chalumeau instruments were described in the comprehensive music dictionary of the Dutch lawyer and writer J. V. Reynvaan (1795). The second and third instruments mentioned in his definition of the chalumeau resemble respectively the mock trumpet and Majer's tenor chalumeau:

CHALUMEAU. (French) in the plural, Chalumeaux, in Latin, *Fistula Pastoritia*. It is a small shepherd's flute about the length of a foot. There are several different kinds which are large and small and high and low in pitch. They are made of reeds or beechwood, with and without keys. Those made of reeds have the width of a man's thumb. They are closed off in front with a cork and given a movable tongue, which is made by making a small cross cut in the reed behind the main cut. This makes the tongue thinner from below towards the small

---

[53] 'Die Menschenstimm / eine kurze Pfeiffe / hat ein Mundstück wie das Klarinetel.'

[54] 'Der Ton desselben hat so viel Interessantes, Eigentümliches, unendlich Angenehmes, dass die ganze Scale der Tonkunst eine merkliche Lücke hätte, wenn diess Instrument verloren ginge.'

cross cut and then splits it away from the main tube along the small cross cut. Those made of beechwood have a mouthpiece made of reed, some instruments have a key on top near the mouthpiece. Furthermore, this instrument has six finger-holes and one thumb-hole. Its range is not much more than one octave, and everything above this becomes very hard to play. The fingering on this instrument is a lot like that of the recorder. Look at the scale for the chalumeau with one key at the top by the mouthpiece on the accompanying plate [Fig. 1.10]. One can also play it a third lower as can be seen by the lower scale. This enables one to play pieces for the violin or transverse flute on it, without having to rewrite them. Actually the scale really starts with f as its sounding pitch, one octave lower than the upper scale shows.[55]

Reynvaan's first chalumeau, a shepherd's flute about the length of a foot, corresponds to the first chalumeau in Walther's definition. The different sizes and tunings discussed by Majer seem to be alluded to by 'several different kinds which are large and small and high and low in pitch'. His second chalumeau, the width of a man's thumb with an idioglot reed, reminds us of the mock trumpet. A third chalumeau (Fig. 1.10) has the same number of finger-holes (seven) as the mock trumpet and, according to Reynvaan's engraving, an idioglot reed as part of its wood mouthpiece. One key provided an additional note but the range of this instrument encompassed about one octave less than the chalumeau in the *Encyclopédie*. However, the notes that it produced sounded one octave lower. Therefore it was a longer instrument than the chalumeau described in the *Encyclopédie* or the mock trumpet and corresponds to Majer's tenor chalumeau in range.[56]

A one-key chalumeau was coincidentally mentioned by the Norwegian band-

---

[55] pp. 118–19: 'CHALUMEAU. (Fransch.) In het meervoudige, *Chalumeaux*. In het Latijn, *Fistula Pastoritia*. Het is een zekere kleine herdersfluit, omtrent ter langte van één voet, welke dien naam gegeven wordt: men heeft er onderscheidene soorten van, grooter en kleiner, en des, hooger of laager in toon; met en zonder kleppen: dezelven worden gemaakt, of van riet, of van beukenboomhout: die van riet, hebben doorgaands de dikte van een mans duim; zijnde van vooren met eene kurk gestopt, en daar voorzien van eene beweegbaare tong, vervaardigd door een dwarskefjen in het riet, achter de kerf, te snijden; hetzelve van onderen naar het kerfjen dun te maaken, en dan de tong langs het kerfjen optesplijten: die welke van beukenboomhout gemaakt zijn, hebben een rieten mondstuk, en hebben sommigen vaan boven bij het mondstuk een klepjen; zijnde er echter ook die dat niet hebben: verders is dit speeltuig voorzien van zes vingergaten, en één duimgat; deszelfs omtrek is al niet veel meer dan één *Octaaf*, en al wat daar boven gaat, wordt zeer bezwaarelijk om te blaazen. De *Applicatie* daarop komt meerendeels overeen met die der fluiten: zie de schaale, voor die met ééne klep boven aan het mondstuk, op de hier nevenstaande Plaat 9; kunnende men die ook een *Ters* laager speelen, zo als bij den ondersten *Muzijkbalk* te zien is, wanneer men dan stukjens voor de *Viool* of *Dwarsfluit*, zonder die te moeten verschrijven, daarop kan speelen; want anders begint eigenlijk de schaale met f, zo als de bovenste *Muzijkbalk* aanwijst; en wel volgens deszelfs eigenlijken toon, een *Octaaf* laager.' Trans. Dr Roelof Wijbrandous, Defense Language Institute, Monterey, Calif.

[56] The 2nd edn. of Reynvaan's dictionary was never completed and ended with 'Muzijkgedacht' (a register of the organ). It is often confused with an earlier incomplete edn. of 1789–90 (*Muzijkaal Konst-woordenboek*), which was entirely revised in 1795. See *NNBW* 'Reynvaan, Mr. Joos Verschuere'.

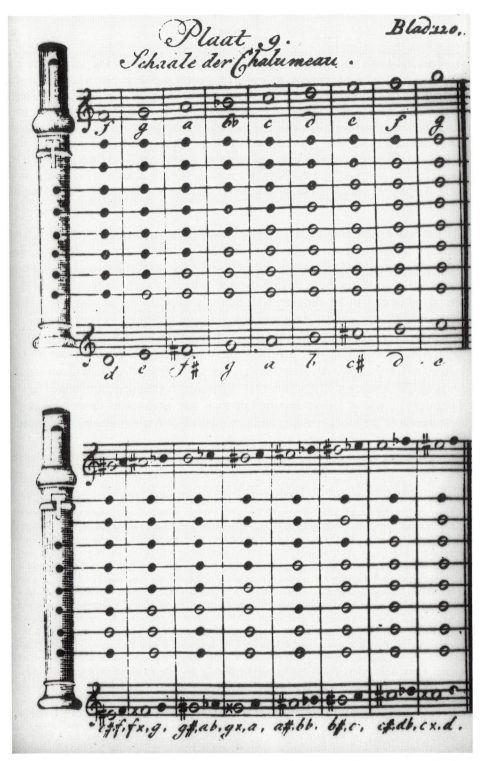

FIG. 1.10. A fingering-chart for a one-key idioglot-reed chalumeau (Reynvaan 1795, Pl. 9)

master Lorents Nicolai Berg in his instrumental treatise of 1782. At the beginning of his chapter on the clarinet he states: 'At one time a type of reed instrument with one key existed. I saw them once in the grammar school in Odense lying among several old instruments like remains of their dead ancestors. The chalumeau, along with others, was also a lovely sounding instrument back then' (Rice 1979–80: 45).[57] Since Berg's 'Scharmeyen' was associated with the clarinet, we may assume that it had a single reed and was similar to Reynvaan's idioglot instrument.

Extant Chalumeaux

Eight surviving instruments have been identified as chalumeaux. Three are preserved in the Stadtmuseum, Munich (on permanent loan from the Bayerisches Nationalmuseum), four in the Statens musiksamlingar Musikmuseet, Stockholm, and one in the Museum Carolino Augusteum, Salzburg. Previously, it had been thought that chalumeaux were not extant (Carse 1939: 149–50) or that none larger than a soprano survived (Baines 1966: 112), because seven of the now-acknowledged chalumeaux had been mistakenly identified as clarinets, and one as a dulcian or sordun. These eight chalumeaux are listed in Table 1.1 in an approximate chronological sequence; they were made between the beginning of the eighteenth century and about 1760.

TABLE 1.1 *Extant Chalumeau Instruments*

Maker	Length	Type	Construction	Location
J. C. Denner	500 mm.	Tenor	3 joints, 2 keys	Munich, SM, No. 136
W. Kress	140 cm.	Bass	4 joints, 5 keys	Salzburg, MCA, No. 8/1
Liebau	330 mm.	Alto	3 joints, 2 keys	Stockholm, MM, No. 139
Klenig	486 mm.	Tenor	3 joints, 2 keys	Stockholm, MM, No. 141
Klenig	490 mm.	Tenor	3 joints, 2 keys	Stockholm, MM, No. 142
Anonymous	290 mm.	Soprano	2 joints, 2 keys	Munich, SM, No. 137[a]
Anonymous	399 mm.	Alto d'amour	3 joints, 3 keys	Munich, SM, No. 134[b]
Muller	321 mm.	Alto	2 joints, 7 keys	Stockholm, MM, No. 140[c]

[a] Attributed to 'Stuehnwal' in earlier printed discussions, but Munich, SM states that the maker's mark is barely legible: 'STV . . . H . . . A . . . X(?)'.

[b] Tentatively attributed by Munich, SM, to a maker from the Walch family.

[c] A missing tenor chalumeau by Liebau (formerly Stockholm, MM, No. 143) was 526 mm. long and had 3 joints and 2 keys. See Becker 1970: 37 and Karp 1972: 82.

[57] Berg 1782: 48: 'Den het været et Slags saadanne Rør-Instrumenter til med een Klap i forrige Tider, dem jeg engang paa den latinske Skole i Oddense kom over at see iblandt endeel gamle Instrumenter, som Levninger at ligge efter deres afdøde Formænd. Scharmeyen var og i de Tider liflig m.f.' A 'Paar Chalimö in C' was listed in the church band inventory of 1781 at Markt Gaunersdorf (now Gaweinstal) in Lower Austria; see Fitzpatrick 1968: 87 n. 8.

A total of five makers (including J. C. Denner and two who are anonymous) are represented by these instruments. Each chalumeau is made of boxwood, except for the Kress instrument, which is probably made of maple, and each includes two brass keys near the mouthpiece, which are opposite each other on the frontal and dorsal sides of the tube. Although the tone-holes for these keys are not always directly opposite each other, none of the instruments has a metal tube inserted into the upper dorsal hole or 'speaker' hole found on all eighteenth-century clarinets (Ross 1985: 57, 73).

The J. C. Denner instrument (Fig. 1.11)[58] includes six finger-holes, another for

FIG. 1.11. Tenor chalumeau by Johann Christoph Denner (Munich, SM, No. 136)

---

[58] A very clear colour photo of this instrument is in Young 1980: 26, No. 52.

the thumb, and a double hole for the lowest finger—resembling an alto recorder.[59] Its head-joint, 187 mm. in length, consists of a mouthpiece and lower section forming a base for its two keys. The Liebau chalumeaux share this characteristic of construction, but Nickel (1971: 213) considers the Denner instrument to be the earliest on the basis of its more primitive mouthpiece. Each instrument, excluding the examples by Klenig, Kress, and the three-key unmarked chalumeau, includes a double hole for the lowest finger to aid in producing the two lowest semitones. The Klenig chalumeaux, similar to early clarinets, have a head-joint formed from a mouthpiece and a pear-shaped socket with the keys mounted on the middle joints. Their mouthpieces also have continuous grooves for the string used in binding the reed to the mouthpiece. This suggests a later date of manufacture than that of the Liebau instrument, whose mouthpiece has irregular notches.

Because of the length of the touchpiece of the keys on the Denner chalumeau, its mouthpiece must be turned so that the reed is placed against the upper lip. If the mouthpiece is turned so that the reed is placed against the lower lip, the touchpiece of the key previously on the frontal side obstructs the thumb-hole. Furthermore, when the mouthpiece is positioned with reed uppermost, the maker's stamp on the head-joint corresponds to the frontal position of the stamp on the lower joints (Eppelsheim 1973).[60] The anonymous soprano chalumeau, previously attributed to Stuehnwal, is only 290 mm. in length. Its two keys are positioned on the finger-hole joint, which may indicate a date of manufacture later than those of the Denner and Liebau instruments (cf. Lawson 1981a: 13). The mouthpiece-socket of this chalumeau is not original, having a much smaller bore than the main joint (12.50 mm. compared with 14.85 mm.), and is constructed from a wood different from the boxwood of the main joint (Ross 1985: 61).[61]

The anonymous three-key alto chalumeau in Munich is distinguished by a pear-shaped, incurved bell, as found on the *clarinette d'amour*, and the presence of a third key manipulated by the thumb of either hand (depending on which was placed lowest). As on the three-key clarinet, the lowest hole for the little finger has been duplicated to give the option to the player as to which hand was placed lowest, the unused hole being stopped by wax or a wooden plug. According to Birsak (1973a: 497), the third key and the 'd'amour' bell is enough evidence to suggest a date of manufacture between 1750 and 1760. Further evidence for a dating after the mid-century lies in the use of horn mounts and the shape and size

---

[59] Resemblance noted by F. Geoffrey Rendall in his 'Historical Sketch' for Thurston and Frank 1939: 4.

[60] Both of these characteristics are also apparent on the alto chalumeau by Liebau; see Karp 1986: 547, illus. 2.

[61] The fact that this mouthpiece-socket is not original has recently been noted on the descriptive label at Munich, SM.

of the mouthpiece (Ross 1985: 63–4).[62] Muller's chalumeau is unusual; it appears to be experimental because of the unique position of its seven keys and the lack of any foot-joint (Becker 1970: 36, 38–9; Lawson 1981a: 15; Karp 1986: 546, 547 illus. 3). The position of its lowest doubled finger-hole requires the use of the right hand below the left. Besides the usual frontal and dorsal keys a third key is positioned for the right-hand thumb. There are four more keys, two of which are positioned vertically on either side of the finger-holes. Because of the position of the touchpieces of these four keys, the finger-holes would need to be covered by the middle joints of the fingers, the tips of the fingers controlling the touchpieces themselves. This instrument also has a metal tube in the lower tone-hole of its two highest keys, presumably a feature borrowed from the early clarinet (Ross 1985: 67–8).[63] Becker (1970: 39) suggests the first quarter of the eighteenth century as a likely date of manufacture. However, Ross (1985: 68–9) shows a similarity in the arrangement of some of its keys to those on the chanters of a musette illustrated in the *Recueil de planches* (1767) in Diderot and d'Alembert's *Encyclopédie*.

It was previously assumed that the bass chalumeau was the same size as a tenor recorder.[64] The estimates and bills for instruments by Jacob Denner, however, show a rather sharp difference in price between the 'Chalimou basson' and the smaller sizes of chalumeau. Several Viennese opera scores of the period also specify a continuo part with 'basson di chalumeau', perhaps indicating an instrument capable of playing the bass-line at pitch (and thus with a probable range of F to c) (*NGDMI* 'Chalumeau'). Recently, a bassoon-shaped bass instrument capable of playing in this range (excluding the high c) has been identified as a bass chalumeau (Eppelsheim 1983: 86–90, 1987: 94; Nagy 1987: 97–8).

This instrument is found in the Museum Carolino Augusteum at Salzburg (No. 8/1), catalogued as a 'sordun' and bearing the mark of 'W Kress' (Birsak 1973b: 31; see Figs. 1.12 and 1.13). No specific information is available concerning where or when Kress was active. Only five other extant instruments are recorded which bear his stamp: two three-key oboes in the Stadtmuseum, Munich (Nos. 38 and 39), a one-key basset-flute in the Städtisches Museum, Brunswick (No. 821), a three-key tenor oboe in the Musikhistorisk Museum, Copenhagen (No. 103), and another in the Oberösterreichisches Landesmuseum, Linz (No. 121); all appear to have been made during the early eighteenth century. Birsak (1973b:

---

[62] Jürgen Eppelsheim has suggested to the author that the mouthpiece-socket of this instrument is not original.

[63] Karp (1986: 547 illus. 3) suggests that the Muller instrument cannot be positively identified as either a chalumeau or a clarinet.

[64] From the early 1950s, the late Otto Steinkopf (who worked from 1964 for the Moeck Verlag in Celle, Germany) made 4 sizes of chalumeaux based on the Stockholm instruments. Moeck's bass size (called tenor) is equivalent in length to a tenor recorder. See Baines 1960: 79.

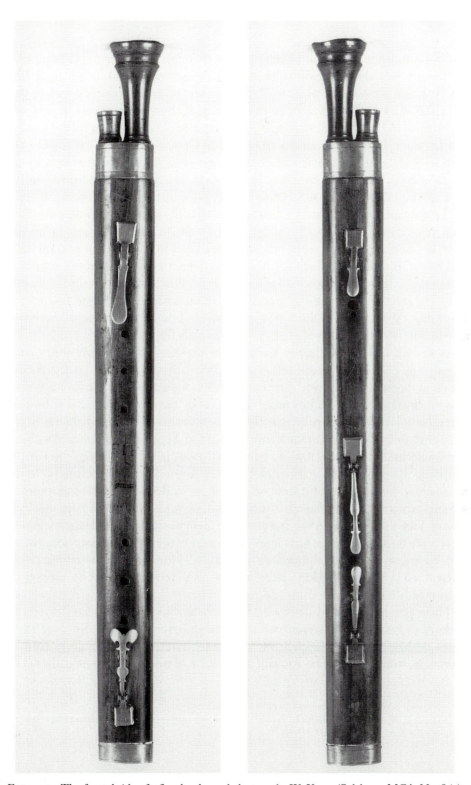

FIG. 1.12. The frontal side of a five-key bass chalumeau by W. Kress (Salzburg, MCA, No. 8/1)

FIG. 1.13. The dorsal side of a five-key bass chalumeau by W. Kress (Salzburg, MCA, No. 8/1)

84–5) believes the sordun in Salzburg dates from not later than the beginning of the century (see also Langwill 1980: 97 and Young 1982b: 76). It is made in the form of a dulcian—in one piece with two parallel bores which double back so that the end of the bore is next to the initial opening. A short bell section is inserted in the bore on the top of the instrument; at the beginning of the bore on the top is a smaller wood insert, presumably made to hold a curved or bent crook. On the lower end of the instrument is a brass capsule covering the bend in the bore. There are nine finger-holes and five brass keys, two on the front side and three on the back, mounted on metal platforms called 'saddles' such as were commonly used on the dulcian and bassoon.[65] There are keys for the notes *a* and *F* (on the front side); *bb*, *E*, and *C*, and tone-holes for *D* and *Bb'* (on the rear). The touchpiece for the *F* key is in a 'butterfly' shape, allowing the player to have the left or right hand lowermost. Birsak found that the fingering of the Kress instrument was similar to that of the sixteenth-century sorduns in the Kunsthistorische Museum of Vienna (Nos. A. 226–A. 229), but the arrangement and design of the four keys on the latter differ from those of the Kress instrument. The natural range of the Kress instrument is given by Birsak (1973b: 31, 84–5) as *Bb'* to *bb*.

As in clarinets of the period, the bore of the Kress instrument is primarily cylindrical. The ratio of its diameter (19 mm.) to its length (140 cm.) is also similar to that found in eighteenth-century basset horns. Consequently, Birsak suggested that this instrument could be considered an early bass clarinet and that its bore diameter corresponds more to that of the chalumeau than to the diameter of the bass sordune in *C* (8 mm.) in the Vienna collection. He also experimented with the Kress instrument by fitting it with a bent metal crook (similar to those found on the clarinette d'amour) and a clarinet mouthpiece. Even though his results were not satisfactory, his playing test cannot be conclusive evidence since the instrument's original crook and mouthpiece are missing (cf. Birsak 1973b: 85, 87, 90–1). John Henry Van der Meer (1977; 1987: 65–8) believes the Kress instrument was played as a bass chalumeau, but identifies it as the earliest bass clarinet because the register key is positioned higher than the *a'* key.[66] However, his reasoning may be questioned because these keys were not always exactly opposite one another on chalumeaux instruments.

Three other unstamped single-reed instruments have been reported by several authors to be bass chalumeaux or early bass clarinets (Berlin, SI, No. 2810; Brussels, MI, No. 939; Museo Storico, Lugano). Each has been made, possibly in Germany, from what may be described as a plank of wood covered in leather. The

---

[65] The use of saddles as mounts is discussed by Carse (1939: 54–5).

[66] Weber (1987) also stated that it is a bass clarinet but does not concede the possibility that it is a bass chalumeau.

bore of the example in Brussels (*c.*18 cm.) runs along one side of the plank with the thumb-hole opening directly on it (see Fig. 1.14). Seven finger-holes enter on the upper surface, bored at oblique angles for convenient reach of the fingers like the finger-holes on the wing-joint of the bassoon. There is also a long, curved crook for the mouthpiece and an upturned widely flared bell (cf. *NGDMI* 'Chalumeau'; Rendall 1971: 140). The earliest of these instruments was destroyed in World War II but is photographed in Sachs' catalogue of the Berlin collection (1922: 299, Pl. 29; Young 1981: 40). It had only one key for its lowest pitch (presumably *E*) and was designed to play only in its lowest register. Rendall (1971: 140) suggested that this instrument was made before 1750 and could have been a bass chalumeau (*NGDMI* 'Chalumeau'). It had previously been part of the collections of Edmond de Coussemaker (1877: 205–6, No. 32) and Césare Snoeck (1894: 172–3, No. 910). Coincidentally, the lexicographer F. J. Fétis wrote (1830: 167) that the earliest clarinets had one key; however, he probably did not know of the Berlin instrument, and his statement has not been corroborated by other evidence.

The instrument in Brussels has three brass keys: the register key, *a′* key, and *e/b′* key; it was meant to play in the overblown register with the use of its register key.[67] The curator of the Brussels Conservatoire collection, V. C. Mahillon (1893–1922: ii. 220), described it as being pitched in *a* and stated that its quality was bad, lacking in timbre and accuracy of intonation. It was probably made about 1750 (Van der Meer 1979: 138). The third unstamped instrument, in Lugano, had three keys (but is now missing the register key, mouthpiece and neck) and was built with a long, straight wooden tube and a downward-pointing bell. Because of the superior workmanship and construction of this instrument, Kalina (1972: 10–12, 12 n. 2) believes that it is probably of later eighteenth-century origin than the other two instruments. (A similar instrument mentioned by Young (1981: 40), Florence, MSM, No. 160, also has a downward pointing bell, but it carries six keys and was made about 1780 (Van der Meer 1979: 138; cf. Young 1981: 40)).[68]

As long ago as 1884, in the article 'Oboe' in the ninth edition of the *Encyclopaedia Britannica*, V. C. Mahillon correctly identified as chalumeaux the instrument made by J. C. Denner and another attributed to Stuehnwal. Referring to the single-reed chalumeau, he stated: 'The present writer has had the good fortune to find quite recently two examples in the National Museum [Bayerisches Nationalmuseum] at Munich, and has been kindly authorized by Herr von

---

[67] Photo and description in Day 1891: 123, Pl. V, reproduced in Rendall 1971: 139–40, Pl. 7 a; another photo in Young 1980: 197, No. 243.

[68] Another description in Gai 1969: 221–2; photo in *Antichi strumenti* 1980, Pl. 108, No. 160. According to Kalina (1972: 12 n. 3), Van der Meer disputes Arnaldo Bonaventura's attribution (1928: 9–10) of the instrument to Domenico Del Mela.

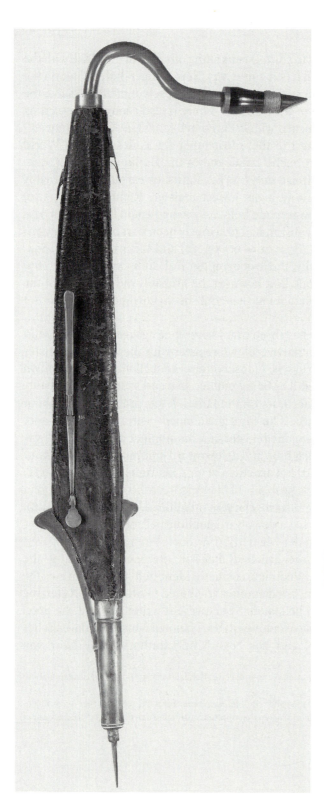

Fɪɢ. 1.14. An unmarked three-key
bass chalumeau or bass clarinet
(Brussels, MI, No. 939)

Hefner-Alteneck, director of the museum, to reproduce them for the museum of the conservatoire at Brussels.'[69]

The engraving of an instrument depicted in Mahillon's article is of such unique construction that it is without doubt the J. C. Denner chalumeau. Mahillon's facsimile (Brussels, MI, No. 911), made between about 1882 and 1884, was later included in the Royal Military Exhibition held in London in 1890. It was photographed for the exhibition catalogue (Day 1891, Pl. IV B) and identified on the 'Errata' page as a chalumeau in c'.[70] A reconstruction of the soprano chalumeau attributed to Stuehnwal was also carried out, probably during the period 1882 to 1884. In his catalogue of 1892, Mahillon described these facsimiles of instruments by Stuehnwal and Denner as chalumeaux (p. 163, No. 906 and p. 165, No. 911 respectively) while cautiously labelling both instruments as 'clarinette'. In his catalogue of 1893–1922 he applied Majer's terminology (1732), describing these instruments as soprano and tenor chalumeaux. Here he incorrectly stated that the tenor chalumeau bore the stamp 'I. [Jacob] Denner' (i. 210). Mahillon's errors were undoubtedly the source of many subsequent erroneous descriptions of these instruments, which have persisted in print as late as 1976.[71] Subsequently, various copies of the J. C. Denner chalumeau were made; they may be found in the Museum of Fine Arts, Boston, No. 17. 1871 (Bessaraboff 1941: 97, No. 108; Lambert and Quigley 1983: 29, No. 18; Galpin 1910, Pl. 34, No. 11), the Metropolitan Museum of Art, New York, No. 89.4.1845 (*Catalogue* 1901–14: i. 134, No. 1845), the Musikhistorisk Museum, Copenhagen (Hammerich 1911: 33, No. 121), the Heckel Collection, Biebrich (*MGG* 'Klarinette', Pl. 43, No. 9), the Museum für Hamburgische Geschichte, Hamburg (Schröder 1930: 74, No. 1926,374), and the Musikinstrumentenmuseum, Karl-Marx-Universität, Leipzig (Schultz 1929: 46, No. 1468a).

Among the makers of extant chalumeaux listed above, J. C. Denner is the only one who also made clarinets. Four clarinets formerly attributed to him have been lost. A three-key specimen (at Berkeley, UC) is discussed in the next chapter. In addition to the evidence that Jacob Denner made both clarinets and chalumeaux (discussed above, pp. 21–3), there is documentation which indicates that two additional makers made these instruments: Philipp Borkens (1693–1759) and Jeremias Schlegel (1730–92). Unfortunately none of their chalumeaux are extant. In 1759, according to the auction catalogue of his property, the Dutch musician

[69] Subsequently Mahillon (1892: 163, 165; 1893–1922: i. 210) acknowledged his use of the Munich, SM instruments in building reproductions. According to Ignace De Keyser of Brussels, MI both of these reproductions have been stolen from the museum.

[70] Day acknowledged Mahillon's assistance in his preface (1891: IX). A photograph of the Brussels fac. is in Kappey *c.*1894, Pl. VI, No. 10.

[71] Beginning with the definitive works by Sachs (1913: 251a, 1930: 339). Later writers include Baines (1967, Pl. XXX, No. 5); Marcuse (1975: 721); and the Diagram Group (1976: 40).

Nicolas Selhof, owned the following instruments: '[No.] 166 Deux Clarinettes de Borkens, 167 Cinq Chalumeaux, dont 1 de Borkens & 1 de deBye' (1973 edn.: 256). A two-key clarinet by Borkens is preserved in the Gemeentemuseum of The Hague (No. Ea 306-1933), but chalumeaux by Debey are not extant. Schlegel stated in a document of 1759 that he made 'Bassoons, oboes, transverse flutes, recorders, clarinets, chalumeaux, flageolets, harps, etc. and operates this business with great success'.[72] Schlegel's extant clarinets include four 'classical' clarinets with four or five keys and two clarinettes d'amour with four and five keys (Küng 1987: 85–6, Young 1982b: 119).[73]

Conclusion

The single-reed chalumeau of the late seventeenth century and eighteenth century was built in a variety of sizes and tunings with one, two, three, five, or seven keys, or none at all. There are also several differences in construction among the extant instruments noted above. A recent description by Anthony Baines of the stages in the development of the chalumeau includes pictures of three instruments: a keyless mock trumpet; a two-key soprano chalumeau; and a two-key tenor chalumeau (*NOCM* 'Clarinet', Fig. 2). On the basis of the evidence presented here it is clear that Baines' description is somewhat oversimplified.

Our foregoing survey of the chalumeau is essential to a discussion of the origins of the clarinet, since several extant two-key chalumeaux of the eighteenth century are quite similar in appearance to contemporary two-key clarinets. Indeed, because of these similarities one might assume that the two-key clarinet was developed from the two-key chalumeau. However, the evidence for this assumption is inconclusive. The clarinet differs from the chalumeau in that the key on the clarinet's dorsal side is positioned higher and is given a smaller tone-hole, with a register tube to assist in producing the overblown register. In addition, the construction of the clarinet mouthpiece makes it more effective in producing the overblown register, and the bell is larger and has a definite flare to its bore, unlike the recorder-like foot of many chalumeau instruments. In the next chapter, we begin our discussion of the clarinet by tracing the earliest instruments to the Nuremberg workshop of Johann Christoph and Jacob Denner, and describing in detail the construction of the two- and three-key clarinets.

---

[72] Staatsarchiv Basel, Bürgerrecht F 2.9, Geschau um Bürgeraufnahme 1759: 'Fagots, Hautbois, fleutes travers und à becq, Clarinettes, Chalumeaux, flacholettes, harffen (etc) . . . und treibt diesen Beruf mit "guthem Success"'. Cited in Küng 1987: 77.

[73] 2 unsigned 4-key clarinettes d'amour in Munich, SM, can be attributed to Jeremias Schlegel on the basis of documents of 1772–3 and a similarity of their key-covers to other Schlegel instruments. See Rice 1986: 98 and Shackleton 1987: 22 n. 45; see also Weber 1986. Jan Steenbergen (before 1700–1752) and Andrea Fornari (1753–1841) also made chalumeaux (see Jonxis 1983 and Bernardini 1989: 53–5).

2

The Earliest Instruments

THE makers, design, and construction of the clarinet with two or three keys, known as the baroque clarinet, are the subjects of this chapter. Such instruments were initially made during the first decade of the eighteenth century and continued to be constructed and played throughout the eighteenth century and into the nineteenth. Many common characteristics of construction shared by the extant baroque clarinets are discussed below, along with differences in construction which appear to reflect, the preferences and techniques of their makers.

In the list below, makers of extant baroque clarinets are grouped under the modern-day name of their countries, where known; the figures in brackets indicate the number of clarinets preserved (for more detailed information see Appendix).[1]

Two-key Clarinets (31)

Germany (17)

Crone, Gottlieb. Leipzig (1)

Denner, Jacob. Nuremberg (3)

Oberlender, Johann Wilhelm I. Nuremberg (2)

Oberlender, Johann Wilhelm II. Nuremberg (1)

Scherer, Georg Heinrich. Butzbach (6)

Walch, Georg. Berchtesgarten (2)

Wietfeld, Philipp Gottlieb. Burgdorf (1)

Zencker, Johann Gottfried. Leipzig (1)

Belgium (6)

Rottenburgh, Godefroid-Adrien. Brussels (2)   Willems, Jean Baptiste. Brussels (4)

Netherlands (2)

Boekhout, Thomas Coenraet. Amsterdam (1)   Borkens, Philip. Amsterdam (1)[2]

Unknown origin (6)

Deper, M. (Germany?) (1)

IGH (J. G. Heinze? Germany?) (1)

Kelmer, G. N. (Germany?) (1)

Unmarked (3)

---

[1] The most important published sources concerning these instruments are Young 1982b and Langwill 1980. Additional information was generously provided by Drs David Ross and Nicholas Shackleton.

[2] An error in Langwill (1980) led Van Acht (1988: 89) to list an additional clarinet by Borkens.

THREE-KEY CLARINETS (13)

Germany (5)

Denner, Johann Christoph. Nuremberg (1)   Scherer, Georg Heinrich. Butzbach (1)
Kenigsperger, Johann Wolfgang. Roding (1)   Walch, Georg. Berchtesgarten (2)

Austria (1)

Paur, R. (Rocko?) Austria (1)[3]

Czechoslovakia (1)

Friderich, J. Prague (1)

Unknown origin (6)

GRFUES (G. R. Fues? Germany?) (1)   Strehli, I. G. (Germany?) (1)
I$W (Johann S. Walch? Germany?) (1)   Unmarked (3)

German makers are predominant in this list; the maker of the largest number of extant two-key clarinets is Georg Heinrich Scherer (1703–78; see Young 1986: 120–1). Those instruments made during the first half of the eighteenth century are seven two-key clarinets—three by Jacob Denner, two by Johann Wilhelm Oberlender I, one by Thomas Conraet Boekhout, and an unmarked clarinet in the Rubin collection in London resembling the Denner instruments—and the three-key clarinet attributed to Johann Christoph Denner (see Ross 1985: 92–114).

Clarinets Made by the Denners: Documentation and Attribution

The most important and often-cited attribution of the invention of the clarinet to Johann Christoph Denner (1655–1707) appeared in J. G. Doppelmayr's *Historische Nachricht von den Nürnbergischen Mathematicis und Künstlern* of 1730. Doppelmayr credited Denner with the invention of the clarinet and improvement of the chalumeau at 'the beginning of the present century' (i.e., the eighteenth). He probably knew the Denners personally, but his statements cannot be accepted without reservation because he made factual errors in the entry on Denner and exaggerated the achievements of other Nuremberg artisans. Nevertheless, his account was adopted by dozens of later writers,[4] who occasionally added details not found in the original sketch. For instance, the idea that J. C. Denner invented

---

[3] Stamp identified as R. Baur by Ross (1985: 158–60). Cf. Van der Meer 1982: 74. A three-key clarinet by G. N. Kelmer, formerly in Berlin, SI (photographed in Kroll 1968: fig. 6), was destroyed during World War II.

[4] Including Walther (1732), Majer (1732), Zedler (1731–54), Barnickel (1737), Gottsched (1760), and Jablonski (1767).

the clarinet by improving the chalumeau can be traced to the third edition of F. A. Brockhaus' well-known *Conversations-Lexikon* (1814–19: iv. 100).[5] This statement was repeated by countless authors and led to a confusion of the physical differences between the eighteenth-century chalumeau and clarinet.

E. L. Gerber repeated most of Doppelmayr's information in his dictionaries but specified 1700 as the year of the invention of the clarinet (1790–2: i/2. Instrumenten Register, 80; 1812–14: ii/1. 871).[6] Some authors mistook Doppelmayr's mention of 'the beginning of the present century' for a reference to the seventeenth century. The first of these was probably John Farey, who wrote the article 'Clarinet' in David Brewster's *Edinburgh Encyclopædia* (1808–30).[7] C. G. von Murr, however, suggested 1690 as the year of invention (1778: 740).[8] This date came to be widely popularized, owing to its inclusion in the *Biographie Universelle* by F. J. Fétis (1860–5: ii. 469).[9] Other specific dates of invention suggested by later writers are 1696, by O. Paul (1874: ii. 649),[10] and 1701, by the clarinettist F. T. Blatt (1839: 3).[11] Still other nineteenth-century sources state that the date of invention was between 1690 and 1700.[12]

The account books in the Nuremberg archives for 1710 show that Jacob Denner (1681–1735), the son of Johann Christoph Denner, received an order for several instruments from the Duke of Gronsfeld, a resident of Nuremberg, which included '2 Clarinettes'.[13] According to Gottron (1959: 115–16), a document in the Wiesbaden Stadtarchiv shows that during 1710 six clarinets by an unknown maker were bought from Mainz for Eberbach abbey in the region of Rheingau. The archival records of the abbey also show that in 1710 a clarinet (perhaps one of the six?) was repaired in Mainz.[14] Thus, of a total of eight or nine clarinets known to have been made in 1710, two were definitely made by Jacob Denner. Not long afterwards, two churches in Nuremberg ordered clarinets from Jacob Denner. Between 1 May 1711 and 30 April 1712, four clarinets were made for the

---

[5] For an account of the history of this dictionary see Collinson 1966: 156–73.

[6] 1700 was also given in the clarinet method by Lefèvre (1802) and the dictionary of inventions by Busch (1802–22).

[7] 1600 was also given in the dictionaries ed. Brande (1842), Colange (1878), and Ripley and Taylor (1873).

[8] Other authors who gave 1690 include Lipowsky (1794), Busch (1801), Keess (1829), and Klosé (c. 1844).

[9] Curiously, Stainer and Barrett (1889: 97) state: 'Most authors relate that Denner invented the instrument in 1659, at which date he was four years old; but it was made by him after his residence in Nuremberg, in 1690.'

[10] Repeated in *ADB* 'Denner, J. C.'

[11] Repeated in Lavoix 1878: 119.

[12] These include Andersch (1829), Gathy (1835), Bernsdorf (1857), and Baermann (1864–75).

[13] Staatsarchiv Nuremberg, Stadtrechnungsbeleg in Repertorium 54 a II, Nr. 1282; quoted in Nickel 1971: 251–2.

[14] Wiesbaden Haupt-Stadtarchiv, Archiv der geistlichen Institut, Abt. 22, Rechnungsbuch des Kloster Eberbach, Rheingau 1710, 39ᵛ: 'Vor ein Clarinett restituire dem Keller zu Maintz den 24. Jan. 1711 3 fl.'; quoted in Nickel 1971: 454 n. 1247. The 'Keller zu Maintz' handled the exchange of goods between the city of Mainz and Eberbach abbey.

'Music-Chor' of the Frauenkirche;[15] two years later, the Sebaldkirche also ordered two clarinets.[16] On the basis of these documents, Nickel (1971: 211) and Lawson (1981a: 9) suggest that the invention of the clarinet should be credited to Jacob Denner and the distinction of improving the chalumeau to Johann Christoph Denner. However, evidence suggesting that Johann Christoph constructed clarinets before 1710 is provided by a photograph of a two-key clarinet destroyed during World War II and by an actual surviving three-key clarinet (fully described later in this chapter).

Several writers have mentioned clarinets made by J. C. Denner, some examples of which were probably misidentified instruments by Jacob Denner; others cannot now be identified. For example, sixty-six instruments in the Germanisches Nationalmuseum in Nuremberg were listed in an anonymous article in the *Anzeiger für Kunde der Deutschen Vorzeit* ('Sammlung' 1860: 46); No. 59 was a 'Clarinette von J. C. Denner' with a length of 1 ft. 8 in. (508 mm.). Today, one clarinet by Jacob Denner is found in this museum in Nuremberg (No. 149). Van der Meer (1983: 127), however, stated that of eighteen instruments lent to this museum by the Lutheran Church administration at Fürth, two clarinets were made by either Jacob or J. C. Denner. For an unknown reason, seventeen of these instruments, including the clarinets, were returned to Fürth in 1932 and cannot be located today. Several years earlier, F. Jahn (1927–8: 109) mentioned 'some well-preserved examples of clarinets by J. C. Denner' in the Nuremberg museum but did not provide further details. In a later manuscript catalogue of this collection, Jahn (n.d.) listed three clarinets (Nos. 149, 196, 197) as the work of the elder Denner. Two of these (Nos. 196 and 197), which were also attributed to Johann Christoph Denner by Van der Meer (1968: 208), were destroyed during World War II; this attribution is supported by Martin Kirnbauer (1987: 451–3), who found a photograph of No. 197 in Nuremberg and determined that it was a clarinet in *c'*.[17] Finally, a letter quoted by Young (1967: 15–16) contains a reference to three clarinets attributed to J. C. Denner. These were owned by Clarence A. Lyle of New York City and were stolen from his home in 1918. While these reports suggest that several clarinets were made by J. C. Denner, they cannot be offered as proof. Some reports have been shown to be mistaken and, until further corroborating evidence is presented, the extant instruments by the Denners must be considered to be: one tenor chalumeau by Johann Christoph, three two-key clarinets by Jacob, and a three-key clarinet attributed to Johann Christoph.

[15] Landeskirchliches Archiv, Nuremberg, Kirchenrechnung Vereinigtes protestantisches Kirchenvermögen der Stadt Nürnberg 228, Nr. 3, 70; cited in Nickel 1971: 454 n. 1246.

[16] Landeskirchliches Archiv, Nuremberg, Kirchenrechnung 228, Nr. 5, 78; cited in Nickel 1971: 454 n. 1246.

[17] The sound produced by fingering a written *c'* on a clarinet is the pitch referred to as the tonality of the instrument.

Design and Construction

Descriptions

Descriptions from the eighteenth century provide important information regarding the design of the baroque clarinet. Buonanni's article 'Oboè' in his *Gabinetto Armonico* (1722) includes a description of the *clarone*:

An instrument similar to the oboe is called the *clarone*. It is two and a half palms long, terminating in a bell like the trumpet three inches in width. There are seven [finger-] holes in front and one behind. [Above these] there are two others opposite each other, but not diametrically. They are closed and opened by two keys pressed by the fingers when it is necessary to vary the notes, which are much lower than the sound formed by the oboe.

I have not found the inventor of this instrument referred to by any author.[18] Since no one has shown a trace of its antiquity, it is modern, originating from recorders. Because it has a high and vigorous sound it is not as easy to explain in writing, or to perceive as it is when you hear it. It is easy to recognize, even when mixed with the sounds of other instruments in symphonies.[19]

Buonanni's *clarone* was similar to the oboe but ended in a wider bell, three inches in width. He also emphasized that the two holes near the top of the clarone were not diametrically opposite each other as on his second type of *scialumò*, called the *calandrone*. These two physical characteristics—the wide bell and non-diametrical keys—are the most important features distinguishing the baroque clarinet (*clarone*) from the keyed chalumeau (*calandrone*). Furthermore, the latter was designed to play only in its fundamental register; the clarinet, on the other hand, had a register or speaker key operated by the thumb which when pressed, opened a small hole further up the bore, causing the instrument to produce easily the pitches of the interval of a twelfth above the notes in the fundamental register (*NGDMI* 'Clarinet'). The length of Buonanni's *clarone*, 'lungo palmi due e mezzo', was less than the oboe's 'circa due palmi e otto oncie' (1722: 67). Yet its range of notes descended much lower than that of the oboe. Its 'high and vigorous sound' was so characteristic of this instrument that Buonanni made a special point of mentioning it. On the basis of these points we see that the *clarone* was probably a

---

[18] This is understandable since Doppelmayr, the earliest to mention the 'inventor' of the clarinet, published his book in 1730.

[19] pp. 67–8: 'Un Istromento simile all' Oboè nominato Clarone è lungo palmi due e mezzo, termina con bocca di Tromba larga oncie 3. E bucato in sette luoghi nella parte superiore, e in uno parte opposta inferiore. Oltre a questi buchi ne hà due altri laterali con due molle calcata con le dita, quando bisogna variare li tuoni, li quali sono più basso della voce formata dall' Oboè. Chi sia stato il primo inventore di tal' Istromento non l'hò trovato riserito da alcuno scrittore, siccome da niuno sù descritto, segno manifesto non esser antico, mà moderno dedotto dalli Flauti, per avere voce più alta, e vigorosa, ne è si facile e spiogarsi colla penna, come la comprede l'udito, da cui si distingue, a conosce, benchè confusa nelle Sinfonie con la voce di altri Istromenti Musicali.' Cf. the trans. in Rendall 1971: 68–9 and Baines 1967: 297.

small, high-pitched clarinet in *d'* or *f'*. Its physical similarity (aside from its bell, mouthpiece, and two keys) to the recorder prompted Buonanni to suggest its origin to be from that instrument.

Ten years after the publication of Buonanni's book, the first definition of the clarinet appeared in J. G. Walther's well-known dictionary of terms and biography, the *Musikalisches Lexicon* of 1732. Like Buonanni he used the oboe for a comparison: 'Clarinet, a woodwind instrument invented at the beginning of this century by a Nuremberger. It resembles a long oboe, except for its wide mouthpiece; from afar the instrument sounds not unlike a trumpet. Its compass extends from *f* to *d'''*, as shown in Table IX, Fig. 1.'[20]

Walther's words 'at the beginning of this century' were obviously derived from Doppelmayr's biographical account of J. C. Denner; he also quoted Doppelmayr and cited his book in a biographical entry on Denner. His clarinet, resembling a 'long oboe', presumably was longer than Buonanni's *clarone*; the 'wide mouthpiece' is a characteristic of the earliest extant two-key clarinets (discussed below). Walther's observation that from afar the clarinet sounds similar to the trumpet is significant, for much of the music for the baroque clarinet relies upon a style similar to that used for the trumpet: repeated notes, fanfare motifs, incomplete arpeggios, and restricted use of the low register. (Its Italian name, *clarinetto*, is clearly a diminutive of 'clarino', or trumpet; see Altenburg 1795: 12; *Dizionario* 1975.) The range that appears in Walther's Table IX was described as *f'* to *d'''*, with all the chromatic notes except for the *c♯'''*; the lowest octave of *f* to *f'*, though included in the quotation cited here from Walther's text proper, appears to have been unintentionally omitted from his table.[21]

The earliest mention of the clarinet in a French publication is found in a brief entry (1753) in Diderot and d'Alembert's *Encyclopédie* (1751–65: iii. 505). Here the instrument is described as a 'sorte de hautbois'; the reader is referred to the article 'Hautbois' (Oboe) and to the 'Lutherie' plates.[22] There is no information on the clarinet in the article on the oboe, however, and the drawing of the two-key clarinet in the *Recueil de planches* (vol. v, Pl. 8; see Fig. 2.1) resembles the outline of the conically bored oboe (see Halfpenny 1954: 333). None the less, this engraving is accurate enough in its structural detail to be useful for making a comparison with photographs of some extant two-key clarinets given in the following section.

---

[20] p. 168: 'Clarinetto, ist ein zu Anfange dieses Seculi von einem Nürnberger erfundenes, und einer langen Hautbois nicht ungleiches hölzernes Blaß-Instrument, ausser daß ein breites Mund-Stück daran befestiget ist; klingt von ferne einer Trompete ziemlich ähnlich, und gehet von f bis ins d''' durch die Tab. IX. F. 1. angezeigte Klänge.' Cf. the trans. of a similar passage in Majer 1732: 32 in Kroll 1968: 21.

[21] The incomplete range was repeated in Wolf 1787 (p. 34) as well as in the edns. of 1792 (p. 34) and 1800 (p. 23). Walther (1732) corrected this error in his list of 'emandanda'.

[22] Diderot's definition is repeated in Boyer 1768 and Chambaud 1778.

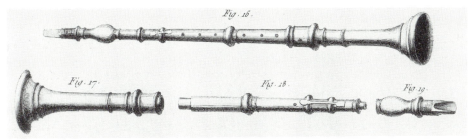

FIG. 2.1. A two-key clarinet made in three sections (Diderot and d'Alembert 1762–72, vol. v, Pl. 8, s.v. 'Lutherie, suite de instruments á vent')

Materials

The baroque clarinet was usually made of European boxwood, *buxus sempervirens*. It is wood of a delicate yellow colour, which darkens with age to a honey hue. Other materials used to construct the body of the instrument were ivory, plum, ebony, and pear (see Appendix and Zadro 1975: 249). Clarinets were usually divided into three sections: (1) mouthpiece with a large socket; (2) a middle joint with two non-diametrical keys placed on the frontal and dorsal sides of the tube, with one hole for the thumb on the dorsal side and six finger-holes on the frontal side; and (3) a lower stock combined with a bell, having one hole for the little finger which could be rotated to allow either hand to be placed lowermost. These instruments were also made in four sections, with the middle joint divided after the third finger-hole (cf. Rice 1984a: 22).[23] The sections were joined together by tenons fitting into corresponding sockets. To make a tenon, the end of one piece was thinned to about half its normal thickness; a corresponding amount was taken away from the inside of the piece which received the tenon, thus forming a socket. In order to give it greater strength, the wood round the socket was turned rather thicker than the rest of the tube and the end was often protected against strain and consequent splitting by a ring or ferrule of ivory, bone, or metal. (These ferrules, however, are lacking in some of the earliest clarinets, notably those by Jacob Denner.) The tenon was wrapped with waxed thread in order to make the joint airtight (Carse 1939: 58).

Mouthpiece

Fig. 2.2 shows a typical mouthpiece with its large socket from a two-key *d'* clarinet—part of an instrument made by Jacob Denner (Nuremberg, GN, No.

[23] A unique 2-key clarinet by Wietfeld (in the private collection of Keith Puddy) has the 7th tone-hole positioned for the right-hand little finger on the same joint as the other finger-holes, and a short stock-bell (cf. Young 1988: No. 22). One unmarked 3-key clarinet (Nuremberg, GN, No. MIR 426) is divided into 6 sections and was probably made during the early 19th cent. (Ross 1985: 167).

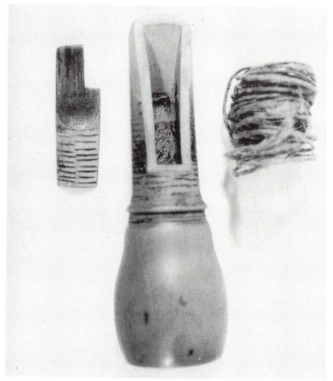

FIG. 2.2. Mouthpiece-socket joint, reed, and string from a clarinet in *d'* by Jacob Denner
(Nuremberg, GN, No. 149)

149).[24] We see a large opening or window bordered by thin 'rails', on which the
reed vibrated. It is interesting to note that the reed found with this mouthpiece is
known to have been made in the eighteenth century (*NGDMI* 'Clarinet'). Several
irregular shallow notches are carved on the outside of the mouthpiece, above and
below the window, as well as on the butt or lower end of the reed (as may be seen in
Fig. 2.2) to facilitate its binding to the rails by a string or twine.[25] At least four
ornamental rings of varying sizes have been turned just below the window. The
socket does not have a ferrule at its end, but its bulging outline indicates a
characteristic thickening of wood just below its mid-point (cf. Halfpenny 1965:
47). The mouthpiece of the clarinet in the *Recueil de planches* (marked 'Fig. 19' in
Fig. 2.1) has a smaller V-shaped window, a large ornamental ring followed by a

[24] The complete instrument is seen in Baines 1966, Pl. 621 (dated *c.*1730); *NGDMI* 'Clarinet', Pl. 3b; Van
der Meer 1982: 61–2 (dated *c.*1715).
[25] The lower horizontal rail of the baroque clarinet mouthpiece was replaced during the middle of the 18th
cent. with a longer flat area of wood called the 'table'. This helped to support the lower end of the reed.

pear-shaped socket, and what appears to be a ferrule at its end. Both mouthpieces are tapered on the opposite side, like the modern mouthpiece, to fit in the player's mouth, the pointed shape being called the 'beak'.

One interesting aspect of baroque clarinets is that the angle of taper varies from mouthpiece to mouthpiece. Another example of such a taper can be found on a clarinet in c' by Jacob Denner (Berlin, SI, No. 223; see Fig. 2.4). Inside all clarinet mouthpieces, opposite the reed, is a wedge-shaped tone-chamber which is made so that the lower portion of the bore is cylindrical in shape to match the bore of the upper joint (cf. *NGDMI* 'Clarinet'). David Ross points out that all of the mouthpieces made by Jacob Denner have very long window-openings of between 40 and 50 mm. These appear to be characteristic of an early stage of clarinet-making, since later makers, such as G. H. Scherer (*c*.1750), constructed considerably smaller mouthpieces with a window-opening of around 30 mm., a table (a flat area below the window) on which a reed could be more securely placed, and grooves regularly shaped for use in wrapping the reed with string (Ross 1985: 98–9, 120). The taper of the mouthpieces of clarinets by G. Walch and 'IŞW' are made in a long, concave arch called a 'duck bill' shape by Ross. In addition, the windows of these mouthpieces are shorter and narrower than those by earlier makers and include a table with narrower side and top rails. Furthermore, the sockets of the G. Walch clarinets are made with an extremely wide pear-shaped bulge (Ross 1985: 126, photos 40–1; Birsak 1985, photos 1b, 1c).

The various dimensions of the mouthpiece, along with the overall length, bore, and size of the tone-holes, affect the tuning of the clarinet. The drawings and measurements of three mouthpieces from two-key d' clarinets shown in Fig. 2.3 further illustrate variety in design, ornamental turning, and shape of windows. Other aspects of design such as the length and size of the window, the shape of the socket, and the style of ornamental turnings reflect a preference of the maker. Jacob Denner's mouthpiece, shown in Fig. 2.2, is similar in shape and ornamental turnings to the anonymous mouthpiece. Differences in measurements are also found in a reconstruction of a mouthpiece for a copy of the J. C. Denner clarinet in d' (Berkeley, UC, No. 19), based on measurements of mouthpieces by Jacob Denner taken by the modern maker Eric Hoeprich. For instance, the overall length of Hoeprich's mouthpiece is about the same as that of the Crone mouthpiece, but the width of the window is greater at the top (12 mm.) and the bottom edge (10 mm.) than in most of these examples (Hoeprich 1981: 21, 24).

Keys

The keys of eighteenth-century clarinets were forged commonly in brass, occasionally in silver (Rendall 1971: 20). Touchpieces for the thumb or fingers were

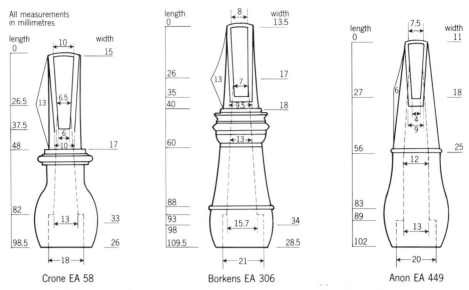

FIG. 2.3. Three mouthpiece-sockets from two-key clarinets in *d'* by Crone, Borkens, and an anonymous maker (The Hague, GM, Nos. Ea 58-X-1952, Ea 306-1933, Ea 449-1933, after Daines *et al.* 1976: 461)

either flat or curved and usually rounded at the upper end, but varied considerably in design. The tone-hole covers or flaps were usually made in a square shape, although a few were round. On the under-surface of each of these flaps a piece of leather was attached in order to make the hole airtight when it was covered (Carse 1939: 50). Carse explains the mechanical actions of the keys (1939: 46–7):

Keys are of two sorts, namely, the open and closed keys. The open key is one which stands open when it is not touched, leaving the hole uncovered; the closed key seals up the hole when the lever is not touched, and only uncovers it when the fingerplate is pressed down. The open key acts in exactly the same way as a finger over a hole, for when a finger falls on a hole, that hole is closed; similarly, when a finger falls on the fingerplate of an open key it causes the hole to be closed. The closed key acts in the opposite way and opens the hole when the finger falls on the fingerplate . . . An open key requires two levers, each pivoting on its own axle, and placed end to end so that one acts on the end of the other; thus, when the fingerplate is up the key-cover [tone-hole-cover] is also up, and the hole is open; conversely, when the fingerplate is pressed down the key-cover descends on the hole and closes it.

A closed key is a single lever rocking see-saw-wise on an axle; when the fingerplate is up the key-cover is down and the hole is covered, but when the fingerplate is pressed down the key-cover rises and opens the hole.

Each key lies in a channel cut in a raised ring or ridge of wood which runs around the instrument, and which has been left standing when the instrument was turned on the lathe. A thin wire of brass, about 1 mm. or less in diameter, acts as the axle on which a key pivots. It is inserted across the channel and through a hole in the middle of the key lever, and often has a hook on one end so one can extract it easily to change the pad (cf. Carse 1939: 53). Both open and closed keys are kept in their normal positions by brass springs, which are attached to the wood (in the earliest clarinets) or riveted to the under-sides of the keys (in the later instruments). The pressure of the spring upwards keeps the touchpiece up until it is depressed (Carse 1939: 47; Young 1982b: p. ix).

A key is commonly named according to the note which sounds when the touchpiece is pressed down. The closed key on the frontal side of the clarinet is usually called an '*a'*' key because on the three-key clarinet and later clarinets of the Classical period (with four to six keys) it produces a written *a'* when its touchpiece is depressed. However, on the baroque clarinet (with two keys) the note most often produced with this key is a written *bb'*. Therefore it will be necessary to refer to this key, when speaking about the two-key clarinet, as the 'frontal' key. The closed key on the dorsal side is called the 'speaker' or 'register' key; when its touchpiece is depressed, an overblown register is produced a twelfth higher than the notes of the fundamental register. The speaker key-hole is always lined with a metal tube, which projects internally about half-way across the bore to prevent the clogging of its tone-hole with moisture (Halfpenny 1965: 47). Fig. 2.4 shows a two-key clarinet in *c'* by Jacob Denner (Berlin, SI, No. 223) and the surviving middle joint (all that remains after the World War II bombing) of a two-key clarinet in *d'* by Johann Wilhelm Oberlender I (Berlin, SI, No. 2870).[26] This photograph clearly shows the tone-hole for the register key on each of these instruments to be higher on the bore than the tone-holes for the frontal keys.[27] Another photograph illustrates these keys on the Denner clarinet and on an unidentified nineteenth-century five-key clarinet (Fig. 2.5).

Looking now at the upper joint of the Jacob Denner instrument (in four sections) and the middle joint of the Oberlender clarinet (formerly in three sections, Fig. 2.4), we see that the upper turned ring carries the speaker key on the dorsal side. The lower turned ring has been channelled to provide room for the touchpiece of the speaker, so that it can be depressed by the thumb of either hand

---

[26] A photo of the complete clarinet is in Sachs 1922, Pl. 29, No. 2870 and Kroll 1968, Pl. 5.

[27] The placement of the tone-holes of these instruments is erroneously described in Rendall 1971: 68. Sachs (1922: 289, No. 2870, 291, No. 223) noted that the keys produced *a'* (frontal key) and *b'* (speaker), which Rendall seems to have interpreted to indicate that they were positioned diametrically opposite each other. Furthermore, Rendall may have been influenced by the descriptions of Altenburg (1904: 3) and Snoeck (1894: 165, No. 870), who both stated that the Oberlender clarinet was similar to the chalumeau and primitive in construction.

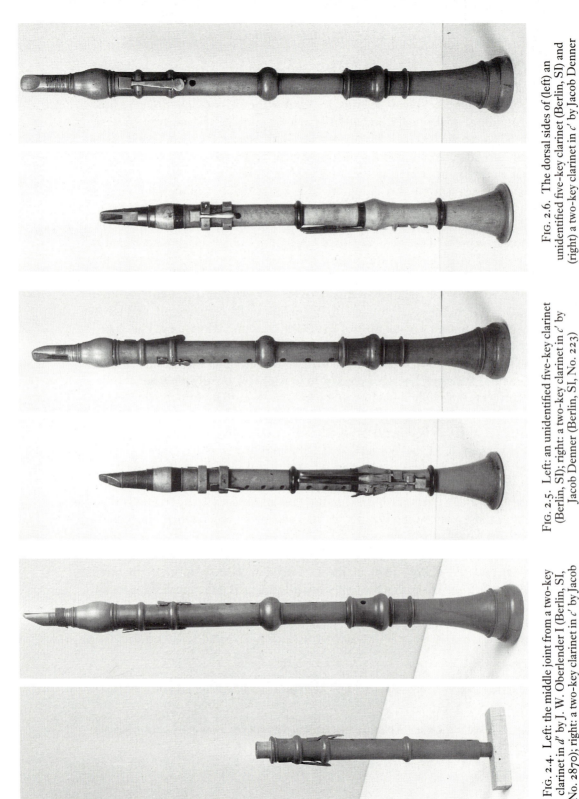

FIG. 2.6. The dorsal sides of (left) an unidentified five-key clarinet (Berlin, SI) and (right) a two-key clarinet in *c'* by Jacob Denner (Berlin, SI, No. 223)

FIG. 2.5. Left: an unidentified five-key clarinet (Berlin, SI); right: a two-key clarinet in *c'* by Jacob Denner (Berlin, SI, No. 223)

FIG. 2.4. Left: the middle joint from a two-key clarinet in *d'* by J. W. Oberlender I (Berlin, SI, No. 2870); right: a two-key clarinet in *c'* by Jacob Denner (Berlin, SI, No. 223)

FIG. 2.7. The mouthpiece-socket and upper joint of a two-key clarinet in *c'* by Jacob Denner (Berlin, SI, No. 223)

FIG. 2.8. The middle joint of a two-key clarinet in *d'* by Johann Wilhelm Oberlender I (Berlin, SI, No. 2870) (see Fig. 2.6 and cf. Fig. 2.1). Both rings on the joints of the Denner and Oberlender clarinets are rounded and have lathe centre-marks as a guide for boring the fulcrum pins on which the keys pivot (see Figs. 2.7 and 2.8; cf. Halfpenny 1965: 47). Some instruments have rings which are much squarer in appearance, and later three-key instruments have the *e/b'* key mounted on a small block of wood called a 'knob'. In Figs. 2.7 and 2.8 the different styles of ornamental turning and design of the frontal keys are also clearly seen.

Maker's Stamps

Makers of baroque clarinets often placed a distinctive stamp with their name, or an abbreviated version of it, on every section of the clarinet except the mouthpiece-socket.[28] Jacob Denner's stamp, as seen in Fig. 2.7, consists of 'I Denner' in a scroll with a pine-tree beneath separating the initials 'I. D.' The use of a pine-tree was a pun on the low German word *Denner*, which had the same meaning as the High German *Tanner* or *Tannenbaum*—a pine-tree (Fitzpatrick 1968: 81). Denner's contemporary Johann Wilhelm Oberlender I used a stamp showing 'J. W. Oberlender' in a scroll with the letter O beneath (Fig. 2.8). Oberlender's son Johann Wilhelm Oberlender II made use of a scroll encircling his name but included a pine-tree beneath it, similar to that found on Jacob Denner's instruments.[29] G. Walch, G. N. Kelmer, ISW, and I. G. Strehli also made use of scrolls encircling their names (Langwill 1980: 222; Ross 1985: 408, photo 52; Birsak 1973b, *Taf.* XVI, 40; Heyde 1979, *Abb.* 6). Two Dutch makers, Thomas Boekhout and Philip Borkens, made use of their surnames and first initials in their stamps, but each included the symbols of a crown above the name and a lion rampant below (Langwill 1980: 216).[30] The German maker Georg Heinrich Scherer also included a lion rampant or a fleur-de-lis beneath his surname on his two- and three-key clarinets. He added the letter D on all the joints of one two-key clarinet and T on those of another two-key clarinet, including the front and back of its mouthpiece (Hoeprich 1984a: 55 n. 5; Young 1986: 120–1).

During the second half of the eighteenth century, several English and French makers added their stamps to the mouthpieces of their clarinets and occasionally stamped a date of manufacture on some of the joints. The earliest known clarinet bearing a date is a five-key instrument by Thomas Collier; it is inscribed 'London 1770' on its stock-bell, and a star and the maker's stamp are placed higher on the

---

[28] A comprehensive listing with illustrations of such stamps is given by Langwill (1980: 211–27, 304); this is made up mainly of the information assembled by Huene (1974).

[29] Nickel (1971: 278–99) suggests that J. W. Oberlender II took over Jacob Denner's workshop on the latter's death in 1735.

[30] For photos of the stamps used by Denner and Boekhout see Hoeprich 1983: 60.

stock-bell.[31] An incomplete five-key a' clarinet by Jacob Grundmann in Poznan (MN, No. 184) was mistakenly reported to be dated 1759 on one joint and 1795 on another. A photograph of the instrument reveals that the date is actually 1795 (Young 1978: 128).[32]

The Middle Section and the Stock-bell

In Fig. 2.5 we notice a large, bulging socket, which is the upper ferrule of the lower finger-hole joint. This 'bulb-shaped' socket is found on several two- and three-key clarinets, including the instrument pictured in the *Recueil de planches* (Fig. 2.1). The clarinet by Oberlender is made with one joint for both its right and left-hand finger-holes. It carries only an ornamental ring, since this section is in one piece and does not need reinforcement such as is found on the finger-hole joints of Denner's clarinet. Three finger-holes are on the lower joint of the Denner clarinet (not clearly visible in the photograph). The stock-bell of this instrument has a large socket boss with a seventh finger-hole bored at a slanted or oblique angle, intended to allow the hole to be comfortably reached by the little finger of either hand. The section beneath the bulging socket appears to have a diameter similar to that of the lower joint, forming a bell from a gradual flaring and expansion. This section too is similar to its corresponding section on the instrument pictured in the *Recueil de planches*. According to Hoeprich (1984a: 53), another Jacob Denner clarinet in Brussels (MI, No. 912) is slightly conical in its exterior despite a cylindrical bore.[33]

The Jacob Denner clarinet in Nuremberg (GN, No. 149) and an anonymous clarinet in the Rubin collection each include a tuning-hole, placed half-way down the stock-bell on the back. These holes may have been an original feature of construction or a later adjustment to raise the pitch of the instruments: tuning-holes are found in the bells of oboes and oboes d'amour of the period. Ross (1985: 104, 112) states that the Denner clarinet in Nuremberg played much better in tune (at a pitch level equivalent to $a' = c.415$) than a Denner clarinet without the tuning-hole (Brussels, MI, No. 912).

Composite Instruments

Woodwinds assembled with sections from other instruments are called 'composite instruments'. Fig. 2.9 shows an unmarked two-key clarinet in the Musik-

---

[31] Now in Kneighly, England, Cliffe Castle Art Gallery and Museum, see Halfpenny 1965: 52 and *NGDMI*, 'Collier, Thomas'.

[32] A photo of the clarinet was sent to the author by Dr Benjamin Vogel of Warsaw University.

[33] Illus. in Hoeprich 1983: 60. A stock-bell by Johann Wilhelm Oberlender I is preserved at the Fürstliches Hohenzollernisches Museum, Sigmaringen (No. 306 K), see Bär (1989). The author wishes to thank William Waterhouse for this information.

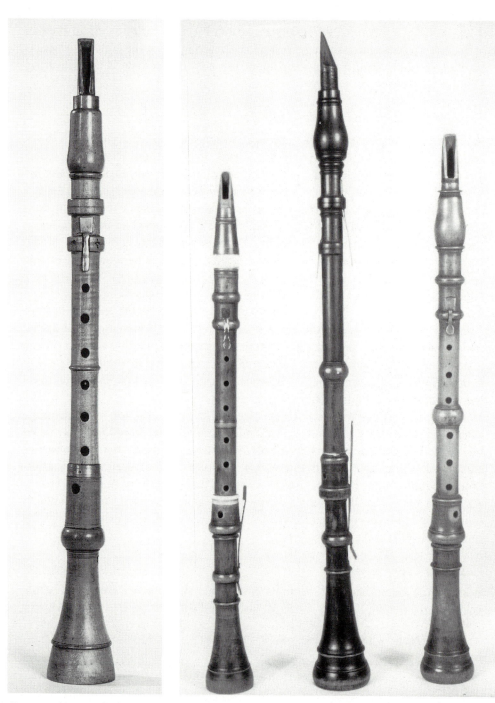

FIG. 2.9. An unmarked two-key
clarinet (Leipzig, KMU, No.
1457) composed of sections
from different instruments

FIG. 2.10. Left to right: three-key clarinet in *d'* by Georg
Heinrich Scherer (*c.* 1760, Brussels, MI, No. 924); unmarked
three-key clarinet in *a'* with the *e/b'* key placed on the back
(Brussels, MI, No. 913); two-key clarinet in *c'* by Jacob Denner
(*c.*1720, Brussels, MI, No. 912)

instrumentenmuseum Karl-Marx-Universität, Leipzig (No. 1457). This instrument was thought to be a chalumeau on the basis of a description of the notes produced by its two keys, *a'* (frontal key) and *b'* (speaker key) (Hochstrasser 1979: 14–15).[34] Dr Hubert Henkel, formerly director of the museum, stated that the register key is 23 mm. higher than the frontal key, indicating that it is a clarinet (personal communication). The photograph reveals that this instrument was assembled from sections that do not match in colour or grain of wood. For instance, the stock-bell, with a large metal ferrule on its upper end, is much darker in colour than the single middle section. The separate barrel is also darker than the middle section. Since these sections were not all made together, the instrument should not be understood as typical of most extant two-key clarinets.

It also appears that the original mouthpiece-socket was damaged on the top or beak and then cut off at the level of the turned ring. A socket was sunk in the upper end of the remaining piece and a metal ferrule added to take the tenon of a replacement mouthpiece. Mouthpieces of many baroque clarinets are not in their original state, because they were altered for particular players or refashioned following damage (cf. Halfpenny 1965: 45). The organologist H. Heyde (1970: 122, 124 n. 14) described the mouthpiece of this clarinet as being made of metal (see also Hochstrasser 1979: 15). Unfortunately, the material used to construct it cannot be identified from this photograph; only the uneven rails can be seen. A three-key clarinet in *a'* (Brussels, MI, No. 913; see Fig. 2.10), which was attributed to Lindner for many years, has been shown to be a composite instrument (Rendall 1971: 70, Pl. Id; Young 1982b: 80). Shackleton (1985) found that only the unmarked stock-bell of this instrument was originally part of a three-key clarinet. The lower joint, marked 'Lindner', is from a *c'* clarinet of the late eighteenth century, and the upper joint and mouthpiece-socket are modern reproductions.

The Third Key and Additional Aspects of Design

By 1750 several woodwind makers had added a third, open-standing key to the stock-bell, supplying the note *e* or the note *b'* (the latter produced with the aid of the register key) and linking the fundamental and overblown registers. This long '*e/b''* key was mounted on a ring of the bell-joint and, on the earliest clarinets, positioned on the back of the instrument to be operated by the right or left thumb (depending on which hand was placed lowermost). Such three-key clarinets were always built with a second or alternative hole on the stock-bell that could be

---

[34] Hochstrasser based his identification on a description by J. Zimmermann (1967: 67), who quoted Georg Kinsky's unpublished MS of vol. iii of his 'Katalog des Heyer-Museums in Köln'.

reached by the little finger, enabling the player to choose which hand would be uppermost; the hole which was not needed was then plugged by wax or a spindle-shaped wooden stopper (Kroll 1968: 19 n. 2). A few clarinets made at a later date have their *e/b'* key on the left side of the instrument to be operated by the left-hand little finger, and include one tone-hole on the stock-bell for the right-hand little finger. Fig. 2.10 shows both types of three-key clarinet and a two-key clarinet: a three-key clarinet in *d'* by Georg Heinrich Scherer (*c.*1760, Brussels, MI, No. 924); three-key composite instrument in *a'* (lower joint stamped Lindner) with the *e/b'* key on the dorsal side (Brussels, MI, No. 913); and two-key clarinet in *c'* by Jacob Denner (*c.*1720, Brussels, MI, No. 912) (cf. the dates given by Ross for the title-page of *The Clarinet*, 1983, 1). Both of the alternate holes are seen on the composite instrument, and the *e/b'* key on the left side of the Scherer clarinet is visible.[35] The extra length of the stock-bell of each three-key clarinet extended directly below a ring for mounting the lowest key.

A few three-key clarinets have an extra section added to the levers of the thumb key so that, when the stock-bell is turned around, this key is within reach of the left-hand fourth finger.[36] The redundant hole is now in the rear and may be permanently blocked. An anonymous three-key instrument (Nuremberg, GN, No. 150), as noted by Kroll (1968: 19 n. 2), is exceptional in regard to its possibilities for the use of the *e/b'* key (see Montagu 1974: 51, Pl. 35; Stubbins 1965, Pl. IV). It is pitched in *eb'* and consequently shorter than most three-key clarinets. Its *e/b'* key, mounted to a block on the stock-bell, is very long and accessible to either the left-hand fourth finger (when the left hand is higher) or the left thumb (if the right hand is higher). Montagu (1974: 51) wrongly assumed that both of these fingering positions are possible on every three-key clarinet. Unless the clarinet is very short, the *e/b'* key must be lengthened in order to be reached by the left-hand fourth finger.[37]

The Scherer clarinet in Fig. 2.10 has ivory ferrules on the top of its stock-bell and at the end of its mouthpiece-socket. Ivory ferrules are occasionally found on early eighteenth-century instruments but more commonly on clarinets built during the last third of the eighteenth century.[38] Scherer is the only known maker

---

[35] In a private letter David Ross states that this key was originally much longer than its present appearance would indicate. According to Ross (1985: 153), several 3-key clarinets play the note *b'* with either the third key or the frontal and dorsal keys.

[36] Examples are a clarinet by G. Walch (Salzburg, MCA, No. 18/2), a clarinette d'amour by ISW (Salzburg, MCA, No. 18/6), and 2 3-key clarinettes d'amour by P. Paur (Vienna, Gesellschaft der Musikfreunde, No. 130, and Vienna, Technisches Museum). See Birsak 1973b: 113 and *NGDMI* 'Clarinet'. At least 19 three-key clarinettes d'amour have been recorded in museum and private collections.

[37] David Ross, in a personal communication to the author, came to this conclusion after an examination of many 18th-cent. instruments. See also Ross 1985: 168.

[38]Ivory mounts are found on 5 2-key clarinets by T. Boekhout, G. H. Scherer, J. W. Oberlender II, J. B. Willems, and P. G. Wietfeld.

who constructed two-key clarinets made entirely of ivory. These two *d'* clarinets are constructed with two finger-hole joints, presumably because of the difficulty of procuring and working with a suitably long piece of ivory. Clarinets built during the mid-century differ in several respects from the earliest instruments. For example, Denner clarinets are characterized by a somewhat wide bore, approximately equivalent to that of the modern *bb* clarinet, as wide a mouthpiece, and large finger-holes. Later in the century, instruments were built with a smaller bore, favouring the higher part of the range, and with a very much narrower mouthpiece and smaller finger-holes. A good example is a two-key clarinet in *d'* by Zencker (Nuremberg, GN, No. 424) dated *c.*1765 by Martin Kirnbauer (1989: 427; cf. *NGDMI* 'Clarinet').[39]

Pitch Levels and Pitch Designations

Two-key clarinets are recorded in museum catalogues and in this book as being constructed in *d'* and *c'*, less often in *eb'*, *f'*, and *g'*. One exception is a two-key instrument in *bb* by Jean Baptiste Willems (Brussels, MI, No. 2573). The three-key instruments have a greater variety of pitches: *a* or *bb*, *c'*, *d'*, *f'*, and *g'* or *ab'*. As in the case of two-key clarinets, the greater number of pitch designations are *d'* and *c'*. The accuracy of pitch designations given in museum catalogues, however, is often questionable, particularly if an instrument is not playable or has not been tested with an electronic tuner. Furthermore, a designation may be given only relative to the modern standard of *a'* = 440 or the usually accepted baroque standard of *a'* = 415.

During the eighteenth century, the pitch used for tuning the clarinet varied according to the time and place. This diversity was not peculiar to the clarinet. The general situation was commented upon by the important German writer Johann Joachim Quantz (1752, 1966 trans.: 267):

The pitch regularly used for tuning an orchestra has always varied considerably according to the time and place. The disagreeable choir pitch prevailed in Germany for several centuries, as the old organs prove. Other instruments, such as violins, double basses, trombones, recorders, shawms, bombards, trumpets, clarinets, &c., were also made to conform to it. But after the French had transformed the German cross-pipe into the transverse flute, the shawm into the oboe, and the bombard into the bassoon, using their lower and more agreeable pitch, the high choir pitch began in Germany to be supplanted by the chamber pitch, as is demonstrated by some of the most famous new organs. At the present time the Venetian pitch is the highest; it is almost the same as our old choir pitch.

---

[39] See Kirnbauer's forthcoming catalogue of the wind instruments in Nuremberg, GN.

The Roman pitch of about twenty years ago was low, and was equal to that of Paris. At present, however, the Parisian pitch is beginning almost to equal that of Venice.[40]

Quantz states that the best tuning is the 'so-called German A chamber pitch' (1966 trans.: 268); this was the mean between the French and Venetian pitches and convenient for both wind and string players. Modern makers who construct reproductions of baroque clarinets, such as Eric Hoeprich of Amsterdam and Brian Ackerman of London, make their instruments at a pitch level between $a' = 415$ and $a' = 420$ and at the modern $a' = 440$ (cf. Ackerman 1989: 38). Ross (1985: 104–5, 132), however, found other pitch levels, although most of the extant baroque clarinets produce a sounding pitch of $a' = 415$. One example by Walch plays in the upper register as low as $a' = 405$, and the Jacob Denner clarinet in Berlin plays well in tune at about $a' = 440$. One solution to the problem of varying pitch levels was the use of extra finger-hole-joints (*corps de rechange*) for woodwinds, primarily flutes. Two joints are known to exist for two d' clarinets by Scherer (Hoeprich 1985: 435), and two three-key clarinets by G. Walch were formerly provided with joints for tuning to c' (Birsak 1985: 26).

Makers began indicating the pitch of their clarinets during the last half of the eighteenth century, by comparing the pitches produced in the upper register (the one most frequently played) to those of the oboe (cf. *NGDMI* 'Transposing instruments'). The sounding pitch of the clarinet when fingering the note c'' (the same fingering as the oboe's c') was then marked on the instrument with a single letter. For example, the clarinet pitched in c' was marked 'C', the clarinet in d' marked 'D', and the clarinet in bb marked 'B' (the German for B♭). The letter was carved or stamped on the upper section of the instrument just below the mouthpiece-socket and occasionally on every section. An early and atypical example is the three-key clarinet by J. W. Kenigsperger (Munich, SM, No. 110) marked 'G' on most of its sections.[41] This instrument is 518 mm. in length with a bore diameter of 12.5 mm., and appears to be too short to be a low clarinet in g and too long to be a clarinet in g'.

---

[40] Quantz 1752: 184: 'Der Ton, in welchem die Orchester zu stimmen pflegen, ist nach Beschaffenheiten der Orte und Zeiten immer sehr verschieden gewesen. Der unangenehme Chorton hat einige Jahrhunderte in Deutschland geherrschet, welches die alten Orgeln sattsam beweisen. Man hat auch die übrigen Instrumente, als: Violinen, Baßgeigen, Posaunen, Flöten a bec, Schallmeyen, Bombarte, Trompeten, Clarinetten, u.s.w. darnach eingerichtet. Nachdem aber die Franzosen, nach ihrem angenehmen tiefern Tone, die deutsche Querpfeife in die Flöte traversiere, die Schallmey in den Hoboe, und den Bombart in den Basson verwandelt hatten hat man in Deutschland auch angefangen, den hohen Chorton mit dem Kammertone zu verwechseln: wie auch nunmehr einige der berühmtesten neuen Orgeln beweisen. Der venezianische Ton ist ißiger Zeit eigentlich der höchste, und unserm alten Chortone fast ähnlich. Der römische Ton war, vor etlichen und zwanzig Jahren, tief, und dem Pariser Ton dem venezianischen fast gleich zu machen.'

[41] Visible in the photo in Young 1980: 26, No. 100.

A solution to this problem appears in the treatise of the Italian writer F. Antolini (1813: 18–19 n. 2), who stated that makers constructed clarinets in pitches determined by their fingerings for the notes *c″* and *f″*. On the basis of this evidence, it is likely that Kenigsperger identified the pitch of his instrument by the fingering for *f″*, indicating that it was tuned one whole tone higher than the clarinet in *c′* and thus was actually pitched in *d′* (according to the present-day method of pitch designation).[42] The length and bore of other *d′* clarinets are similar to those of this instrument, supporting this assumption.

The J. C. Denner Clarinet

It has been suggested (Hoeprich 1981) that an unusual and controversial three-key clarinet (Berkeley, UC, No. 19) is the work of Johann Christoph Denner. This instrument was formerly owned by Michel Harry de Young (1849–1925), the editor and publisher of the *San Francisco Chronicle* and a collector of all types of art and musical instruments. De Young was named commissioner from California to the Paris Exposition in 1889, and in 1892 he was selected as commissioner and vice-president of the World's Columbian Exposition in Chicago. Upon returning to California, he organized the California Midwinter Exposition in San Francisco, which utilized four buildings for exhibitions and opened to the public on 29 January 1894 (*National Cyclopædia* 1898: i. 269; Johnson and Malone 1930: v. 283–4; Driscoll 1921). Its four buildings formed the nucleus of the present-day De Young Museum (owned by the city and county of San Francisco). The Denner clarinet was exhibited with several other instruments during the Midwinter Exposition. From 1962 to 1968, seventy instruments owned by the De Young Museum were loaned to the music department of the University of California at Berkeley. On 19 April 1968 forty-one of these, including the Denner clarinet, were purchased from the museum by the university.[43]

The Berkeley three-key clarinet is incomplete, consisting of only a middle section and a lower stock-bell (see Fig. 2.11). The third key is mounted for use by the thumb, and double finger-holes are bored for the third, fourth, sixth, and seventh hole positions, with the bottom set duplicated to allow for left- or right-handed players (see also Fig. 2.12). The author found the maker's mark on this clarinet illegible; only a scroll is visible with a letter D beneath. J. C. Denner's

---

[42] Shackleton has stated in a private letter that he is sure that this instrument is pitched in *d′*; Ross (1985: 158), however, thinks that it is pitched in *eb′* at *a′* = 440.

[43] Photocopies of the loan form (1962) and purchase order (1968) were supplied to the author by Jeff Davis of the Department of Music and Ms Keith Stetson of the Music Library.

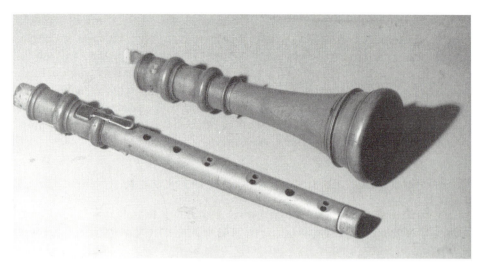

FIG. 2.11. A three-key clarinet in *d′* attributed to J. C. Denner (Berkeley, UC, No. 19)

stamp usually consisted of 'I C Denner' in a scroll, sometimes with 'D' or 'I D' beneath the scroll (Nickel 1971: 255–6; Langwill 1980: 217).[44]

Lawson (1980) and Young (1982b: 23, 25) have expressed reservations about accepting the attribution of this clarinet to J. C. Denner, basing their arguments mainly on the identity of the maker of the bass recorders sold in 1720 to Göttweig Abbey, near Vienna. These instruments bear the name 'I C Denner' in a scroll with the subscript 'ID'. Fitzpatrick (1968: 81, 85–6) suggests that Jacob Denner continued to use his father's stamp on his own instruments after his father's death in 1707, the subscript being Jacob's initials. Van der Meer (1970: 118), however, rejects this hypothesis, proposing rather that Jacob added his initials to instruments made and stamped by his father and subsequently sold these. However, another explanation for these initials, suggested to the author by Martin Kirnbauer, is that they were stamped by an official who regularly approved the instruments of woodwind-makers in Nuremberg.

If one accepts the Berkeley clarinet as being made by J. C. Denner, there can be no doubt according to Hoeprich (1981: 24, 27), that the third key was J. C. Denner's invention and not added at a later time. Indeed, the construction of the ring in which this key is mounted is not merely ornamental but clearly an original part of the bell. Although the bell section is not stamped, its colour, ornamental turnings, and key-mounts are identical to those of the middle section. Hoeprich believes that it is unlikely that this bell was made by Jacob Denner because of its

---

[44] A 3rd mark of J. C. Denner shows interlocking initials without a scroll.

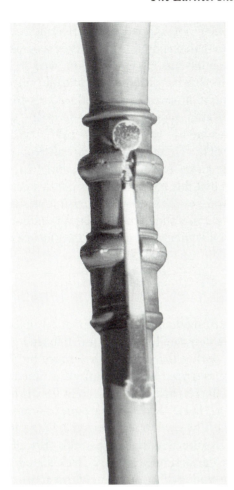

FIG. 2.12. The *e/b'* key on the dorsal
side of a three-key clarinet in *d'*
attributed to J. C. Denner (Berkeley,
UC, No. 19)

uneven profile, which is typical of earlier baroque instruments. The touchpiece
and round cover of the key on the bell (Fig. 2.12) are exactly the same shape as
those found on a number of extant bass recorders by J. C. Denner, and, moreover,
the extant instruments by Jacob Denner do not have two-piece, open keys of this
shape.

The unusual number of double holes on the Berkeley instrument, for the third,
fourth, sixth, and seventh positions, is notable. Indeed, in this respect the clarinet
is more typical of clarinets made during the last third of the eighteenth century.
Double holes are found, however, for the seventh positions on the J. C. Denner
chalumeau (Munich, SM, No. 136) and for the third and fourth positions of
several oboes by this maker. Furthermore, a recently found unique ivory recorder
by J. C. Denner has double holes for the sixth and seventh hole positions, making

it easier to accept the profusion of double holes found on the Berkeley clarinet (Young 1982a: 84). Clarinets with more than one double hole were recognized by J. E. Altenburg in his manual for trumpet and timpani players, written about 1770. He stated: 'The clarinet . . . can also be played chromatically, since it is provided with all half tones, and can thus modulate to a multitude of keys and play along in them. This may have motivated some composers to write special concertos and sonatas for [this instrument]' (1974 trans.: 14).[45] Finally, a three-key instrument attributed to one of the Denners was mistakenly recorded in the catalogue of the Brussels Conservatoire instrument collection (No. 913). Shackleton (1985) has recently shown that this instrument was not by one of the Denners but is actually a composite three-key clarinet with its lower joint stamped 'Lindner'. In my opinion the Berkeley clarinet should be accepted as authentic; it is then the only extant clarinet by J. C. Denner, and probably the oldest existing clarinet (cf. Hoeprich 1984b).

Keyless Clarinets

Keyless clarinets have occasionally been made as non-functional art objects. A clarinet made of faience (earthenware decorated with opaque coloured glazes) was part of the collection assembled during the nineteenth century by Savoye (1882: 14, No. 118), and as recently as 1979, a photograph of a nineteenth-century instrument made of faience appeared in an advertisement for the firm of Sotheby's in London (*Early Music* 7: 151). 'Keyless' baroque clarinets are depicted and described in four sources. The earliest is an engraving (*c*.1720–30) of several woodwind instruments by the German artist M. Engelbrecht (1684–1756).[46] In his commentary to a facsimile, Sydney Beck stated that a keyless clarinet was pictured on a table among other instruments, next to a seated gentleman playing a recorder. But on examining the orginal engraving at the New York Public Library, the author found that the touchpiece of the frontal key is visible, and that Engelbrecht was probably portraying a two-key instrument.[47] Another keyless instrument is found near the bottom of an English engraving of the title-page to Handel's opera *Alexander*, published in London by John Cluer in 1726 (Fraenkel 1968, Pl. 153). Coincidentally, this is the same year as the first known appearance of the clarinet in London (Rice 1988a: 389), although Handel

---

[45] Altenburg 1795: 12: 'Die Clarinette . . . auch dabey chromatisch blasen, indem sie alle halbe Töne darauf haben, und daher in die mehresten Tonarten ausweichen und daraus mit blasen können. Dies mag wol einige Componisten bewogen haben, besondere Concerte und Sonaten darauf zu setzen.'

[46] *Flötten, Hautbois, Flachinett, Fagot, und Clarinette &c.*, from the series, 'Varii generis instrumenta musica'. See Beck and Roth 1965: 30, 32.

[47] In a private letter David Ross suggested that this would be the case.

did not use clarinets in this work. Despite the lack of keys and the inaccurate number of finger-holes, the exterior turning and joint division clearly identify the instrument as a clarinet (Ross 1985: 82).

The next two sources are catalogues in which instruments are reported as being keyless. In the catalogue of the Stearns collection at Ann Arbor, Michigan, a keyless alto clarinet in *f* was described as being covered with leather on two of its four sections and having seven finger-holes and a length of 83 cm. (Stanley 1921: 95, No. 628). This instrument, however, was recently re-catalogued as a fake and attributed to the forger Leopoldo Franciolini (Borders 1988: 39, No. 628). The second catalogue is that of the private collection of Natale Gallini (now in the Museo Strumenti Musicali, Castello Sforzesco, Milan), which includes a photograph of a keyless eighteenth-century (?) soprano clarinet, described as a primitive clarinet 655 mm. in length, its wood covered in leather (Gallini 1953: 34, Pl. XXVII, No. 148). This report, however, is questionable, as many descriptions of instruments in catalogues have been shown to be erroneous. Furthermore, the construction of this instrument must be verified by photographs or a personal inspection. Thus of four reports of keyless clarinets, none can be considered conclusive.

Conclusion

The baroque clarinet has been documented from at least as early as 1710 in Nuremberg. Forty-four two- and three-key instruments have been identified as having been made in present-day Germany, Belgium, the Netherlands, Austria, and Czechoslovakia, and the many variations in design of the clarinets among the twenty-two makers respresented are typical of this period of hand-craftsmanship. By about 1760, several makers in major European cities had altered the design of the clarinet, creating an instrument that could easily respond to the increased technical demands of composers. This instrument with four to six keys is the clarinet of the Classical period.

3

Playing Techniques for the
Baroque Clarinet

The Two-Key Clarinet

THERE are two main written sources concerning the playing techniques of the two-key clarinet—the German treatises by J. F. B. C. Majer (1732, 2nd edn. 1741) and J. P. Eisel (1738, 2nd edn. 1762). Both include sections devoted to music theory and provide elementary instructions or general comments regarding a variety of wind, keyboard, percussion, and stringed instruments. These books are the earliest and most important published sources dealing with the baroque clarinet.

Range, Mouthpiece Position, Embouchure, and Articulation

In his *Museum Musicum Theoretico Practicum* (1732: 39) Majer writes a brief description of the instrument and includes what is now the earliest known fingering-chart for the two-key clarinet.[1] The chart shows separate fingerings for many notes of the range by the use of filled-in dots, indicating which finger-holes are to be covered and which touchpieces pressed (see Fig. 3.1). Majer's information on the clarinet (which occupies only a single page) is identical with one exception to that found in J. G. Walther's *Musikalisches Lexicon* of the same year (1732: 168). The exception is that Majer describes the range of the clarinet as extending from tenor *f* to *a″* and sometimes to *c‴*, whereas Walther (who does not provide a fingering-chart) specifies *f* to *d‴*. Heinz Becker notes in the 'Nachwort' to the reprint edition of Majer's treatise that the section on the clarinet was placed next to Majer's remarks on the trumpet, not on the basis of a similar playing technique, but because the clarinet sounds like a trumpet from a distance ('von ferne einer Trompete ziemlich ähnlich': Majer 1732: 39).[2] Eisel's *Musicus Autodidaktos* is arranged according to a format of questions and answers; his text (pp. 76–8) includes more information than is found in Majer's treatise.[3] The third

---

[1] All these details are unchanged in the 2nd edn. (p. 52).

[2] The Württembergische Landesbibliothek in Stuttgart owns a copy of this book with MS additions in Majer's hand (p. 71), none of which concern the clarinet. Cf. Warner 1967: 15.

[3] This remained unchanged in the 2nd edn. (pp. 54–7).

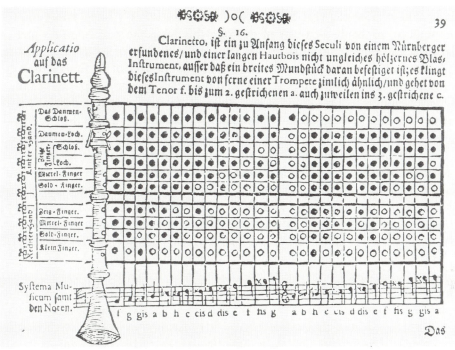

FIG. 3.1. The earliest fingering-chart for the two-key clarinet (Majer 1732: 39)

question in Eisel's chapter on the clarinet refers to a fingering-chart showing a range of *f* to *c'''* 'although it is not impossible for some virtuosos to play a fifth or sixth higher' [to *g'''* or *a'''*] (p. 76).[4] Diderot's *Encyclopédie* (iii. 505) includes only a brief mention of the clarinet, but the plates published in the separate *Recueil de planches* include a table which indicates the range of notes available on the majority of instruments illustrated (v, Pl. 8). Here, the range of the two-key clarinet is almost identical to Eisel's, staring on *f* and ascending to *b''*.[5]

Majer's illustration of the two-key clarinet in his fingering-chart is rather crudely drawn, but does indicate a flared bell and a bulbous barrel, typical of many instruments (Rice 1984*a*: 22). The position of the mouthpiece shows that the reed would have to be placed towards the upper lip, contrary to the usual playing technique of today. This position, however, was probably not the only one used by players of the baroque clarinet. For example, Hoeprich (1984*a*: 55 n. 5) noted that a two-key clarinet by Scherer, in a private collection in the Netherlands, is stamped as usual on all joints except the mouthpiece with the maker's name and

---

[4] 'Doch ist es manchen Virtuosen nichts unmögliches, eine 5te oder 6te höher zu blasen.'

[5] 'Table du Rapport de L'Etendue des Voix et des Instruments de Musique comparés au Clavecin ... clarinette; elle a d'étendue une 24eme'.

mark—the symbol of a lion. Scherer also added the letter T on all joints and the mouthpiece, probably as a way of marking this instrument as one of a pair of clarinets; the other, formerly in the same collection (now in the Rosenbaum collection), is identified by the letter D. On the mouthpiece of the first clarinet the letter T appears on both the reed side and the side opposite, clearly indicating a choice of mouthpiece position. Indeed, this conclusion is supported by a body of written evidence in treatises and clarinet tutors from the last half of the eighteenth century and the beginning of the nineteenth century which, while showing a preference for one mouthpiece position, does not rule out the opposite (see Charlton 1988: 397–9). Heinz Becker has suggested (*GLM* 'Chalumeau', 'Klarinette') that the German terms denoting mouthpiece position, *übersichblasen* (upper-lip playing) and *untersichblasen* (lower-lip playing),[6] should be replaced by phrases using the more precise anatomical terms 'maxillary' (with the upper jaw) and 'mandibular' (with the lower jaw),[7] which have been adopted for this study.

The French word 'embouchure' is now commonly understood to refer to the shape of the lips and their position over the teeth while playing a wind instrument. During the eighteenth century this term was sometimes used to indicate the mouthpiece (Jaubert 1772–3: ii. 184).[8] Players of the baroque clarinet probably would not have placed their teeth on the side of the mouthpiece which carried the reed, since this would inhibit its vibration. Instead, they would cover the teeth with the lip which lay against the reed to cover both the upper and lower teeth. The widespread use of this embouchure is supported by a general lack of tooth-marks upon surviving mouthpieces of eighteenth-century clarinets (see Hoeprich 1984a: 51). Both of these embouchures are described in later tutors for the classical five-key clarinet by several authors, including Vanderhagen (*c.*1785), Blasius (*c.*1796), Michel (*c.*1801), Lefèvre (1802), Backofen (*c.*1803), and Fröhlich (1801–11) (see Rice 1987: 332–45; Charlton 1988: 403–4).

Three possible methods of articulation are described in contemporary documents: with the chest, the throat, and the tongue. Valentin Roeser came from Germany to Paris as early as 1754 and was active as a composer and clarinettist. He mentioned the chest articulation in his treatise of 1764, near the end of the section on the clarinet: 'Many repeated sixteenth-notes are not used on the clarinet, since the chest has to substitute for the tongue stroke, owing to the reed's position beneath the palate of the mouth.'[9]

---

[6] First found in Backofen *c.*1803: 37.

[7] The terms 'suprajacent reed' and 'subjacent reed' were applied to these mouthpiece positions by Ligtvoet n.d.: 46.

[8] 'Embouchure' is also occasionally used today to refer to the mouthpiece of the clarinet or the head-joint of the flute. See Apel 1972: 287.

[9] p. 12: 'Beaucoup de doubles Croches dans le Mode parallele ne sont point en usage sur la Clarinette,

This type of articulation was used with the reed placed against the upper lip, as is indicated by Roeser's description and the maxillary position of the mouthpiece in his fingering-chart (*c*.1769) for a four-key clarinet.[10] It is possible that the playing practices of clarinettists in Paris influenced visitors from other countries. For instance, a letter from Johan Miklin (*director musices* in Linköping, Sweden) to A. A. Hülphers, dated 31 August 1772, mentions large clarinets 'used in concerts in Paris' and describes a manner of articulation similar to that mentioned by Roeser: '. . . The reed is not like that used for the oboe; instead one places a thin, flat, wide reed over an oblong opening. It is always stationary, and is lightly pressed by the lips, but never touched by the tongue. One must, so to speak, puff out the wind, but it is not heavy or hard to play.'[11]

The chest articulation used by the Würzburg clarinettist Philipp Meissner (active in Paris in the 1770s) is noted by Joseph Fröhlich in his extensive *Musikschule* (1810–11). He describes Meissner's use of chest articulation as resulting in 'a lively and brilliant playing style, coupled with a full tone capable of the most delicate shadings . . .' (Waterhouse 1986).[12] Fröhlich clearly explains how this articulation is accomplished when coupled with the maxillary position of the mouthpiece: 'To obtain this advantage one speaks a light h (ha) into the instrument, more firmly spoken only in lower notes, in whose performance one also gets support through the help of the lips' (Charlton 1988: 400).[13] This type of articulation would obviously limit the speed at which the performer could play. Fröhlich illustrates three types of articulation using the 'ha' syllable, but mentions that the placement of the mouthpiece with the reed above does not allow for the tongue to be used precisely and securely.[14]

Throat articulation is mentioned by several authors, such as Vanderhagen (*c*.1785: 9), Lefèvre (1802: 10), and Backofen (*c.* 1803: 11–12). This sort of articulation resembles the 'stroke of the glottis' advocated by Garcia in his treatise on singing (1970 edn.: 13) as 'The neat articulation of the glottis that gives a precise and clean start to a sound' (cf. Charlton 1988: 401). It seems possible that

attendu que la Poitrine doit substituer au coup de Langue, à cause de la position de l'Anche qui se trouve sous le Palais de la Bouche.'

[10] In his *Gamme de la clarinette* (Paris: Le Menu, [*c*.1769]); see Rice 1984a: 23–4, Pl. V.

[11] '. . . Röret är ej som på hautbois; utan öfver den aflånga öpningen lägges och inskjutes et tunt, platt bredt rör, som altid sitter fast, hwilket löst tryckes med läpparne, men aldrig får röras med tungan, utan måste man liksom flåsa fram wädret; är dock icke tungeller hårdspelt.' Quoted in Norlind 1937: 56–7. Cf. the author's earlier interpretation of this passage in Rice 1984b: 429, 431.

[12] p. 14: '. . . ein lebendiger brillanter Vortrag, verbunden mit einem vollen, der sanftesten Schattirungen fähigen Tone . . .'.

[13] p. 14: 'Um diesen Vortheil zu erhalten, spreche man in das Instrument ein leichtes h (ha) welches nur bey tiefern Tönen härter angesprochen wird, bey deren Vortrage man sich auch etwas Vorschub durch das Nachhelfen mit den Lippen verschafft.'

[14] See Charlton 1988: 400–1 for these and additional descriptions of the chest articulation.

the technique was used with faster passages that could not be played with chest articulation.

The use of the tongue for articulation, with the reed placed against the upper lip, was prescribed by the majority of writers from Vanderhagen (1785: 5–9) to Willman (1826: 24–5). These authors suggested that the player make use of several different syllables when tonguing, such as 'd', 't', 'tu', 'té', 'tú', 'tü', 'ti', and 'di' (Charlton 1988: 402, Table 1; Backofen *c.* 1803). The tongued articulation with the mandibular mouthpiece position was first recommended by the Norwegian bandmaster Lorents Nicolai Berg in his treatise of 1782 (discussed below). This mouthpiece position is noted by many of the authors who mentioned syllables used with the reed placed on the upper lip; after about 1830, the majority of players normally used the tongue when articulating notes, only occasionally making use of chest or throat articulation.

It is important to keep in mind that the blowing resistance on both baroque and classical clarinets is considerably less than on the modern clarinet. This is a result of the design of the early mouthpiece, which requires a reed (described by players as 'light' or 'soft'), with less wood in its width in order to respond easily in all registers. The pressure of the lips is also less when playing the early clarinets. Poor tone quality and erratic intonation are sometimes obtained if the player of the early clarinet is not aware of these differences. The mouthpiece of the modern clarinet requires a heavy or stiff reed in order to produce a resonant and brilliant quality which will easily be heard in today's large concert-halls. These observations have been verified by several players who perform on the early clarinets, such as Hans Rudolf Stalder, Alan Hacker, Eric Hoeprich, and David Ross (1985: 50–1; see Ackerman 1989: 40).

Hand Position and Fingerings

Eisel (1738: 76) states that the hands are placed as on the oboe, with the left hand above and the right below.[15] Apparently it has always been usual with woodwind instruments to place the right hand in the lower position because the work of the lower hand is slightly more complex than that of the upper hand (*NGDMI* 'Fingering', § III, 1). Eisel's fingering-chart is reproduced in Fig. 3.2 from a copy in the Bibliothèque Nationale, Paris, which includes unique handwritten additions and an inaccurate drawing of the clarinet.[16] His horizontal arrangement of filled-in circles indicates which finger-holes are to be covered and which touch-

[15] '. . . das Clarinett wird wie ein Hautbois mit Anseßung der lincken Hand oben, und der Rechten unten tractiret'.
[16] See the comments on this copy by Haynes (1978: 74).

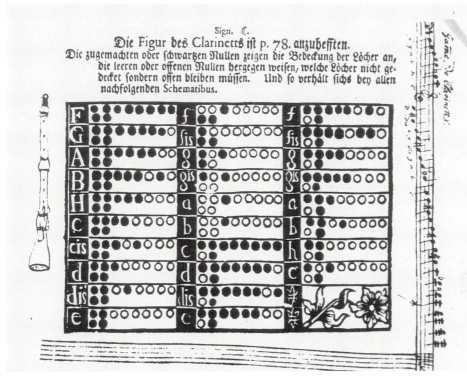

FIG. 3.2. Fingering-chart for the two-key clarinet (Eisel 1738, between pp. 78 and 79, Bibliothèque Nationale, Paris), showing handwritten additions

pieces pressed.[17] Eisel also gives a separate description of each fingering from *f* to *c'''*, correcting errors which incidentally occur in his fingering-chart for *f'* and *g♯''* (pp. 76–8). In Fig. 3.2 a handwritten scale entitled 'Gamme de Clarinett' appears vertically next to the fingerings. This scale, from *f* to *g'''*, excludes Eisel's *c♯'* and *g♯'*, but extends his range by four more notes from *d'''* to *g'''*. Whoever drew the clarinet here appears to have confused it with the oboe; its two keys are mounted in the same position as the oboe's *d♯'* (with the left hand lowermost) and *c'* keys on the lower section, and the finger-holes for the upper hand are too widely spaced. The oboe's double reed, however, seems to have been replaced by a single reed or clarinet mouthpiece.[18]

[17] This arrangement had previously appeared in the fingering-charts of Daniel Speer's treatise (1697). It would seem that Eisel partially modelled his treatise on this, since Speer's discussion also takes the form of questions and answers. See Speer's fingering-chart for the cornett in *NGDMI* 'Cornett', Illus. 2.

[18] A considerably more accurate and detailed drawing of the oboe is found in this copy of Eisel's treatise, along with additional fingerings for high notes; see Haynes 1978: 74.

All of the fingerings given in the charts by Majer and Eisel are compared in Table 3.1. The letter T denotes the thumb; the numbers 1, 2, and 3 represent the holes covered by the fingers of the upper hand, and 4, 5, 6, and 7 those covered by the lower. The letter S indicates the speaker key, and F the frontal key. Note the similarities for most notes in the low register *f* to *bb'*. Surprisingly, in the second or overblown register all of Majer's fingerings from *b'* to *a''* appear in Eisel's chart but produce pitches from a semitone to a minor third lower. It appears that the pitches given for one set of these fingerings are incorrect. The

TABLE 3.1. *Majer's Fingerings for the Two-key Clarinet Compared with those of Eisel*

Pitch	Fingering	
	Majer	Eisel
First register:		
f	T 123 456 7	
g	T 123 456	
g♯	T 123 45 7	Omitted
a	T 123 45	
bb	T 123 4 6	
b	T 123 56	T 123 4
c'	T 123	
c♯'	T 12 4	
d'	T 12	
d♯'	T 1 3	
e'	T 1	
f'	T 2	
f♯'	FT 12	T
g'	FT 2	2
g♯'	Omitted	S 2
a'	F	SF 2 (probably an error)
bb'	SF	SF 2
Second register:		
b'	ST 123 456 7	Omitted
c''	ST 123 456	ST 123 456 7
c♯''	ST 123 45 7	Omitted
d'	ST 123 45	ST 123 456
d♯''	ST 123 4 6	ST 123 45 7
e''	ST 123 56	ST 123 45
f''	ST 123	ST 123 4 6
f♯''	ST 12	ST 123 56
g''	ST 1 3	ST 123
g♯''	ST 1	ST 12 4
a''	ST 2	ST 12
bb''	Omitted	ST 1 3
b''	Omitted	ST 1
c'''	Omitted	ST 2

Note: Eisel's fingerings are shown only where they differ from Majer's. Cf. a similar table in Rice 1984a: 36–7.

fingerings for Eisel's second register are equivalent to those normally utilized on all later types of eighteenth- and nineteenth-century clarinets. Majer's fingerings for the upper register are quite logical (omitting only ST 12 4), yet when used with two-key clarinets they do not produce these pitches. Thus it appears that he was provided with fingerings for the entire range of the instrument (from *f* to *c'''*), probably by a musician, and mistakenly attempted to fit them into a range extending only up to *a''* (see Ross 1985: 76–8).

The lack of a fingering for *b'* in Eisel's chart prompted Baines (1967: 298) to suggest that 'the *b'* was made by squeezing the *bb''*'—that is, by tightening the lips. However, the majority of extant baroque clarinets played by Hoeprich and Ross are fully chromatic and capable of producing the note *b'*. The usual fingering-pattern for the notes making use of the two keys is S (*a'*), F (*bb'*), SF (*b'*) (Ross 1985: 102; Hoeprich 1981: 28).[19] Ross found only one two-key clarinet which produces a *bb'* by using both keys (by Crone, in The Hague, GM). Yet the mouthpiece of this instrument appears to have been modified recently, possibly affecting the pitch of this note (cf. Ross 1985: 140 n. 47). Significantly, the addition of the thumb on some clarinets with each of the keys lowers these three pitches by a semitone, corresponding to the pitches produced without the thumb on the three-key clarinet and later Classical-period clarinets (with four to six keys).[20]

The use of additional fingers may be necessary to obtain small pitch corrections to Majer's and Eisel's fingerings. For instance, what were considered errors in Majer's chart (the inclusion of the *a'* key and the use of the thumb for *f♯'* and *g'*) might have been very appropriate for a particular two-key clarinet (cf. Birsak 1973b: 120). Majer omitted a fingering for *g♯'*, a note which might have been provided by the use of Eisel's fingering for *g♯'* (S 2). The lack of a *c♯''* in Majer's chart might have been solved by covering half of the seventh finger-hole. Half-hole fingerings were surely known among the wind players who performed on the clarinet, since they are found in the fingering-charts for the flute by Hotteterre (*c.* 1728: 12–15; Pl. 1) and Quantz (1752: 35) (cf. Birsak 1973b: 124). Eisel's omission of a fingering for *b'* is not surprising considering that the notes produced by each of the two keys are the most unstable within the clarinet's range. A probable error in Eisel's chart is the inclusion of the speaker with the fingering for *a'* (cf. Birsak 1973b: 120). Eisel also omitted a fingering for *g♯*, a note which possibly could have been provided by the use of Majer's fingering for *g♯* (T 123 45 7).

---

[19] Hoeprich's chart of fingerings for the Denner clarinet (1981: 31–2) shows 4 half-hole fingerings using the double holes.

[20] Ross (1985: 160) noted these pitches while playing the 3-key clarinet by R. Paur and a few other instruments.

The Three-Key Clarinet

Two sources which include material pertaining to the three-key clarinet have recently been discovered by the author (see Rice 1984a: 23). They include the only known fingering-charts for the three-key clarinet as well as other unique historical evidence. Both were written after 1780 and testify to the continued use of this instrument alongside the more advanced four-, five-, and six-key clarinets. Their charts are, however, much less important and detailed than that found in Eisel's treatise, which served several early makers, according to Birsak (1973b: 132–3), as a model for tuning clarinets. The first three-key chart is found in the treatise by L. N. Berg (1782), written in Norwegian and entitled *Den første Prøve for Begyndere udi Instrumental-Kunsten* (*The First Training for Beginners in Instrumental Music*). Berg's book is similar in organization to the treatises by Majer and Eisel; he included a section devoted to music theory and discussed several stringed, keyboard, and wind instruments. In his chapter on the clarinet, Berg actually describes the five-key instrument (the most popular clarinet of the time) but provides as well the only fingering-chart known for the three-key clarinet with an *e/b'* key positioned for the left hand (pp. 48–52; Fig. 3.3 and Rice 1979–80). He

FIG. 3.3. The earliest fingering-chart for the three-key clarinet, with an *e/b'* key positioned for the left-hand little finger (Berg 1782: 50)

explains that this chart can serve as a model for all types of clarinet and recommends a less expensive three-key clarinet for the beginner (see Rice 1979–80: 49).[21] In this unique chart, Berg makes use of the numbers 1 to 7 to represent the fingers, and o for the thumb. The letter A denotes the *a'* key, and L the *e/b'* key, which was operated by the left-hand little finger. The vertical line above the o indicates the use of the speaker key. Berg's range is from *e* to *e'''*, greater than those in the charts for the two-key clarinet but simplified for beginners by excluding chromatic notes except for Bbs. His fingering for *bb'* (AT 2) appears to be in error; it should include the speaker key rather than the thumb, as found in all later sources.

Berg's Instructions

The reader will note that Berg specifies the sixth finger (ring finger of the right hand) in almost every fingering. This additional supporting finger, called a 'buttress finger' or 'Stutzfinger', is mentioned in tutors for the recorder, flute, and oboe of the seventeenth century onwards (see Hudgebutt 1679; Freillon Poncein 1700; Haynes 1978: 81–90). It is not surprising, therefore, that players of the baroque clarinet made use of the technique too. The employment of a buttress finger improved the resonance and tuning of certain notes; its use on the oboe, according to Halfpenny (1956: 51), was primarily for the purpose of eliminating unnecessary finger shifts and thus facilitating smoother playing.[22] Berg made the earliest known recommendation for the use of a mandibular mouthpiece position, stating that with its use a good tone would be produced, and that notes would be easily articulated by using the tongue (Rice 1979–80: 47). There seems to be a direct relationship between the mandibular position and the need for a buttress finger, since some instruction books by German authors of the nineteenth century advocate both (see Rice 1984a: 20).

Additional evidence concerning these playing techniques is found in a fine mezzotint (*c.*1750–60) by the Augsburg engraver Johann Elias Ridinger of a boy playing a clarinet in a pastoral setting (Fig. 3.4).[23] Ridinger's depiction of the clarinet shows a number of carefully drawn details which imply that it was copied from an actual specimen. For instance, the *a'* key is clearly shown, and a long cylindrical section below the lowest finger-hole includes a ring for the lowest key, situated appropriately on the back of the instrument. A wooden peg for the unused

[21] Berg appears to have been influenced by the treatise of J. D. Berlin (1744), the first music instruction book in Norway, since he praises (p. 59) Berlin's fingerings for the dulcian. See Græsvold 1976: 117.

[22] Berg's experience as an oboist, noted in his ch. on the clarinet, is reflected in his frequent use of the same buttress finger in his chart for the oboe (1782: 46).

[23] Photos also in Ross 1979: 34 and Hoeprich 1984a: 48, illus. 1.

FIG. 3.4. Engraving by J. E. Ridinger of a boy playing a three-key clarinet (*c*.1750–60)

little finger-hole is also evident, as well as an accurately drawn bell. The only questionable details are a somewhat truncated barrel and several over-sized tone-holes (Ross 1979: 34–5). Interestingly, it appears that the back of the mouthpiece is curved, suggesting that this is an early example of a player using the mandibular mouthpiece position in order to press the reed against the lower lip (cf. Ross 1979: 35; Hoeprich 1984a: 53). Furthermore, the position of the fingers suggests the use of a buttress finger (the sixth finger) to produce the notes *eb'* (T 1 3 6) or *f♯'* (1 3 6).

The 'Gamut for the Clarionet'

The second chart for the three-key clarinet appears on the flyleaf of a copy of *The Compleat Tutor for the German Flute* (*c.*1810).[24] It is a single page entitled 'Gamut for the Clarionet', with the fingerings and notes written out by hand (Fig. 3.5). The letters indicating the names of the notes and the text in the left-hand column appear to be printed. This is the only chart of its sort which seems to have been meant for an instrument with an *e/b'* key positioned to be operated by the thumb, as indicated by the listing of that key below the *a'* key and above the left hand. The

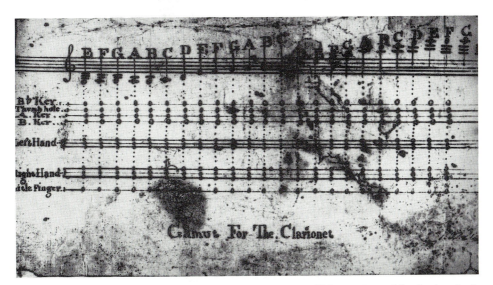

FIG. 3.5. A fingering-chart for the three-key clarinet with an *e/b'* key positioned for the thumb of either hand (*Compleat Tutor c.*1810)

[24] Reproduced on microfilm in the series Woodwind Instruction Books,'1600–1830: Music 3141; photo in Rice 1984a, Pl. VI.

range ascends to *f‴*, one half-step higher than that given by Berg, but its range is more limited than Berg's because all chromatic pitches, including *bb′*, are omitted. The fingering given for *f″* (ST 123 5) is probably erroneous, since it actually produces an *f♯″* on eighteenth- and nineteenth-century clarinets (Rice 1984a: 23).

A comparison of all of the fingerings in this chart and those given in Berg's treatise are listed in Table 3.2; this uses the same abbreviations as Table 3.1, with the addition of A (*a′* key) and B (*e/b′* key). The fingerings are almost identical if we

TABLE 3.2. *Berg's Fingerings for the Three-key Clarinet Compared with those of the 'Gamut for the Clarionet'*

Pitch	Fingering	
	Berg	'Gamut for the Clarionet'
First register:		
e	T 123 456 7 B	
f	T 123 456 7	
g	T 123 456	
a	T 123 45	
bb	T 123 4 6	Omitted
b	T 123 56	T 123 4
c′	T 123 6	T 123
d′	T 12 6	T 12
e′	T 1 6	T 1
f′	T 2 6	T 2
g′	2 6	Open
a′	A 2 6	A
bb′	AT 2 6	Omitted
Second register:		
b′	ST 123 456 7 B	
c″	ST 123 456 7	
d″	ST 123 456	
e″	ST 123 45	
f″	ST 123 4 6	ST 123 5 (probably an error)
g″	ST 123 6	ST 123
a″	ST 12 6	ST 12
bb″	ST 1 3 6	Omitted
b″	ST 1 6	ST 1
c‴	ST 2 6	ST 2
d‴	ST 23 4 6 B	ST 23 4 6
e‴	ST 23 B	ST 23
f‴	Omitted	ST 12

Note: Fingerings in the 'Gamut for the Clarionet' are shown only where they differ from Berg's.

ignore the consistent use of the sixth finger as a buttress finger and the *e/b'* key (for *d'''* and *e'''*) in Berg's chart. Those in the lower register are similar to those of Majer and Eisel, and those in the upper register to those of Eisel (cf. Table 3.1).

Kurt Birsak's investigation of the baroque clarinet involved playing two-key and three-key clarinets by G. Walch (Salzburg, MCA, Nos. 18/1 and 18/2, both *c*.1760), noting the pitches and frequencies on an electronic tuning device, and providing fingering-charts for the instruments (1973b: 120–33). It must be noted that the tunings determined by Birsak are atypical of clarinets from the period. He found the two-key instrument essentially in tune with itself except for the note *f*, which was too low in pitch. Overblowing this note by using the register key produced a *b'*, following Majer's fingering. On Walch's three-key clarinet, Birsak found that the placement of tone-holes for the two lowest notes, *e* and *f*, is such that they actually produce *f* and *f♯*. When overblowing the lowest note, *e*, he produced a *b'*. This result suggests that on this instrument the third key was added only in order to obtain a *b'*. Its *b'*, at 434 Hz, tuned well with its *a'* but was low in pitch in relation to its *c''* at 450 Hz. Birsak (1973b: 124, 128) suggested as an explanation for this that when Walch added the third key, Eisel's fingering was probably not known, or its principles rejected. He concluded that the tuning of both of these instruments was based on Majer's fingerings for the upper register.

Another three-key instrument—a clarinette d'amour in *ab* by ISW (Salzburg, MCA, No. 18/5)—revealed the same tuning in the low register as the three-key clarinet by Walch: *f* and *f♯* for the usual *e* and *f*. This instrument, however, was tuned according to Eisel's fingerings in the second register, and when overblown it did not produce *b'* with the third key in the upper register, but *c''* instead. A third three-key instrument—a clarinette d'amour stamped 'Ioseph/SW/Trifftern' (Salzburg, MCA, No. 18/4)—followed Eisel's fingerings in the upper register, producing a *c''* with the third key. But in the chalumeau register this key produced an *e* (Birsak 1973b: 128–9, Table VI, n. 163). Birsak's playing of these instruments indicates several differences from the usual tuning of other baroque clarinets. He attributed these differences to the instrument-makers' practice of tuning according to the fingerings given by Majer or Eisel in the upper register. However, another explanation of these peculiarities is that they may have been the result of enlarged tone-holes or alterations in the size of the bore.

Ross (1985: 130–6) has criticized Birsak's findings in several areas, which it will be useful to paraphrase here. Although Birsak does not state this in his catalogue, he found the facings on the original mouthpieces of the Walch clarinets unplayable and made use of reproductions for his playing tests. These may have produced results quite different from those intended by the makers of the clarinets. Birsak's tables make use of cents to show absolute pitch or frequency readings, but a more useful measuring unit for indicating pitch tendencies throughout the range is the hertz (used by Ross).[25] In Tables II and III of Birsak's catalogue, the pitch readings are given in reference to a standard of 440 Hz. The pitches of different fingerings are noted: some are transposed a full tone higher to correspond with the pitch of the *d'* clarinet, but others are mistakenly transposed by only a semitone. Thus the pitch tendencies of the clarinets studied are not clearly shown. Ross concludes his study of the clarinets by Walch at Salzburg (1985: 123–36) by stating that they have more intonation problems than other baroque clarinets tested, and that it would be unwise to take their tunings and particular fingering-patterns as a standard for the baroque clarinet.

Conclusion

The baroque clarinet should be viewed as a capable member of the woodwind family during the first half of the eighteenth century. It can be played chromatically from *e* or *f* to *d'''* or higher. Its mouthpiece is often positioned so that the reed may be placed against the upper lip, but the player always has the option to turn the mouthpiece so that the reed will be against the lower lip. The blowing resistance is greater than that experienced by playing the recorder but less than that of the modern clarinet. Its limitations of technique are certainly no greater than those of any other baroque woodwind instrument (see Hoeprich 1983: 62). Indeed, the composers who wrote for the clarinet, who are discussed in Chapter 4, made effective use of the instrument's distinctive and variable tone-quality.

---

[25] The cent is the unit of a scientific method of measuring musical intervals introduced by A. J. Ellis (1814–90); it has been widely adopted in acoustics and ethnomusicology. The cent is equal to 0.01 of the semitone of the equal-tempered scale; thus the octave equals 1,200 cents. The Hz is a unit of frequency equal to 1 cycle/sec. See Apel 1972: 140 and *Webster* 1973: 537.

4

Music for the Baroque Clarinet

MUSIC with parts intended specifically for the baroque clarinet began to appear during the second decade of the eighteenth century. The majority of these parts exhibit a style of writing characterized by repeated notes, incomplete arpeggios, fanfare motifs, a limited range, and restricted use of the low register. In works composed after about 1730, other characteristics which take on a greater import-ance are a lyrical style of melodic writing, scale passages, leaps of an octave or more, and a more frequent use of the low register. The following discussion of manuscript and published music covers the period from about 1712 to 1756, when the baroque clarinet was played by soloists and orchestral musicians. (The baroque instrument continued to be used primarily by military musicians and amateurs until the end of the eighteenth century and at the beginning of the nineteenth, but the majority of their music was not published or preserved.) Music written in France and England from the 1760s onwards is not included; this was probably played on 'classical' clarinets having four, five, or six keys, as is shown by a number of extant instruments, particularly from Belgium, Germany, and England. This is also supported by the lack of extant examples of baroque instruments made or preserved in England or France. Moreover, a general change in musical style occurred during the 1750s and 1760s which coincided with the emergence of the 'classical' clarinet.

The Early Duos

The earliest known musical works calling for clarinets were published by the Frenchman Estienne Roger in Amsterdam between about 1712 and 1715. They are an anonymous collection of duos in two volumes entitled *Airs à Deux Chalumeaux, Deux Trompettes, deux Haubois, deux Violons, deux Flûtes, deux Clarinelles, ou Cors de Chasse.*[1] Only a second edition, published by Roger and M. C. Le Cène (*c.*1717–22), is extant (see Dart 1951: 40).[2] The name 'clarinelles' in the

---

[1] Dated in Lesure 1969: 84. Dr Shackleton has informed the author that Roger did not mention the clarinet in an advertisement of 1706–8 (cf. *NGDMI* 'clarinet').

[2] Nos. 1, 2, 3, 24, and 60 ed. H. Becker in *Klarinetten-Duette* 1954: 3–6.

title is surely a printer's error since the catalogues of Roger (1716)[3] and his successor Le Cène (1737)[4] advertised these duos using the word 'clarinette'. Another book of duos, not known to be extant, was advertised in Roger's catalogue of 1716 (No. 358) as *Airs à 2 Clarinettes ou deux Chalumeaux &c. Composées par Mr. Dreux*. Walther (1732: 218) identified the flautist Jaques (*sic*) Philippe Dreux (by then deceased) as both the composer of these airs and the editor of three books of *Fanfares pour deux Chalumeaux ou deux Trompettes*. In another catalogue by Roger from 1716 appears the heading: 'Pieces pour la clarinette et le cor de Chasse'.[5]

The anonymous *Airs* of *c.* 1717–22 were published in two volumes, each having two part-books named 'premier dessus' and 'second dessus' respectively. The first volume contains thirty-four airs and the second forty-four, numbered consecutively from 1 to 78 (Dart 1951: 40; Lawson 1981a: 36, 188 n. 16). The music in both volumes requires a diatonic range of d' to b'', omitting e' but with an occasional $g\sharp'$, while the upper part includes one a in No. 78. About two-fifths of these duos may be played using only notes from the harmonic series and are therefore suitable for brass instruments (Lawson 1981a: 37; cf. *NGDMI* 'Harmonics', Table 1). The last two airs in the second volume (Nos. 77 and 78) contain an unfigured bass part using only the notes A and d which, according to Dart (1951: 40), was probably intended for the timpani. Lawson notes, in No. 78 (1974: 127–8, Ex. 2), the wide range of the 'premier dessus', a to a'', and the exclusive use of the notes of the D major arpeggio, suggesting that this piece was written for a brass instrument.

According to Lawson (1981a: 37), alto chalumeaux pitched in *Chorton* with their lowest note sounding d' could play all of the duets except No. 78; conventional soprano chalumeaux with a doubled seventh finger-hole could also be used for all but three. The inclusion of violins and flutes in the titles of the *Airs* was probably intended to secure a wider sale, since the music includes repeated notes and broken-chord figures more typical of idiomatic brass writing (Lawson 1981a: 37). For example, the third duet (Ex. 4.1) illustrates the trumpet-like character of many of these pieces and a popular echo effect. Although this music was not intended exclusively for the clarinet, some of its stylistic characteristics are similar to those found in later music which is designated as being for this instrument alone. Two-key clarinets pitched in d' (transposing the parts into C major) are best suited for the technical demands, because they would require fewer awkward cross-fingerings than clarinets pitched in c'.

---

[3] *Catalogue de Musique* (appended to Vairasse 1716: 310), Nos. 348–9.
[4] *Catalogue des livres de Musique* (repr. in Lesure 1969), 19.
[5] *Catalogue de Musique* (appended to Aubin 1716), [1].

Ex. 4.1. *Airs* (*c.*1717–22), No. 3

Vivaldi: Juditha Triumphans

In his oratorio *Juditha Triumphans* (RV 644, 1716), Antonio Vivaldi (1678–1741) included two 'clareni' in the nineteenth piece—a chorus entitled 'Plena nectare'.[6] One part is written for two instruments in unison in B flat major with a one-octave range of *bb'* to *bb"* (Ex. 4.2). It might be thought that Vivaldi's use of the term 'clareni' suggests that trumpets, not clarinets, were intended. Although the part exhibits a trumpet-like character in its use of repeated notes and triadic figures it would not have been playable on trumpets of Vivaldi's time, which were pitched in *d'* and *c'* (see Bate 1978: 114). Furthermore, during the eighteenth century, German composers (not Italians) used the term 'clarino' to refer to the trumpet as

---

[6] Autograph in the Biblioteca Nazionale Universitaria, Turin, Collezione Foá 28. See the fac. edn. (1948) and modern edn. (1971).

Ex. 4.2. Vivaldi (1948), *Juditha Triumphans*, chorus 'Plena nectare': 'clareni' part

well as to a specific register of the trumpet (Kolneder 1951: 187, 1955b: 209–10; Talbot 1978: 162–3).[7] For instance, J. Mattheson (1713: 265) defined the trumpet as 'die Trompete/Ital. Tromba oder Clarino'. A part for the *tromba* is also included by Vivaldi in the overture, and several scholars have associated the designation 'clareni' with other names used in reference to the clarinet by Vivaldi. For instance, Kolneder (1955b: 209–10) and Talbot (1978: 163) cited 'clarinet-(ti)' in the concertos RV 559 and 560, 'claren(i)' in the concerto RV 556, and 'clarini' in the slow movement of RV 556. *Clarone*, a term similar to those used by Vivaldi, was used by Buonanni (1722), as noted in Chapter 2, in reference to the two-key clarinet. Selfridge-Field (1975: 256–7, 1979: 139) also believes that the parts for 'clareni' were meant for clarinets, and has mentioned Vivaldi's manifest interest in and access to novel instruments. He travelled extensively in the German-speaking domains, Holland, perhaps France, and much of Italy, where he may have heard the clarinet. In addition, the Pietà audience regularly brought

[7] This interpretation is supported by a definition of 'clarino' as a 'klarinet' by the Dutch writer Reynvaan (1789: i. 150) who cites an Italian derivation.

gift-bearing European nobility of many nationalities into its midst. If we are correct in assuming that Vivaldi's 'clareni' were clarinets, then these parts are the earliest known instance of orchestral music for the clarinet. Two-key clarinets pitched in *bb*, as suggested by Talbot (1978: 163), are well suited for the cross-fingerings required in this work. Clarinets in *c'*, however, could also have been used for these very restricted parts, and are more likely to have been played, since the earliest extant instruments are pitched in *c'* and *d'*.[8]

Interestingly, in *Juditha* Vivaldi employed almost every instrument that was in use at the Pietà. The score calls for two recorders, two oboes, a soprano chalumeau, two clarinets, two trumpets with timpani, a mandolin, four theorbos (playing in two parts), an obbligato organ, five violas *all'inglese*, and a viola d'amore in addition to strings and continuo. Some players probably doubled on more than one instrument since, for example, only one kind of woodwind instrument is heard at a time (Talbot 1978: 196). Evidence presented in the next section and in Chapter 5 shows that the baroque clarinet was often played by a musician whose main instrument was the flute, oboe, bassoon, or French horn. The music for clarinet in Vivaldi's concertos is stylistically more advanced than the parts in *Juditha* and therefore is discussed later in this chapter.

Caldara

The prolific composer Antonio Caldara (*c.*1670–1736) was born in Venice and held important appointments in Mantua, Rome, and Vienna. He may have become acquainted with the clarinet through performances of Vivaldi's works in Venice. After his appointment in 1699 to the court of Ferdinando Carlo in Mantua, he undertook additional work in Venice, Florence, Genoa, and Rome between 1699 and 1707. On 1 January 1717 Caldara was officially appointed vice-Kapellmeister to the court of the Emperor Charles VI in Vienna (*Grove 6* 'Caldara, Antonio').

On 4 November 1718 Caldara's opera *Ifigenia in Aulide* was produced in Vienna, and it was revived there on 22 November 1723 (Loewenberg 1978: 136).[9] In one manuscript of this opera, a sinfonia, the alto solo 'Asia tremi', and the chorus 'Nel Nome Augusto sonori' in act I scene ii, two parts are found for 'Clarinetti' with trumpets and timpani (cf. Lawson 1986: 554).[10] The use of the

---

[8] For the view that these parts were meant for the trumpet see Lebermann 1954.

[9] The suggestion that it was first performed in Vienna in 1714 is probably erroneous, since Caldara is known to have been in Rome during this time. Cf. *Grove 6* 'Caldara, Antonio'.

[10] MSS of *Ifigenia in Aulide* are in the Österreichische Nationalbibliothek, Vienna, and the Conservatoire Royal de Musique, Brussels. The author thanks Colin Lawson for the use of photocopies of act I of the Brussels MS at the Open University, Cardiff.

Ex. 4.3. Caldara (1718), *Ifigenia in Aulide*, act I scene ii, contralto solo 'Asia tremi', measures 46–57: clarinet, trumpet, and timpani parts

term 'clarinetti' in the manuscript from the Brussels Conservatoire library may indicate the clarinet rather than the clarino, an instrument used extensively at the Viennese court. However, unlike Vivaldi's 'claren' part in B♭ major, these parts in C major are playable on *C* trumpets of the time. Thus an exact identification of them must remain speculative. The Viennese practice of trumpet playing for liturgical and court functions and Caldara's writing for trumpets, clarini, and timpani from 1709 to 1736 is documented by Brown (1987).[11] It is possible,

[11] In a personal communication to the author, Professor Brown has stated that he is unaware of any Viennese MS by Caldara which specifies 'clarinetti' rather than 'clarini'.

however, that the clarinet was used as a special instrument in a later version of the opera, since players of the chalumeau were not listed in the Hofkapelle orchestra, but Caldara and other Viennese composers of the period wrote for it in several operas and oratorios (see Lawson 1981a: 177–8; Selfridge–Field 1987: 138; Kubitschek 1987: 109–19). The pairing of clarinets and trumpets may have been prompted by their similar tone-colours, not unlike Telemann's later use of the instrument (discussed below). The three sections are written in C major for clarinets in *c'*, with restricted ranges from *c'* to *b''* for the first clarinet and *c'* to *g''* for the second. The parts do not include the note *b'* or any accidentals; they consist mainly of stepwise motion and triadic figures and are easily played on two-key clarinets of this period (see Ex. 4.3).

Conti

Francesco Bartolomeo Conti (1681–1732) became associate theorbo player at the Habsburg court in Vienna in April 1701. He was officially designated court composer in 1713 and continued to perform on the theorbo (*Grove 6* 'Conti, Francesco Bartolomeo'). Like Vivaldi, he wrote for the chalumeau in several cantatas (see Lawson 1981a: 62–3) and for 'clarinetti' in *c'* in at least one version of the comic opera *Don Chischiotte in Sierra Morena* (1719).[12] This work was particularly popular and was given in Brunswick from February 1720 until 1738 and in Hamburg from 5 October 1722 until 1737.[13] The manuscript in which the clarinet is specified may have been produced in Brunswick or Hamburg.

Telemann

Georg Philipp Telemann (1681–1767) wrote for the chalumeau from 1718 onwards; he was one of the earliest composers to write for the clarinet, beginning in 1721. According to Lawson (1983: 18), the chalumeaux called for in Telemann's cantatas, oratorios, and serenatas were clearly regarded as desirable for their delicate tone-colours and were often reserved for poignant dramatic moments. In contrast, the clarinet assumed a less important position in his music. Presented here is a list of Telemann's works employing the clarinet, including in each case the key and range of the parts, the tonality of the clarinets required, and

[12] Title-page and opening of the 'Ouvertura Andante' reproduced in *MGG* 'Conti'. This version of the opera has not been available to the author. A copy in the Österreichische Nationalbibliothek, Vienna (Sig. 17.207), does not include clarinet parts.

[13] German texts were provided for some of the arias in Brunswick by J. S. Müller and in Hamburg by Plochäu and Mattheson. See Loewenberg 1978: 140; *MGG* 'Conti'; '*Grove 6* 'Conti, Francesco Bartolomeo'; and Gerber 1812–14: ii/1. 771–2.

comments on the writing.[14] Items 1, 2, and 5 include autograph parts; the parts in items 3 and 4 are copied in later hands.

1. Cantata, 'Wer mich liebet, der wird mein Wort halten' (1721).[15] C major; *c'* to *a''* for clarinet in *d'* (the orchestral score is written in D major). One part is marked 'Clarinetto et Corno da Caccia' (see Ex. 4.4). Here the clarinet appears in the second aria and a 'Corno da caccia ex f' in the third aria; the instruments were probably intended to be played by the same musician (piccolo parts are also included for oboes 1 and 2). The writing for the horn is considerably more difficult than that for the clarinet, requiring a range ascending to *e'''*, the twentieth harmonic. Telemann's clarinet part is technically more demanding than that found in the anonymous *Airs*, Vivaldi's *Juditha*, and Caldara's *Ifigenia in Aulide* discussed above, including several leaps of as much as a ninth. Together with this larger range we find dynamic markings for *forte* and *piano*. Two alternative clarinet parts for this cantata are extant; they appear to have been written at a later date and introduce a more elaborate version with the use of triplets to replace groups of eighth-notes.

2. Cantata, 'Christus ist um unsrer Missetat willen' (1721). C major; first clarinet, *c''* to *c'''*; second clarinet, *c'* to *g''*; for clarinets in *d'*. Clarinets are called for in the second and fourth arias and in a concluding choral section. The first clarinet part includes some thirty-second-notes, turns, trills, and the notes *f♯''* and *bb''* in the fourth aria (see Ex. 4.5). The two clarinets are often paired in thirds or fifths, and there are additional parts in D major for clarinets in *c'*, which have been crossed out. Alternative autograph parts for 'Oboe I^mo obligato', 'Oboe 2do obligato', and 'Pro Organo' include the stipulation 'In Ermangelüng der Clarinetten' (in the absence of clarinets). Thus it appears that during the 1720s the clarinet was not always available to Telemann.

3. Cantata, 'Jesu, wirst du bald erscheinen' (first performed in 1719). B flat major; *f'* to *bb''* for clarinet in *c'*. One of the orchestral parts for the first and second arias is marked 'Cornettino vel Clarinetto' (Ex. 4.6). It is in a different (and probably later) hand from the autograph parts, though this is not identified in the catalogue by Süss and Epstein (1926; see Lawson 1981b: 316). The consistent employment of broken-chord figures and repeated notes is stylistically appropriate for the baroque clarinet. It is less likely to be for a 'cornettino' because of its low range and awkward key, even though it is marked for this instrument and the words 'vel Clarinetto' seemed to have been added as an afterthought. This part is

---

[14] While most of the comments in this list are based on the author's own study of the music, in some cases he has adopted Lawson's observations in 1981b: 315–16, 318, and 1983: 18. For further information on the cantatas see Menke 1982–3: i. 16, No. 151; 41, No. 434; 91, No. 988; 145, No. 1589.

[15] The beginning of the 2nd aria in its full autograph score is reproduced in Lawson 1979: 352.

Ex. 4.4. Telemann (1721b), 'Wer mich liebet, der wird mein Wort halten': 'Clarinetto et Corno da Caccia' part

Ex. 4.5. Telemann (1721a), 'Christus ist um unsrer Missetat willen': 'Clarinetto 1' part

Ex. 4.6. Telemann (1719), 'Jesu, wirst du bald erscheinen': 'Cornettino vel Clarinetto' part

Ex. 4.6. – *cont.*

slightly awkward in fingering on a *c'* clarinet and could have been played on a *bb* instrument, transposing at sight. Autograph parts for 'cornetto' and three trombones in A major are extant, as well as a score in C major including these parts. Clarinet parts do not appear in this score.

4. Cantata, 'Ein ungefärbt Gemüte Aufgenommen' (first performed in 1722). F major; first clarinet, *f'* to *f'''*; second clarinet, *f'* to *bb''*; for clarinets in *d'*. These are additional parts in a later hand which double the horn parts in three arias and a concluding choral section. The use of pitches above *c'''* (as in the third aria) is more commonly found in parts from the mid-eighteenth century. Clarinet parts do not appear in two scores of this work.

5. 'Serenata, zum Convivio der HH Burgercapitains' (1728). D major; *e'* to *g''* for clarinet in *d'*. After 1721, when Telemann moved to Hamburg, he was required once a year to entertain the guests of the commandant of the city's militia by producing a 'Kapitänsmusik' consisting of an oratorio and a serenata (*Grove 6* 'Telemann, Georg Philipp'). In the bass solo with chorus 'Der höhe Schutzherr dieses Staats', the orchestra comprises a *tromba, clarinetto*, second oboe, and strings.[16] The clarinet and trumpet parts are stylistically indistinguishable from each other and at some points in the score even share the same stave. Indeed, here

[16] Part of the score of this aria is in Lawson 1981b: 319, Ex. 6, and 1983: 19, Ex. 1.

the clarinet seems to have been a genuine substitute for an unavailable second trumpet rather than offering a subtle contrast of timbre; it must have been played by the first oboist (Lawson 1983: 18).

Telemann wrote for the clarinet in *d'* in his autograph parts (items 1, 2, and 5 above) and restricted the range of each part to the interval of a thirteenth. It is notable that the note *b'* was purposely avoided, as well as the chalumeau notes below *c'*. He was aware that the note *b'* was not reliable on some two-key clarinets and that the notes below *c'* did not resemble the trumpet's sound. Furthermore, in respect to range, he treated the clarinet as if it were identical to the oboe. The non-autograph clarinet parts in two cantatas (items 3 and 4 above) were probably written and played during Telemann's lifetime, but it is also possible that they were added after his death by his grandson Georg Michael, who became Kantor at Riga in 1773 and undertook extensive revisions of the cantatas from 1776 to 1827 (Petzoldt 1974: 75; *Grove 6* 'Telemann, Georg Philipp').

Faber

The lexicographer F. J. Fétis (1860–5: iii. 173) cited an early use of the clarinet by Jean-Adam-Joseph Faber, a priest of the Church of Notre-Dame at Antwerp. Faber's Mass 'pour l'Assomption' is scored for five voice parts and an orchestra of two violins, viola, two cellos, oboe, two flutes, clarinet, double bass, and harpsichord in a manuscript copy dated July 1726. In his treatise of 1885 (p. 177) F. A. Gevaert published the first twenty-one measures of the contralto solo 'Qui tollis peccata mundi' from an unidentified Mass by Faber of 1720, which included the clarinet (see Ex. 4.7).[17] Gevaert had received this excerpt and descriptive information from the musicologist Léon-Philippe-Marie Burbure de Wesembeek, who is known today for cataloguing the archives at Antwerp (*Grove 6* 'Burbure, Léon-Philippe-Marie'). It is not clear whether Gevaert's example comes from the Mass 'pour l'Assomption' referred to by Fétis. Van der Linden called it 'Maria Assumpta' in his article 'Antwerpen' in *MGG*.[18] The solo contralto in the 'Qui tollis' is accompanied by two flutes, clarinet, and harpsichord. A two-key clarinet in *c'* is appropriate for this part, which features the earliest known use of arpeggios in the chalumeau or low register, descending to *f*; the highest note is *bb''*. The part is slightly more demanding in its frequent leaps than Telemann's music and includes a wide leap of two octaves and a third (from *f* to *a''*) in the fourteenth measure. The manuscript of the Mass was reported by the

---

[17] See also Gevaert n.d.: 177–8, Ex. 264.

[18] His bibliog. includes writings by Burbure which were not available to the author.

Ex. 4.7. J. A. J. Faber (1720), unidentified Mass, contralto solo, 'Qui tollis peccata mundi', measures 1–21 (Gevaert 1885: 178, Ex. 264)

archivist of Antwerp Cathedral to have been lost, according to Kroll (1968: 46 n. 1).

Some composers at this time were acquainted with two different approaches to writing for the clarinet. For example, the sixth question concerning the clarinet in J. P. Eisel's *Musicus Autodidaktos* (1738) is: 'What type of clef is used for the clarinet?' Eisel replies that 'One usually used the G clef, in which case the instrument is treated in the clarino or trumpet style, yet sometimes the soprano and alto clefs are found, in which case the clarinet is handled as a chalumeau.'[19] Although soprano and alto clefs are rarely found in parts for the baroque clarinet, Eisel's statement is substantiated by the trumpet-like clarinet writing in several works, such as Telemann's, and by the extended use of the chalumeau register in Faber's Mass. These two approaches may explain how the term 'chalumeau' came to be applied later in the century to the lowest register of the clarinet (cf. Lawson 1983: 18).

Rathgeber

The earliest known concertos probably intended for the clarinet were written by Johann Valentin Rathgeber (1682–1750), a Benedictine priest and choirmaster at Banz near Coburg in southern Germany. A popular composer of church music, he had much of his music published during his lifetime by the Augsburg firm of Lotter. From 1729 to 1738 Rathgeber left his post and travelled throughout Germany—without permission from his abbot—where he gathered information about performance conditions and liturgical customs in the Roman Catholic areas. Although he was reinstated as choirmaster after his return to Banz, he produced no more church music after 1738. His works include three collections of secular instrumental music (see *Grove 6* 'Rathgeber, Johann Valentin'). The first of these was his Op. 6, published by Lotter in 1728 and entitled *Chelys Sonora Excitans Spiritum Musicorum Digitis, Auribus, Ac Animis (The Sonorous Lute Stimulates the Musical Spirit of the Fingers, Hearing, and Soul).*[20] The work is in the form of a complete set of part-books, which is held in the Zentralbibliothek at Zurich.[21] It comprises twenty-four concertos divided into two parts, including both solo concertos and concerti grossi. Rathgeber contrasts the scoring for

---

[19] 'Was hat das *Clarinett* vor einen *Clavem?* Das gemeine und ordentliche Zeiten dieses Instruments ist insgemein der *Clavis* G, und so dann wird es auf *Clarino*-Art tractiret, doch kommt auch jezuweilen der *Discant* und *Alt-Clavis*, wenn man das *Clarinett* wie einen *Chalumeaux* handelt, vor.'

[20] *Chelys*, the Greek word for 'tortoise', refers to the tortoiseshell of the lyre, and in medieval and Renaissance writings was used to mean the lyre itself. See *NGDMI* 'Lyre, §2'.

[21] The contents of this work have been incorrectly described in every source consulted by the author (including *MGG* and *Grove 6*).

strings in the first part with that for winds and strings in the second. The first six concertos are for violin solo (marked 'principale'), two violins (a viola part is not included), organ, and cello; each concerto is in a different key. The next six of the first part are for two violins, organ, and cello; again, each is in a different key, except for Nos. 11 and 12, which are both in G minor. The first six concertos of the second part are for two violins, two 'clarini vel Litui obligatis', organ, and cello. In each of these the clarino (trumpet) or *lituo* (identified variously as a cornetto, shawm, horn, and low trumpet; see Walther 1732: 376; Sachs 1921; *NGDMI* 'Lituo') is pitched in a different tonality. Of the final six concertos, the first two, Nos. 19 and 20, are for two violins, 'Clarineto vel Lituo ex C obligato', organ, and cello. Concerto No. 21 is for violin solo, two violins, two 'clarini vel Litui ex C pro libitu', organ, and cello. No. 22 is for two violins, two 'clarini' (designated as in No. 21), organ, and cello. The final two concertos (Nos. 23 and 24) are entitled 'Concerto pastorello' and are for two violins, two 'clarini' (as in the previous work), organ, and cello.

Because of the proximity of Banz to Nuremberg, where the Denners and Oberlenders worked (about 55 miles away), it seems likely that Rathgeber would have known of the clarinet and used it as a substitute for the clarino or *lituo* in Nos. 19 and 20. Each of these works is in three movements: Allegro, Adagio (the 'clarineto' is silent), and Allegro; and Allegro, Adagio (the 'clarineto' plays only a repeated *e'*), and Presto. The ranges employed for the clarinet are *c'* to *a''* (No. 19)[22] and *e'* to *c'''* (No. 20); both works include *f♯''*. These parts are indistinguishable from those for the clarino in Rathgeber's concertos and contain triadic themes and repeated notes, as shown in the first movement of Concerto 19 (Ex. 4.8; cf. No. 15 for two trumpets, 1968 edn.). An indication that Rathgeber's conservative style of writing was a matter of choice is found in his preface to these concertos, entitled 'Ad Philomusum' (To the Music-Lover): 'I decided to provide the easiest possible manner and method, and to that end appeal less to virtuoso skill and more to musical judgement.'[23] His writing for the 'clarineto' in these works is similar to that found in the clarinet part of Telemann's 'Wer mich liebet, der wird mein Wort halten' (Ex. 4.4) in its triadic style, lack of the note *b'*, and omission of all chalumeau notes below *c'*. Rathgeber's concertos are also technically idiomatic for two-key clarinets in *c'*.[24]

---

[22] E. Nowak's edn. (1976) is for trumpet, violin, or recorder; Nowak also suggests the possibility of performing this work on the soprano chalumeau, clarinet, and horn in *c'*.

[23] 'Index docebit omnia; Modum & methodum facillimam subministrare cogitavi, ideò non tam artificio pro solis Virtuosis, quàm aurium judicio pro minùs habituatis placere studui.'

[24] Hans Rudolph Stalder, formerly first clarinettist of the Tonhalle orchestra of Zurich, performed concertos 19 and 20 in 1981 on a reproduction of a 2-key clarinet by T. Eric Hoeprich. See Nicol 1981.

Ex. 4.8. Rathgeber (1728), Concerto No. 19, first and second movements: 'Clarineto vel Lituo' part

Vivaldi: Concertos

Two of Vivaldi's concertos specifying the 'clarinet' (RV 559 and 560) are concerti grossi, as are several of the works in Rathgeber's *Chelys Sonora*. In Vivaldi's concertos two clarinets in *c'* are paired with two oboes and a full complement of strings and basso continuo. The range of each clarinet in RV 559 is *g* to *c'''*; in RV 560 the range of the first clarinet is from *g* to *c'''*, that of the second from *f* to *c'''*. Vivaldi and Faber were perhaps the earliest composers to exploit purposely the distinctive tone-colours of the upper and lower registers of the clarinet. Vivaldi's writing for the upper register is similar to Rathgeber's in its trumpet-like character, as seen in a passage from RV 560 (Ex. 4.9).[25] He also shows an

Ex. 4.9. Vivaldi (1947b), Concerto RV 560, first movement, measures 28–32: clarinet parts

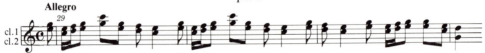

awareness of the aptness of the chalumeau register for lugubrious effects, emphasized by a use of minor inflections in the same movement (Ex. 4.10; see Talbot 1978: 162). This difference in timbre between the upper and lower registers was subsequently noted by the German author J. Adlung (1758), who stated: 'The clarinet is well known. In the low range it sounds differently from in the high range, and therefore one calls it [the range] chalumeau.'[26]

Ex. 4.10. Vivaldi (1947b), Concerto RV 560, first movement, measures 40–3: clarinet parts

Interestingly, when writing in the chalumeau register, Vivaldi employed the bass clef, intending the notes to sound an octave higher (see Exx. 4.11 and 4.13). Such a use of octave transposition is common in writing for the horn, another indication of the connection between the two instruments. During the second movement of RV 560 (Largo), the oboes are featured as a duet with string accompaniment while the clarinets are silent. The second movement of RV 559

---

[25] Several passages copied from the autograph scores of these concertos are shown in Kolneder 1951: 187–90, 1955a: 109, 1955b: 210.

[26] p. 588: 'Clarinet ist bekannt. In der Tiefe lautet es anders, als in der Höhe, und alsdenn nennt man es chalumeau.'

Ex. 4.11. Vivaldi (1947b), Concerto RV 560, first movement, measures 78–81: clarinet, oboe, and continuo parts

Ex. 4.12. Vivaldi (1947a), Concerto RV 559, second movement, measures 89–94: clarinet and oboe parts

(Largo), however, is quite unusual in that the oboes and clarinets play alone in a lyrical dialogue (Ex. 4.12).

Vivaldi's third concerto with clarinets (RV 556) was written for the feast of Saint Lawrence ('per la Solennità di San Lorenzo') and combines aspects of the solo concerto and the concerto grosso. It has a dominant violin solo part with a second concertante violin and an extensive wind section of two recorders, two oboes, two clarinets (marked 'claren') in c', and bassoon. The first clarinet utilizes a range of from c' to d''', extending one note higher than RV 559 and 560; the second clarinet part has a range of g to c'''. In marked contrast to the outer movements, the second movement in its first version was written for solo violin and a bass part played by five instruments. A note written at the beginning of the second movement in the autograph score, to the left of the lower stave and extending downwards, specifies these additional instruments: 'Clarini solo, e | Arpeggio con | il Leuto | Un Violoncello | Un Viol:o piz | zicato | Tutti il Basso'. Talbot (1979) surmised that the bass part was to be played by both clarinets (marked 'clarini') and an additional violin, pizzicato, in the upper octave (normal when these instruments read from the bass clef) and one cello and an archlute, *arpeggiando*, at written pitch. Later, Vivaldi suppressed the clarinet parts, allotting their notes in the outer movements by means of cues to recorders, oboes, or violins as appropriate. In the second version, he reverted to the more conventional solo cello, perhaps with continuo instruments, to play the bass part.[27]

Vivaldi carefully avoided the note *b♮'* in the clarinet parts of each of the three concertos. Two apparent exceptions occur in RV 556 and 559. In Ephrikian's Ricordi edition of RV 556 (1949), the note *b'* occurs once in measures 34, 139, and 142 of the first movement, each time within a dominant seventh framework, on G. Ephrikian notes that the last two were written in the manuscript as *d'*; thus it is likely that the printed *b'* in measure 34 was also originally a *d'*. In the Ricordi edition of RV 559 (1947a), a *b'* is printed twice in each of measures 96 and 97 of the second movement, with the two clarinet parts in unison. Kolneder (1951: 190), however, shows measure 9 of this movement (1947a edn., measure 97) in the autograph version, where both parts are notated in the bass clef (Ex. 4.13), and indicates that they were intended to be played an octave higher. In this and the previous measure, a transposition of two octaves is also musically justified, because of the high tessitura of the oboes and a written *D*. The conspicuous lack of the note *b'* in these concertos strongly suggests a conscious effort by Vivaldi to take into account the insecure intonation of this note on some two-key clarinets in *c'*. Kolneder (1951: 190) dated these works between 1720 and 1740, while Karl Haas (1960, n. 4) suggested 1726 to 1730. Both estimates may be supported by the early

Ex. 4.13. Vivaldi (1947a), Concerto RV 559, second movement, measures 97–8: clarinet and oboe parts

[27] Talbot (1979) refers to fo. 11ᵛ of the autograph at the Biblioteca Nazionale Universitaria, Turin, Giordano collezione 34. Kolneder (1955a: 110–11) stated that a different script was used for the note 'Un violoncello un Viol: o pizzicato Tutti il Basso', and that an upper part is marked 'Violº Solo', indicating a 3rd manner of performing this movement.

use of the single-reed chalumeau (*salmoé*) at the Pietà from 1706 (Talbot 1980: 158–9) and the payment for the repair of two clarinets at the Pietà on 13 March 1740 (Arnold 1965: 78).[28]

Paganelli

Giuseppe Antonio Paganelli was born in Padua in 1710 and died probably in Madrid about 1763. His career as a composer and virtuoso musician took him to Venice, Augsburg, Prague, Rheinsburg, Brunswick, and Bayreuth. He wrote several operas, vocal music, and instrumental works, many of which were published in Paris (*Grove 6* 'Paganelli, Giuseppe Antonio'). A concerto in B flat major by Paganelli may have been intended for the clarinet. According to a private letter from Eric Hoeprich this work was composed in 1733, although the author has not been able to verify this dating. Paganelli may have written it in Venice or in Augsburg, where he appeared in 1733 as a harpsichordist with the opera troupe of Antonio Maria Peruzzi (*Grove 6* 'Paganelli, Giuseppe Antonio'), or during the 1750s or 1760s.

The score of the concerto is preserved in Padua at the Archivio Musicale della Cappella Antoniana.[29] Its title appears to read 'Concerto per Clareto', although the last word is not clearly written and could be 'Clarete' or simply 'Claret'. It is in three movements (Allegro in 4/4, Adagio in 2/2, and Presto in 3/8); the solo part is written in B flat major but was probably intended to be played in C major on a clarinet in bb.[30] The total range of the solo part is from f' to bb''. To judge from this small range and the style of the work, the concerto may have been meant for the soprano chalumeau rather than the clarinet.[31] In the first movement the solo line is angular and requires jumps of a seventh and an octave, requiring the awkward notes $c\sharp''$, eb'', and a trill from a'' to bb'' (Ex. 4.14). The Adagio second movement, in G minor, requires several leaps and adds the note $f\sharp'$ to these accidentals (Ex. 4.15). The final Presto is technically the least demanding but requires an ab'' and a trill from b' to c'' which is easier to play on a three-key clarinet (Ex. 4.16). This work makes greater technical demands than Vivaldi's concertos and Kölbel's trio (discussed below), but is more restricted in range than the latter work.

---

[28] Another Italian composer, Nicolò Jommelli, wrote for the 'Clarinette' in his opera *Cajo Mario* (1746). See Abert 1908: 201.

[29] Thanks are given to Eric Hoeprich for a photocopy of this work.

[30] It is possible to perform this work at the written pitch with a 2-key clarinet in c', but the majority of clarinet works at this time were written in C and F major.

[31] In a private letter to the author, Hans Rudolf Stalder notes that the range of this work is appropriate for the chalumeau and points to a similar type of writing in Fasch's Chalumeau Concerto (see Lawson 1981a: 156–9).

Ex. 4.14. Paganelli (1733?), Clarinet Concerto, first movement, measures 14–24, 36–41: solo part

Ex. 4.15. Paganelli (1733?), Clarinet Concerto, second movement, measures 11–37: solo part

Ex. 4.16. Paganelli (1733?), Clarinet Concerto, third movement, measures 26–80, 116–34: solo part

Kölbel

A unique trio for 'Clarinet, Cornu de Schass et Basso' by Ferdinand Kölbel, a hunting-horn player, is found in manuscript parts at Darmstadt.[32] Not much is known of Kölbel's life. About 1724, while he was employed as a player of the hunting-horn by the Duke of Holstein, he went to St Petersburg and remained to become a member of the court orchestra in 1729. In 1740 he presented an application at the court to build a keyed horn 'mit verschiedenen neuen Tönen'. Kölbel travelled to Vienna in 1744; some time between 1741 and 1754 the Dutch ambassador to St Petersburg took him to Constantinople with a number of other musicians (Kölbel 1979: 807). By 1756 he had returned to the Russian court, where he remained for thirteen more years in the orchestra (Mooser 1951: i. 228).

---

[32] Cf. Alfred Berner's description of this work, quoted in Kölbel 1979: 806.

About 1766, Kölbel made a successful début with his keyed horn (which he called the *Amorschall*), playing with his son-in-law Franz Hensel in three trios for two horns and cello in the remote keys (for a brass instrument) of C minor, F minor, and E major. They also played two obbligato horn parts in a concerto with other instruments (Stählin 1769: ii. 175–8, 186–92; see Mooser 1951: ii. 38 n. 1). After this performance his invention was not heard of again.

There are four separate parts to Kölbel's trio but no score. The first part, designated 'Clarinet', is in the key of C; the second, marked 'Cornu', is also in C major. The bass part exists in two versions—one in D and the other in C—and is written in the bass clef without any designation or numbers to indicate a figured bass. It could have been played as a continuo bass-line on a keyboard instrument or on another wind or stringed instrument. It seems likely that Kölbel wrote the D major version to accommodate the use of a woodwind instrument such as a bassoon tuned a major second lower, at *Cammerton* (see Haynes 1985: 64, 102–3); it also allows for a horn crooked in *d'* and a clarinet pitched in *d'*, both of which would play from the C major parts. The trio consists of three movements (Allegro, Adagio, and Allegro), which utilize a clarinet range of from *c'* to *g'''*. Kölbel did not hesitate to use the highest part of this range, from *e'''* to *g'''*, repeatedly in all three movements. His writing for the clarinet is based on triadic themes and mainly relies on scale passages, octave leaps, and arpeggiated figures (Ex. 4.17).

Ex. 4.17. Kölbel (*c*.1740–50), Trio, first and second movements: clarinet part

Ex. 4.17. – *cont.*

This part strongly resembles Vivaldi's parts in the concertos in its scale passages and thematic material, as is shown by a comparison of the beginning of Kölbel's first movement and a few measures from Vivaldi's Concerto RV 560 (Ex 4.18). Kölbel's writing, however, calls for an even greater technical ability and employs a consistently higher tessitura, as shown in a passage from the third movement (Ex. 4.19).

The title-page of Kölbel's trio is marked 'a Wien'. This suggests that the work was written while he lived in Vienna, some time between 1744 and 1756. Rau, in his study of chamber music written for the clarinet (1977: 233–4), suggests a date of composition of *c*.1740–50. In our earlier description of Telemann's 'Wer mich

Ex. 4.18. Kölbel (*c.*1740–50), Trio, first movement, measures 1–4
Vivaldi (1947b), Concerto RV 560, first movement, measures 46–9

Ex. 4.19. Kölbel (*c.*1740–50), Trio, third movement: clarinet part

liebet, der wird mein Wort halten' we noted that the same musician probably played the clarinet and horn parts; we may assume that either Kölbel or his son-in-law played the clarinet.[33]

Handel

Another early chamber work with clarinet is the *Ouverture* (HWV 424) for two clarinets and horn, in four movements, by George Frideric Handel (1685–1759). There are no individual parts but only a score written in D major, showing a range of *c♯′* to *d′′′* for the first clarinet and *a* to *d′′′* for the second. According to Haas (1952 edn.), the score is in Handel's handwriting, with the identification of the instruments ('Clarinet 1', 'Clarinet 2', and 'Corno di Caccia') entered into the autograph by his friend John Christopher Smith, sen.[34] The *Ouverture* was previously thought to be only the wind parts of an incomplete orchestral work; the musical evidence, however, shows that it is a complete work in its harmonic and structural content, and it has no long sections of rests implying that other parts are missing (cf. Fuller-Maitland and Mann 1893; Chatwin 1950: 6–8). The opening section is clearly written in the French overture style, leading into a lively Allegro ma non troppo where imitative, fanfare-like entries abound (Ex. 4.20). A lyrical Larghetto pairs the clarinets in thirds and sixths with the horn in both supportive and imitative roles. Passages for the clarinets alone are contrasted with sections for the horn by itself in the following movement, Andante allegro (Ex. 4.21). The final Allegro in 3/8 is quite brilliant, featuring rapidly moving eighth- and sixteenth-notes in every part (Ex. 4.22).

Ex. 4.20. Handel (1952), *Ouverture*, first movement, measures 1–4, 29–35

---

[33] A further association of musical idiom between the clarinet and horn at this time is implied by an anonymous 'Sonate a 2 Corno o Clarinetti' owned by the Dutch music-collector Nicolas Selhof (see Selhof 1973 edn.: 247, No. 2926). Not surprisingly, he also owned a copy of Rathgeber 1728 (p. 256, No. 1293).

[34] See the reproduction of the beginning of the autograph in Handel 1952 edn.

Ex. 4.20. – *cont.*

Ex. 4.21. Handel (1952), *Ouverture*, third movement, measures 1–6

Ex. 4.22. Handel (1952), *Ouverture*, fourth movement, measures 1–32

The clarinet parts include several chromatic pitches besides the F♯s and C♯s designated by the key signature, such as *g♯'*, *d♯"*, and *g♯"*. Because of the resulting complications in fingering and the poor intonation of some pitches, Halfpenny (1952) assumed that two-key clarinets in *d'* were used in order to play in C major. Chatwin (1950: 7) suggested that a three-key clarinet in *c'* must also be considered as a possibility. Indeed, on the basis of our working knowledge of clarinet fingerings, it is also apparent that these parts were playable on certain two-key clarinets in *c'* and three-key clarinets in *d'*. Baselt (1978–: iii. 208) dated the work *c.*1740–1 on the basis of the date of the paper used for the autograph. This date is supported by the apparent use of clarinets in the Granville copies of the aria 'Par che mi nasca in seno' in Handel's opera *Tamerlano* (first performed in 1724) (cf. Schoelcher 1857: 405; Streatfield 1911: 216; Baselt 1978–: i. 238). According to Larsen (1972: 211–12), the copies made for the Granville collection of Handel's works were completed between about 1744 and 1745.

Molter

A technically most advanced style of writing for the two-key clarinet in *d'* is found in the six concertos by the Kapellmeister of Durlach (the eastern district of Karlsruhe) Johann Melchior Molter (1696–1765), preserved in the Badische Landesbibliothek, Karlsruhe (MSS 302, 304, 328, 332, 334, and 337). Molter is noted for his adventurous writing for the timpani, trumpet (clarino), and horn, as well as his preference for new and unusual instruments like the clarinet, chalumeau, flute d'amour, cornetto, and harp (*Grove 6* 'Molter, Johann Melchior'). Four of his clarinet concertos (MSS 302, 304, 334, and 337) have been edited by Heinz Becker (*Klarinetten-Konzerte* 1957: 1–52); another (MS 332) is the subject of a DMA dissertation (Lanning 1969); and the last (MS 328) has been included in another DMA dissertation (Shanley 1976). Scores (which include five parts) are preserved for all six concertos. MSS 302 and 304 have title-pages which describe the instrumentation as 'Concerto, Clarinetto concertato, Violino primo, Violino secondo, Viola [MS 302; Violetta MS 304], Violoncello e Cembalo'. Only the original cembalo part is extant in MS 302, with additional oboe parts in a later hand. In MS 304, however, all the parts are preserved, including two additional oboe parts. In the scores of MSS 334 and 337 the highest part is designated 'Clarinetto'. The scores of the other two works (MSS 328 and 332) are unmarked, but their highest parts are sufficiently similar in range and style of writing to the solo parts of the clarinet concertos to be identified as such.

All six concertos consistently employ a very high tessitura between *c'''* and *g'''*, and notes below *c"* are usually treated in a purely triadic manner. The technical devices include wide leaps of more than one octave, triplet sixteenth-note figures, and thirty-second- and sixty-fourth-note flourishes as well as a number of grace-notes and trills (Ex. 4.23, MS 304). The music for the clarinet in these works, moreover, cannot be considered appropriate for the clarino trumpet, but represents a mature style of writing for the two-key clarinet. Becker (1955: 287–8) supported this view when he observed that the concertos employ a wider range and

Ex. 4.23. Molter (*c.*1745), Clarinet Concerto in A major (MS 304), first movement, measures 1–71: solo part

Ex. 4.23. – *cont.*

higher tessitura than a clarino concerto by Molter. He also noted that in the latter work and in the Brandenburg Concerto No. 2 by Bach, the clarino rests during the slow movements, but that the clarinet in Molter's concertos plays in all the slow movements. In MS 304, the clarinet begins with a long sustained note of a type that Becker (1955: 287–8) has noted was used in clarinet music by several composers of the nineteenth century (Ex. 4.24). Lanning (1969: 7–9) also found

Ex. 4.24. Molter (*c.*1745), Clarinet Concerto in A major (MS 304), second movement: solo part

Ex. 4.24. – *cont.*

in three concertos for horn, three concertos for clarino, and one for horn and clarino that Molter used a range extending up to *d'''*; *f♯''* was the only chromatic pitch required. Table 4.1 shows the ranges and chromatic pitches found in each of the clarinet concertos (cf. Lanning 1969: 8). It is evident that Molter's playing demands are quite high, considering the awkward fingering and the level of technique required. The range from *g* to *f'''* in MS 328 is the widest, and the use of seven chromatic pitches in MSS 332 and 337 is the most extensive of all of these works (it is noteworthy that both *g♯''* and *ab''* appear in MS 332). An exceptional occurrence of low *g* in the chalumeau register is found in the third movement of

TABLE 4.1. *The Range and Chromatic Pitches Found in Johann Melchior Molter's Clarinet Concertos*

Concerto	Range	Chromatic pitches								
		b'	*c♯''*	*d♯''*	*e♯''*	*f♯''*	*g♯''*	*bb''*	*c♯'''*	*f♯'''*
MS 302 (G major)	*c'–g'''*			√		√	√	√		√
MS 304 (A major)	*c''–g'''*		√	√		√	√	√	√	
MS 328 (D major)	*g–f'''*			√		√		√	√	√
MS 332 (D major)	*d'–g'''*	√	√	√		√	√	√		√
MS 334 (D major)	*c''–f♯'''*		√	√		√		√	√	√
MS 337 (D major)	*g'–g'''*		√	√	√	√	√		√	√

Ex. 4.25. Molter (*c*.1745), Clarinet Concerto in D major (MS 328), third movement, measures 35–58: solo part

the unmarked Concerto in D (MS 328). Here a sequence of eighth-notes leads to a leap of *g* to *c'''*, or two octaves and a fourth (Ex. 4.25). The note *b'* in the first movement of another concerto in D (MS 332) is the only example in Molter's writing of this note for the clarinet (Ex. 4.26).[35]

Ex. 4.26. Molter (*c*.1745), Clarinet Concerto in D major (MS 332), first movement, measures 43–53: solo part

Becker believed that these concertos were written about 1745 during Molter's second Karlsruhe period as Kapellmeister for the court of Baden-Durlach (1742–65) (*GLM* 'Klarinette').[36] In support of this dating, we note that the

---

[35] This concerto was recently recorded with harpsichord accompaniment by Keith Puddy of London on a 2-key clarinet in *d'* by Brian Ackerman and Edward Planas (a copy of a clarinet by Zencker, Nuremberg, GN, No. 424) on a Capriole cassette (CAPT 1994, 1984).

[36] See ch. 5.

opening ritornello of the Concerto in A major (MS 304) appears to be a transposed version of Johann Adolph Hasse's Concerto in B minor for flute, published in London in 1741.[37] This is not surprising, since many composers copied themes from others during this period, and Hasse's music was popular and widely published during his lifetime. Molter's concertos exhibit characteristics of the *galant* style (in his elegant treatment of themes), which he developed from his musical studies in Italy and during his second Karlsruhe period (*Grove 6* 'Molter, Johann Melchior').

Rameau

We have reason to believe that in France the clarinet was first used in the *tragédie en musique Zoroastre* (1749) by Jean-Philippe Rameau (1683–1764). Two clarinettists, Jean [Johann] Schieffer and François [Franz] Raiffer, are listed in a document from the archives of the Paris Opéra entitled 'Instruments Extraordinaires Employés à l'Opéra'. They were paid a total of 168 *livres* 'pour avoir joué de la clarinette dans trois Répétitions et 25 Représentations de l'Opéra de *Zoroastre*, à raison de 6 Livres, chacque fois'.[38] However, neither the engraved score of *Zoroastre* (1749) nor another score (in the Bibliothèque Nationale, Paris), dated 1756, contains parts for the clarinet. This implies that the musicians cited above also played other wind instruments (such as the oboe) in the orchestra, playing the clarinet only when instructed to do so. Their parts probably doubled those for the violin or oboe, as is indicated in Rameau's last work using the clarinet, his *tragédie en musique Les Boréades* (1764). In an autograph score the overture includes various indications: 'clarinettes ou hautbois', 'hautbois et clarinettes', 'h.b. et cl', and 'sans h.b. ni clar' (pp. 1–3), but separate clarinet parts are not found. The clarinets and/or oboes usually double the violin parts, though occasionally the violins move down to other staves, leaving the winds their own part (Stern 1983: 7). Rameau's use of the clarinet is verified in a note on p. 5 of the score which reads: 'If there are clarinets, they will play the violin parts and the bassoons will play the bass parts, all of which will have to be copied out.'[39] Besides the string instruments, the

[37] Compare this concerto's 1st movement in *Klarinetten-Konzerte* 1957 with the opening measures of the flute concerto by Hasse in *Instrumentalkonzerte* 1958: 33. The beginning of the 2nd movement of Hasse's concerto also begins with a sustained note, as in Molter's A major Concerto.

[38] Etat de Payements qui seront faits à plusieurs sujets cy-après nommez, employez à l'Opéra, par extraordinaire, depuis le 29 aoust 1749, Arch. Opéra. A. 19. *Emargements*, 1749–1751, quoted by La Laurencie (1913). This document was not found by Stern (1983: 6–7), who assumed that it was lost during the recent transfer of material from the archives of the Opéra to the Archives Nationales in Paris.

[39] 'S'il y a des clar elles joueront les parties des viol. et les Bassons celles des Basses, qu'il faudra néanmois copier partons.' See Rameau 1982 edn.: 5.

orchestra for *Zoroastre* consisted of two flutes, two horns and two oboes (La Laurencie 1913: 28).[40]

In his *Dernièrs Souvenirs* of 1859 (p. 181), Adolphe Adam stated that Rameau had used the clarinet in his *opéra-ballet Le Temple de la Gloire* of 1745, as an incidental part in the orchestra and in the overture as a curious and special instrument. No other evidence, however, appears to support his statement. In an earlier book (1857: 71), Adam mentioned that the first use of the clarinet in the orchestra had been in Rameau's *pastorale héroïque Acante et Céphise* of 1751. Indeed, Rameau skilfully made use of two clarinets in thirteen sections of *Acante et Céphise*, more specifically in the overture, 'Fanfare', and acts II and III. (The clarinet part-books contain some music which is not indicated in the score; see Stern 1983: 12, app.). For instance, in the 'Feu d'artifice' ('Firework') section of the overture two clarinets in *c'* are given parts which include trumpet-like triadic figures (Ex. 4.27),[41] sixteenth-note ornaments on *a'* and *b'* (Ex. 4.28), and thirty-second-note flourishes in unison (Ex. 4.29). This movement requires a technical facility equivalent to that demanded by some sections of the Molter

Ex. 4.27. Rameau (1751), *Acante et Céphise*, overture, 'Feu d'artifice', measures 1–7

---

[40] The orchestra for the performance in 1756 included 4 oboes, 2 flutes, 5 bassoons, and 1 trumpet; see Noinville and Travenol 1757: ii. 141.

[41] A few measures of the opening are illus. in La Laurencie 1913–31: ix. 2233–4.

Ex. 4.27. – *cont.*

Ex. 4.28. Rameau (1751), *Acante et Céphise*, overture, measures 14–19

Ex. 4.28. – *cont.*

Ex. 4.29. Rameau (1751), *Acante et Céphise*, overture, measures 50–7: clarinet parts

concertos. A wide range from *g* to *e‴* is also required, as well as *g♯′*, *c♯″*, *f♯″*, *g♯″*, and *c♯‴* and trills from *b′* to *c″*, suggesting that three-key clarinets in *c′* were played.

In an orchestral and choral number entitled 'annonce' in act II, clarinet and horn parts are notated on the same line. Since the piece is written in D major, the clarinettists probably played *d′* instruments, transposing the parts into C major or playing from transposed parts. In the next section, called 'Entrée', clarinets in *a* are given a lyrical solo line with the accompaniment of two horns, strings, and basso continuo (Ex. 4.30). The music of the score and the clarinet parts has been

Ex. 4.30. Rameau (1751), *Acante et Céphise*, act II, 'Entrée'

Ex. 4.30. – *cont.*

transposed for the player in a similar manner to that followed in present-day notation. However, in Ex. 4.30 two clefs are notated: a treble clef in F major followed by a soprano clef in D major. The first clef indicates what the player reads, whereas the second clef indicates what is actually heard. According to Pierre (1890: 214–15), Rameau was the first French composer to make use of an additional soprano or alto clef intended for the convenience of the player (see also Stern 1983: 13–14). The theorist Francoeur (1772: 25–9, 32–3) confirmed the practice by giving musical examples transposed into easily played tonalities for six clarinets of different pitches, and wrote a second clef immediately to the left of each clarinet part to indicate the required transposition.

Following the 'Entrée' section is a 'Rigaudon', a dance movement scored simply for two clarinets in *a* and two horns in *d*. This quartet presents a striking and rich blend of tone-colours that was to become a popular and frequently used combination later in the century (Ex. 4.31). (Ten of the thirteen movements with clarinets

Ex. 4.31. Rameau (1751), *Acante et Céphise*, act II, first and second Rigaudons

Ex. 4.31. – *cont.*

in *Acante* include horn parts.) The contrast with the string tone of the second 'Rigaudon' is especially effective. The following section, 'Un chasseur' (A hunter), is a bass aria, 'L'Amour est heureux', which makes use of canonic entries with a combination of clarinets in *d'* and horns in *d* as accompaniment (Ex. 4.32). Here an alto clef indicates the transposition for the clarinets and a supporting basso continuo is notated in the solo bass part. This aria was praised in the *Mercure de France* in December 1751 after the first performance of *Acante et Céphise* on 19 November: 'On à extrémet gouté . . . dans la fête des chasseurs, les airs joués par les clarinettes' (Bobillier 1900: 224–5, 1903: 184). The Entr'acte between acts II and III includes another quartet for clarinets in *a* and horns in *d*, this time in a harmonically and rhythmically simple style (Ex. 4.33).[42] Throughout *Acante*, clarinets in *a* are always featured in soloistic passages accompanied by horns; in the 'Air vif' of act III, for instance, the first clarinet in *a* ascends to high *f'''*. At the beginning of act III the instrumentation is altered to achieve a new blend of tone-colours: two clarinets in *d'* are paired with violins doubled by oboes with a supporting bass-line in a fanfare-like 'Contre-danse'. The choir is added to this instrumentation in the next section of the work.

Ex. 4.32. Rameau (1751), *Acante et Céphise*, act II, aria 'L'amour est heureux', measures 1–18

---

[42] Transcribed to sounding pitch in Masson (1930: 524–5). See also Stern 1984, 1985.

Ex. 4.32. – *cont.*

Ex. 4.32. – *cont.*

- mour est heur-eux par lui meme,_____ sa chai - - - - - -

- - - - - - - - - - - ne est son plus cher tre -

Ex. 4.32. – *cont.*

Ex. 4.33. Rameau (1751), *Acante et Céphise*, Entr'acte between acts II and III

Ex. 4.33. – *cont.*

Some scholars had previously thought that Rameau's parts for 'clarinettes' were meant for the clarino, or high trumpet. For instance, the German writer Mennicke (1906: 278–9), pointing to the fanfare-like style of the 'Feu d'artifice', stated that the parts could all be performed on a natural trumpet. The remaining sections of the overture, however, prove that a natural trumpet could not have been intended, because the thirty-second-notes beginning on *a* and *g* (Ex. 4.30) include many pitches not playable on that instrument. Furthermore, the lyrical nature of the 'clarinette' parts in the 'Entrée' of act II (Ex. 4.31) and elsewhere in *Acante* show that they were meant for the clarinet and not the natural trumpet. Hellouin, the biographer of F. J. Gossec, assumed that the designation 'clarinettes' in *Acante* was equivalent to 'clarini' (1903: 129 n. 1).[43] Bobillier, however, argued against Hellouin's identification by citing the following note, written in Rameau's hand at the end of the second Riguadon in the second act: 'We repeat the first rigaudon after the second, but then very softly, since the clarinets ['clarinettes'] play at the same time.'[44] Surely such a reduction in volume would not have been required if trumpets had been used. On the basis of this document and the musical evidence, Bobillier concluded that clarinets were intended in *Acante et Céphise*.

Johann Stamitz

The important Mannheim composer Johann Stamitz (1717–57) stayed in Paris from September 1754 to September 1755, when he conducted the orchestra of the wealthy patron of the arts A. J. J. de La Pouplinière at his palace (Cucuel 1913b: 312–13). It is quite possible that while there he wrote the three-movement Quartet for two clarinets in *bb'* and two horns in *eb* that was published in 1764 by the German clarinettist Valentin Roeser (1764: 20–1). Roeser's activity in Paris during 1754 and 1755 is indicated by a statement in his manual on instrumentation (1764): 'We played this piece [an untitled quartet for clarinets and horns] in the presence of Mr Stamitz, during his journey to Paris . . .'[45] The quartet is written in three short movements, Adagio, Adagio, and Allegro (Ex. 4.34).[46] The technical demands are modest, and the range is limited for the first clarinet from *f'*

---

[43] L. Stollbrock (1892: 296–7) assumed that J. G. von Reutter referred to the clarinet when he specified 2 'clarini' as well as 2 'trombe' in his opera *La Speranza Assicurata* (1736). This does not appear to be supported by any other evidence, and furthermore an important school of clarino playing was cultivated during the 18th cent. in Vienna, where Reutter's opera was performed. Cf. *NGDMI* 'Trumpet'.

[44] 'On reprend ce premier rigaudon après le deuxième, mais pour lors très doux, parce que les clarinettes le jouent en même tems.' Quoted by Bobillier (1903: 185), who cited the authority of the musicologist Charles Malherbe in identifying Rameau's handwriting.

[45] p. 19: 'Nous avons exécuté ces Pièces en présence de Mr. Stamitz, pendant son séjour à Paris . . . .' Cf. Keillor 1975 and *Grove 6* 'Roeser, Valentin'.

[46] The 1st movement appeared in a version with parts for 2 clarinets in *g* and 2 horns in *c* and a new part for bassoon, as well as additional markings for ornaments, articulation, and dynamics, in Francoeur 1772: 58.

Ex. 4.34. Johann Stamitz, Quartet (Roeser 1764: 20–1)

Ex. 4.34. – *cont.*

Ex. 4.34. – *cont.*

Ex. 4.34. – *cont.*

to *c‴*, and for the second from *a* to *g″*. The first movement is similar in metre and tempo to Rameau's quartet in the Entr'acte at the end of act II of *Acante et Céphise* (Ex. 4.33). The Stamitz work, however, shows a greater independence of part-writing, frequently pairing the second clarinet with the first horn, and an abundance of *forte* and *piano* dynamic markings, occasionally separated by only one beat.[47]

While he was living in Paris, Stamitz also made use of the clarinet in at least three symphonies. In the *Mercure de France* of May 1755 a performance at the Concert Spirituel of 26 March was reviewed at which 'une symphonie de Stamich, avec clarinets et cors de chasse' was performed. A performance at the Concert Spirituel the following night also included a symphony by 'Stamich' with the same instrumentation (Pierre 1975: 269, Nos. 537–8).[48] Wolf believes that these citations refer to one of the symphonies by Stamitz published by Venier of Paris in a collection of six works with the subtitle *La Melodia Germanica* (1758). The title-page of this collection implies a preference for the clarinet, stating, 'in place of clarinets, they may be played with two oboes, flutes or violins'.[49] Indeed, in three extant symphonies by Stamitz from this period, clarinets appear to represent the preferred woodwind (Wolf 1981: 293). It should be noted that they were not officially part of the Mannheim court orchestra until after July of 1759,[50] and may not have been available to Stamitz until his visit to Paris during 1754 and 1755.

The Parisian writer Ancelet was so impressed by the combination of horns and clarinets (probably as a result of hearing Stamitz's works) that he stated the following: 'The horns please still more than when they accompany clarinets, instruments unknown till now in France and which have on our hearts and on our ears rights which were unknown to us. Of what use they could be to our composers in their music!' (Macdonald 1968: i. 172–3.)[51] Another work by Stamitz, a concerto in B flat major for clarinet and orchestra, may have been written during his stay in Paris.[52] Because it is technically much more difficult than the quartet,

[47] Both of these devices are associated with Stamitz's adaptation of the Italian overture style to the symphony; see *Grove 6* 'Stamitz, Johann'.

[48] Another concert there on 30 Mar. included an unidentified 'Symphony avec clarinettes et cors de chasse' probably by Stamitz.

[49] 'Faute de Clarinettes, on pourra les Exécuter avec deux Hautbois, Flutes ou Violons'. The other composers represented are Wagenseil, Kohaut, and Richter. See Johansson 1955, fac. 118; Wolf 1985, Pl. 4b, 36–7, 293, 343 n. 15; Macdonald 1968: i. 298; and Hoeprich 1985, *Abb.* 2.

[50] See the MS salary list reproduced in Münster 1983: 39–40, 41 nn. 5–6. Graupner's last sacred cantata, 'Lasset eure Bitte im Gebet' of 1754, includes a pair of *d′* clarinets. His writing is confined to a simple fanfare style similar to Telemann's (see Lawson 1979: 352, ex. 3; 1981a: 108).

[51] Ancelet 1757: 33: 'Les Cors de chasse plaisent encore davantage, quand ils accompagnent les Clarinettes, instrumens ignorés jusqu'ici en France, & qui ont sur nos coers & sur nos oreilles, des droits qui nous étoient inconnus. Quel emploi nos compositeurs n'en pourroient-ils pas faire dans leur Musique!'

[52] Modern edns. by Peter Gradenwitz (New York: MCA Music, 1953) and Walter Lebermann (Mainz: B. Schott's Söhne, 1967).

exhibiting wide leaps, virtuosic writing, and frequent use of the chalumeau register, it seems to have been meant for a virtuoso playing a 'classical' clarinet with four or five keys (see Gradenwitz 1936 and Rice 1987: 374–5).

D'Herbain and Garsault

The Chevalier d'Herbain included clarinets in his ballet *Célime*, produced at the Opéra on 28 September 1756. They are often paired with horns. Cucuel (1913a: 18 n. 1 and musical exx.) found that at one point in the manuscript score there are parts for clarinets pitched in *f*; in the engraved score these same parts were transposed a minor third lower for 'clarinettes en ré'. Later in the manuscript score (p. 72) we find an ariette accompanied by clarinets in *eb'*.

An interesting description of 1761 appears to verify d'Herbain's use of these high-pitched clarinets. F. A. P. de Garsault included an extensive section on music in his encyclopaedia entitled *Notionaire, ou Mémorial Raisonné* (1761: 601–69). He described forty instruments, dividing them into eight categories according to their different usages. The clarinet is listed among the 'Instruments de Guerre & de Chasse' as 'à vent & embouchure de Chalumeau. Le Clarinet ou Haut-bois de forêts, joue avec les Cors de-Chasse dans les Concerts' (pp. 632–3; cf. Rice 1979).[53] Garsault provided the following description of the clarinet and an engraving of both the clarinet and 'Trompe ou Cors de Chasse' (see Fig. 4.1):

The clarinet is a wind instrument at the fifth, that is, its *a'* is at the fifth below the *a'* of the treble instruments. Therefore, one is always obliged to transpose since it must sound *e'* to play in unison with the violins, oboes, etc. That is why it is still necessary to have, when one is playing this instrument, additional clarinets to match the treble instruments that are pitched on a higher or lower *a'*. It has the advantage of being gay and sonorous and of mixing well with hunting-horns in concerts. It is rarely played alone because of the hardness of its sound, which is difficult to soften. It has a special mouthpiece that is split in its length at the end. This slot, one inch or more in length, is put in the mouth and produces with the breath the sound of the musette or the rural chalumeau. One holds it in front like the oboe.

It is nineteen inches in length and is pierced with ten holes, of which the two highest are covered with keys.

Range
From F below its *a'* to E in the third octave.[54]

---

[53] For a discussion of the woodwind instruments described by Garsault see Eppelsheim 1986.

[54] p. 647: 'Le Clarinet est un instrument à vent, a la quinte des tons, c'est-à-dire, que son *amila* est à la quinte au-dessous de l'*amila* des dessus, ce qui l'oblige à transposer toujours, puis qu'il doit sonner *mi* pour se trouver à l'unisson des Violons, Hautbois, &c. C'est ce qui fait encore qu'il faut être muni, quand on joue de cet instrument, d'autant de Clarinets que les dessus sont montés sur un *amila* plus haut ou plus bas. Il a en récompense l'avantage d'être gai & sonore, & de faire très-bien dans les Concerts mêlé avec les Cors-de-

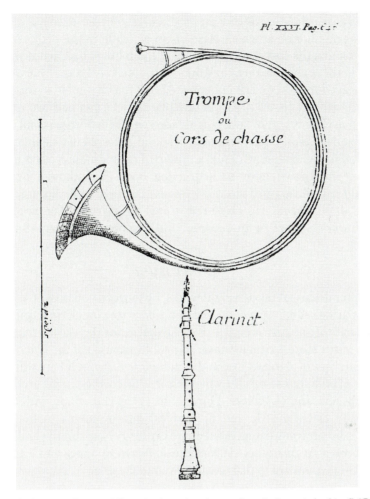

FIG. 4.1. The hunting-horn or 'Cors de chasse' and a two-key clarinet pitched in *f'* (Garsault 1761: 646, Pl. XXXI)

Given the transposition required for its *e'* to sound an *a'* and its length of only nineteen inches, Garsault's two-key clarinet must have been pitched in *f'*, though he stated that there were additional pitches. Walther, Majer, and Eisel did not mention the pitch of the two-key clarinets that they described. Not until Roeser's

Chasse. Il est rare qu'il réussisse seul à cause de la dureté du son qu'il est difficile d'adoucir. Il a une embouchure particuliere, c'est d'être fendu en long par le bout d'en haut: cette fente, longue d'un pounce & plus, mise dans la bouche, rend en soufflant un son de Muzette ou de Chalumeau champêtre. On le tient en avant comme le Haut-bois. Il a dix-neuf pouces de long, & percé de dix trous, dont les deux d'en haut sont bouchés avec des clefs. | *Etendue* | Du *fa* au-dessous de son *amila* au *mi* troisième octave'. Cf. the trans. in Rice 1979: 101.

Essai d'instruction à l'usage de ceux qui composent pour la clarinette et le cor (1764) are the pitches mentioned at which clarinets were made in the eighteenth century. Roeser included the clarinet in *f'* as one of them but stated that it was very high and used in the orchestra only 'for works which are very loud'.[55] He described the more advanced four-key clarinet but stated that the clarinet in *d'* was too small to hold the fourth key (p. 10 n. *); presumably this clarinet had two or three keys. According to Garsault, the *f'* clarinet blended well with horns, a combination used by d'Herbain in *Célime*. The 'hardness of sound' referred to was undoubtedly due to its high pitch. Garsault's brief description of the mouthpiece and its reed is the earliest in any known tutor or instruction book. Yet, though he included a description and illustration of double reeds, he apparently did not fully understand the double reed. He classified it and the clarinet mouthpiece with the 'embouchures en sifflet' of the recorder and flageolet (1761: 627–8).

Conclusion

This chapter discusses twenty-eight works, by thirteen composers, written for the baroque clarinet. A majority of these composers wrote for clarinets pitched in *d'* or *c'*. Many treated the instrument as a replacement for the clarino trumpet, others wrote for it in a more lyrical manner. A notable example of the latter is Rameau's emancipated use of clarinets in *c'* and *a* in *Acante et Céphise*. There will no doubt be a number of additions to this list when music is discovered in the archives of Italy, Czechoslovakia, and elsewhere. During the 1750s and 1760s, with the development of the classical style and mechanical improvements to the instrument, composers became more interested in the expressive capabilities and tone-colour of the clarinet. At this time, clarinet music began to appear on a technical and musical level equivalent to that usually given to the oboe.

---

[55] p. 2: 'pour les pieces à grand bruit'. Eppelsheim (1986: 69) suggests that the unusual term 'Haut-bois de forêts' (Garsault 1761: 633) was used to indicate that the clarinet's *f'* tonality was the same as that of the horn, and that this type of clarinet was associated with the hunt.

5

The Use of the Baroque Clarinet by Amateurs and Professionals

THE use of the clarinet before 1760 is documented in various sources including iconographical documents, concert reviews and notices, listings of orchestral players, and biographical accounts. In this chapter iconographical documents are discussed along with the concert appearances and orchestral posts of several individual clarinettists. Their positions, obligations, and privileges within eighteenth-century society are also noted.

The following ranking of instrumentalists formulated by C. H. Mahling (1983: 255) provides a useful categorization of musicians during the eighteenth century:

1. Travelling virtuoso
2. Court orchestral musician
3. Church and village musician
4. Military musician
5. *Spielmann* or itinerant minstrel

The successful travelling virtuoso was held in the highest esteem, while the wandering *Spielmann* or minstrel was simply tolerated by society. The remaining types of musicians held positions with different requirements and privileges, although there were also village musicians who alternated between music-making as a profession and as an avocation (Krickeberg 1983: 104–6). Musicians who played the baroque clarinet were active in all five categories. Furthermore, there exists a body of evidence showing the use of the clarinet by wealthy aristocrats.

Aristocrats

While written references make no mention of the use of the baroque clarinet by the aristocracy, their interest in the clarinet is shown in documents which indicate that they purchased instruments and included them in their private wind ensembles. For instance, the Nuremberg archival records from 1710 indicate that the Duke of Gronsfeld ordered two clarinets from the maker Jacob Denner (Nickel 1971: 251–2), to be used among the many instruments played by his court musicians.[1] The earliest known representation of a clarinettist shows a well-dressed gentleman playing a two-key clarinet in a luxurious room in what could have been a wealthy residence; this is an engraving by the Nuremberg artist J. C. Weigel from a collection entitled *Musicalisches Theatrum* (Nuremberg, *c.*1722, sheet 14; see Fig. 5.1).[2]

According to Berner (1961: p. viii), a chapter entitled 'Von dem Musikalischen Instrumente' in Johann Mattheson's *Das Neu-Eröffnete Orchestre* (1713) served as a guide for the planning and execution of Weigel's collection of thirty-six engravings depicting musicians. Mattheson evaluated several instruments on the basis of their aesthetic appeal and mentioned their use by different members of society. Weigel's collection reflects Mattheson's approach in that it contrasts a courtly, elegant musical life in its first section with a peasant's or soldier's form of music-making in its second. Indeed, of twenty-three musical instruments described by Mattheson, all but one (the chalumeau) are shown by Weigel, who in its place depicts a similar but more fashionable instrument, the clarinet (cf. Berner 1961: pp. iv, viii). Because these engravings were made in Nuremberg, the depiction of a clarinet, as well as those of several other wind instruments, could have been based on the actual instruments made by the Denners or J. W. Oberlender I (cf. Berner 1961: p. ix). However, the conical outline of the clarinet is similar to that of the oboe, which probably indicates the artist's unfamiliarity with the clarinet. Weigel's illustrations show some independence from Mattheson's book in regard to the evaluation of instruments found in the poetic captions, such as those for the recorder and lute (Berner 1961: p. viii). Another example is Weigel's approval of the clarinet. In his caption to the engraving of the clarinet he provides this favourable description:

> When the trumpet call is all too loud,
> The clarinet does serve to please
> Eschewing both the high and lowest sound,
> It varies gracefully and thus attains the prize.
> Wherefore the noble spirit, enamored of this reed,
> Instruction craves and plays assiduously.[3]

---

[1] The orchestral musician did not specialize in a single instrument until the 19th cent. During the 18th cent. most players were initially trained to play a number of wind, string, and percussion instruments in a *Stadtpfeiferei* (town pipers' school). See Mahling 1983: 231–4 and Schwab 1983: 41.

[2] Dated in *MGG* 'Weigel, Familie'. An earlier engraving by Weigel may have been intended to portray either the clarinet or the recorder. It appeared in Megerle 1709: 295 in a plate entitled 'Music Narr'. The text of this section of the book mentions 'Flauten' and several other instruments but not the clarinet. Cf. Schmid 1985: 7–8.

[3] 'Waan der Trompeten-Schall will allzulaut erthönen | so dient das Clarinet auf angenehme weiß | es darff en honen-Thon auch niedern nicht entlehnen | und wechselt lieblich um; Ihm bleibt hierdurch der preiß. | darum manch Edler Geist, dem dieses werck beliebet. | Sich Lehr-begierig zeigt und embsig darin übet.' Trans. in Kroll 1968: 51.

FIG. 5.1. The earliest representation of a clarinettist (Weigel *c*.1722, sheet 14)

His suggestion that the clarinet is a softer substitute for the trumpet is particularly well illustrated in the compositions of Telemann.

In a similar series of engravings of aristocratic and peasant musicians (*c*.1720 –30), the Augsburg artist Martin Engelbrecht included a well-dressed aristocrat playing a recorder (see Beck and Roth 1965, Nos. 30, 32). A bassoon is also shown resting against a wall, with an oboe, two more recorders, a flageolet, and a two-key clarinet on a nearby table.[4] Another aristocrat actually playing a baroque clarinet is depicted as one of sixteen different scenes of musicians on a single eighteenth-century engraved sheet in the Gemeentemuseum, The Hague (Fig. 5.2). Because of the small size of the original engraving, only a few details of the clarinet are visible. It is shown with a long lower joint, which may indicate that a three-key clarinet (with a thumb key for the note *e* or *b'*) was intended. On the lower left-hand corner of the sheet appears: 'Joh. Pet: Wolff Seel: Erben exc.', which probably indicates that the artist was one Johann Peter Wolff.[5] An aristocratic family is depicted in an anonymous German etching (from the first half of the eighteenth century) with the father playing the cello and the mother singing while a son plays the clarinet (Fig. 5.3). The instrument held by the boy is clearly shown to be a baroque clarinet by the shape of the bell and mouthpiece, in spite of Klerk's identification of it as a recorder (1976: 8). In common with many eighteenth-century depictions, such as that found in the *Recueil de planches* (see Fig. 2.1), this clarinet is conical in its outward appearance. It appears that the etching was part of a series, since it carries the number 3 on the right-hand corner. The accompanying couplet reads: 'I work with true affection, strengthened through music's sound, and bring to the Creator a pure song of praise.'[6]

The Universitätsbibliothek in Munich holds a volume of six Masses by Albericus Hirschberger, published in 1743 by Johann Jakob Luzenberger of Burghausen. The frontispiece illustrates a number of instruments (trumpets, horns, trombone, bassoon, harp, viola da gamba, timpani, transverse flute, post-horn, spinet, pan-pipes), among which are two clarinets (of a somewhat conical outline), each placed diagonally across a recorder (Göthel 1972: 395–6, No. 544, illus. 51). The illustration is small and insufficient in detail but does indicate a key on the upper dorsal side of one of the clarinets. Another interesting German engraving which includes a baroque clarinet is by Johann Christoph Steudner (1710–75), entitled 'Rühmlichster Nachklang die schönste Music. Dulcissimum melos bona fama'. In a room with a view of a garden is a group of musicians: a director with a roll of paper, a clavichord player, viola da gamba

---

[4] This player is portrayed in a strikingly similar manner to Weigel's player of the 'Flûte Douse' in *Musicalisches Theatrum* (sheet 12), and even shows identical fingering.

[5] The engraving was attributed to an anonymous artist; cf. Klerk 1976: 15, see Rice 1988a: Fig. 2.

[6] 'Mit treuen Seelen trieb, gestärckt durch Music klang, bring ich dem Schöpffer dar, ein reines Lob-gesang.'

FIG. 5.2. An engraving of an aristocrat playing the baroque clarinet, probably by Johann Peter Wolff (*European Musical Instruments* 1976, No. 41 (1.4))

FIG. 5·3. An aristocratic family depicted in an anonymous German etching from the first half of the eighteenth century (*European Musical Instruments* 1976, No. 20 (2.5))

player, violinist, three wind players (recorder, oboe, clarinet), a pair of singers, and an audience of a woman and child (Sasse 1966: iv. 124; Göthel 1972: 172, No. 136, illus. 15). Unfortunately the depiction of the clarinet does not show many details of construction. Interestingly, two other German artists appear to have been involved in the previous design and production of this work, since it is signed 'Paul Decker inv. et del' and 'Mart. Engelbrecht esc. A. V.'

An English depiction of what were probably two-key clarinets appears in the upper library of Christ Church in Oxford. Here several woodwind, brass, stringed, and percussion instruments were copied by Thomas Roberts (1711–71) for elaborate stuccoes, completed on 8 November 1753, that decorate the upper walls of the library. Among the instruments which Halfpenny identified were eight 'Schalmeys', which he suggested were Roberts' attempt to show the imperfectly understood clarinet (1975: 81–3). These instruments are not represented in much detail, but they are similar enough to the engraving in the *Recueil de planches* (1767) in Diderot and d'Alembert's *Encyclopédie* (see p. 45, Fig. 2.1 above) to support Halfpenny's suggestion. Finally, an illustration of a two-key clarinet is found in the painting *Portrait of the Perceval Family* by the French artist Guillaume Voiriot (1713–99). Here, a mock concert is given by five children (one of whom holds a clarinet), who perform outdoors in front of their wealthy parents. It is reproduced in Richard Leppert's study of aristocratic musette and hurdy-gurdy playing in pre-Revolution France, although the clarinet is misidentified as an oboe (Leppert 1978: 80, 86, Pl. 39). There is some uncertainty as to whether the artist completed this painting in France or England (Leppert 1978: 122 n. 81).[7]

Travelling Virtuosi

Travelling virtuosi played an important part in introducing the clarinet to the concert-going public in many large cities of Germany, Great Britain, and France during the first half of the eighteenth century. Their performances undoubtedly encouraged aristocrats and town and church musicians to add the new instrument to their musical organizations. The prospect of financial gain led performers to England in particular. Mattheson (1713) observed that most musicians in Europe went to England to earn a good deal of money: 'He who in the present time thinks of playing music travels to England. In Italy and France one plays to hear and learn, in England one plays to gain [money], but in the fatherland it is the best to consume.'[8] Another contemporary writer claimed that the Italian singer

---

[7] Oja (1978: 39, item 207) correctly identifies the instrument as a clarinet.

[8] p. 211: 'Wer bey diesen Zeiten etwas in der Music zu *praesti*ren vermeinet / der begibt sich nach Engelland. In Italien and Frankreich etwas zu hören und zu lernen; in Engelland etwas zu verdienen; im Vaterlande aber am besten zu verzehren'. Cf. the trans. in Sands 1943: 91.

Francesca Margherita de l'Epine had 'since her Arrival in *England*, by Modest Computation; . . . got by the Stage and Gentry, above 10,000 Guineas' (Downes 1708: 46).[9]

The Daily Courant of 24 March 1726 mentioned the first clarinettists to be identified by name, two Germans who gave benefit concerts in London during 1726 and 1727:

For the Benefit of M. August Freudenfeld, and Francis Rosenberg, Clarinets.

At Mr. Hickford's Great Room over against the Tennis-Court, in James's Street, near the Hay-Market, Tomorrow being Friday, the 25th of March, will be performed a Consort of Instrumental Musick by the best Hands. To begin precisely at Seven a-Clock. N.B. You are desired to come in at James's-Street Side.

The same announcement was repeated one year later in *The Daily Courant* of 14 March 1727, with an admission price given as five shillings.[10] A little more than a week later (26 April) the clarinet was included in a benefit concert for Mrs Davies at the York Buildings, probably played by Freudenfeld and Rosenberg (see *London Stage* 1960–8: ii. 921–2). The clarinet was not soon forgotten, for its name was used as a novelty by Gay in 1733, when he chose 'Clarinette' for the title of a tune (Air XXXVII) in his libretto to the ballad opera *Achilles*.[11] Freudenfeld or Rosenberg may have also played the chalumeau in concerts at the Richmond-Wells theatre, for *The Daily Post* of 31 June 1722 announced: 'RICHMOND-WELLS . . . on Mondays will be a select band of Musick from the Opera . . . N.B. There will be several Concerto's every Evening on a new Instrument from Germany call'd *The Shalamo*; never play'd in Publick before' (Weston 1977: 16).

Both the 'shalamo' and clarinet were subsequently played in London, starting in 1737, by another foreign-born virtuoso, a 'Mons. Charle', also known as 'Mr Charles', whose career has been documented in some depth (reconstructed in Weston 1971: 17–28 and Highfill *et al.* 1973: iii. 178–9). Originally from France, he appeared in various cities throughout Great Britain for twenty-two years and made a significant contribution to the clarinet's new-found popularity. He was first mentioned on 6 October 1733 in the 'Third Musick' between the acts of Sir John Vanbrugh's play *The Relapse* at the Haymarket theatre, London. This included: 'I. Concerto for French Horns, the French Horns by Charle and Giay, lately arriv'd from Paris' and 'III. Solo for French Horn by Charle' (*London Stage*

---

[9] Although this particular figure may be an exaggeration, l'Epine was immensely popular and did command high fees. See *Grove 6* 'L'Epine, Francesca Margherita de'.

[10] These players may have also influenced Handel to include two chalumeaux in a sketch for the aria 'Quando non vede' in the opera *Riccardo Primo* (1727). In later versions, Handel replaced the chalumeaux with oboes by inserting a musically similar aria, 'Quell' innocente afflito'. See Lawson 1981a: 145–6.

[11] The other short tunes indicated in this libretto are also named without any apparent purpose. See Fiske 1973: 113.

1960–8: iii. 323). Both Charle and Giay performed again at the Haymarket on 20 October 1733, but this time in a 'Duo for Two French Horns' (*London Stage* 1960–8: iii. 328). Charle's first name is never mentioned in a concert advertisement; he began to call himself 'Mr Charles' on 9 September 1734, when he played a concerto on the horn at Goodman's Fields theatre (*London Stage* 1960–8: iii. 414).[12] He continued to appear as a soloist on the horn, but on 1 April 1735 he gave a benefit concert at the Swan Tavern, performing 'several new Pieces on the French Horn and Clarinet' (*London Stage* 1960–8: iii. 475). It appears that he also used the French form of his name when composing; for instance, *The Daily Advertiser* for 10 October 1735 mentioned the following works to be performed on the flute: 'Solo on the German Flute by Burchinger, *Se Largo* by Burchinger and Charle' (*London Stage* 1960–8: iii. 517). Two years later, he began to play the chalumeau in his concerts. On 11 March 1737, admission to Stationers' Hall was advertised at a cost of five shillings for a concert of music 'By the best Hands, with a Solo; and several new Pieces on the French Horn, Clarinette, and Sharlarno [*sic*] by Mr Charles. Also several pieces on the French Horn by an English Gentlewoman, and a Negro boy of ten years old, both scholars of Mr Charles' (Highfill *et al.* 1973–: iii. 178–9). Charle was now active as a teacher of the horn and possibly also the clarinet.

He may have been the chalumeau soloist in Paris at a Concert Spirituel on 21 February 1728, when it was reported in the *Mercure de France* that 'They played a concerto for chalumeau with the accompaniment of the symphony, who formed the choruses. This instrument, which is greatly used in Germany, imitates the oboe and the recorder. The whole thing had quite a singular effect and gave pleasure . . .'[13]

According to Weston, Charle travelled in March of 1742 to Dublin, where he was heralded as 'the famous French-Horn' and 'Master of Musick from London'. It is possible that he came to Dublin at the suggestion of Handel, who had preceded him there by a few days, and whose works were often included in his concerts. Charle lived in Caple Street at the house of Mr Hunt, an upholsterer; he played in the pit band at the Aungier Street Theatre and is known to have advertised for pupils (Weston 1971: 21). *Faulkner's Dublin Journal* referred to him as 'the Hungarian' (Highfill *et al.* 1973–: iii. 179), and this is how he is described in the *Dublin Mercury* advertisement for his benefit concert on 12 May 1742 (Fig. 5.4). This included popular works such as 'Mr Handel's Water-Music, with the

---

[12] A performer with a similar name, 'Charles, the Merry Trumpeter of Oxford', gave performances during Oct. in 1729–33. See *London Stage* 1960–8: iii.

[13] 'On joua ensuite un Concerto de chalumeau, avec les accompagnements de la Simphonie qui forment les choeurs. Cet instrument, qui est fort en usage en Allemagne, imite le Haut-Bois et la Flûte à Bec. Le tout ensemble parut assez singulier et fin plaisir . . .' Quoted in Bobillier 1900: 135–6; Weston 1971: 20.

At the MUSIC-HALL in Fishmble-street,
To-morrow being Wednesday the 12th of May,
1742.
will be performed
A GRAND CONCERT of MUSIC,
By Mr. CHARLES, the HUNGARIAN, Master
of the French Horn, with his Second; accompanied by all the best Hands in this City.

First ACT,
1. An Overture with French Horns, called, new Pastor Fido;
2. The 6th Concerto of Signior Geminiani;
3. A Solo on the French Horn, by Mr. Charles, to shew the Beauty of that Instrument;
4. A Concerto on the Clarinet.

Second ACT,
1. Mr. HANDEL's Water - Music, with the March in Scipio, and the grand Chorus in Atalanta;
2. A Concerto on the German Flute, by Mr. Levieux;
3. A Solo on the Hautbois de Amour, by Mr. Charles;
4. Signior Hasse's Concerto, with Signora Barbarini's Minuet.

Third ACT.
1. The Overture in Saul, with the Dead March, composed by Mr. HANDEL, but never performed here before.
2. A select Piece on the Shalamo.
3. A Solo on the Violoncello, by Signior Pasqualino.
4. The Turkish Musick in the original Taste, as performed at the Spring Garden, Vaux-hall, London.

The Concert to begin at 7 o'Clock in the Evening.
N. B. The Clarinet, the Hautbois de Amour, and Shalamo, were never heard in this Kingdom before.
Tickets at 5 s. and 5 d. each; to be had at Mr. Neal's and Mr. Manwaring's Musick Shops, at Bacon's Coffee-house, and at Mr. Hoey's in Skinner-Row.

FIG. 5.4. An announcement in the *Dublin Mercury* of Mons. Charle's first concert in Dublin on 12 May 1742 (Weston 1971: 23)

March in Scipio, and the grand Chorus in Atalanta'. Charle himself played a 'Solo on the French Horn', 'A Concerto on the Clarinet', 'A Solo on the Hautbois de Amour', and 'A select Piece on the Shalamo', and according to the announcement in the *Dublin Mercury*, 'The Clarinet, the Hautbois de Amour, and Shalamo, were never heard in this Kingdom before'.

As Charle was himself a composer, it is probable that the clarinet concerto and solos for horn, oboe d'amour, and chalumeau were all written by him. His success at performing on four different instruments was widely noted in the newspapers, where it was announced that he would, at popular request, give a repeat performance. This was given on 2 June at the fashionable Playhouse, or Theatre Royal, in Aungier Street. In November the papers announced that he had taken over 'Mr Geminiani's Concerns and Great Musick Room in Dame Street' (Weston 1971: 25), the violinist Francesco Geminiani having left in 1741 (Highfill *et al.* 1973–: iii. 179). Here, Charle gave lessons to gentlemen 'and others' from 8 a.m. to 3 p.m., stating his terms as follows: 'If to the Room, a guinea entrance, and a guinea for sixteen lessons to a month. If he waits on gentlemen, a Moydore entrance, and a Moydore for sixteen lessons' (Weston 1971: 25). Since the moidore was the equivalent of 27s. 6d., Charle may have made a handsome profit with a large number of students (cf. Flood 1913: 284; Boydell 1988: 90).

After two more concerts, one of which featured the clarinet, Charle gave up his tenure at Geminiani's house and returned to London. His next concert took place on 1 November 1743 in the Assembly Rooms at Salisbury, and included his usual horn solos and works for clarinet, oboe d'amour, and chalumeau. There was an important addition in the form of a trio for three French horns which he played himself, with his wife and son. Handel's music was featured again and, as in Dublin, the clarinet, oboe d'amour, and chalumeau were making their first appearance in the city. By 29 December Charle and his family had travelled to Bristol, where two horns and the oboe d'amour were played as well as a trio on the 'shalmo'.[14] The family gave a similar concert at Hickford's Room, London, on 25 April 1744. Weston suggested (1971: 25–6) that if Mrs Charle or her son was able to perform on the clarinet, Handel's *Ouverture* in D major for two clarinets and horn could have been written for and played by the family trio (see pp. 106–9 above). Charle and his son continued to perform in provincial cities, as the announcement in *Barrow's Worcester Journal* for 1748 shows: 'Mr. Charles, senior and junior, from Vauxhall, performed on the French horn and two foreign instruments, the shallamo and clarinet' (Scholes 1970: 190). At Vauxhall Gardens, London, they were employed as orchestral players, accompanying vocal

---

[14] Advertised in the *Bristol Oracle and County Advertiser*, 24 Dec. 1743; see Hooper 1963: 99. The author thanks Janet Page and Michael Finkelman for this reference.

solos and probably playing concertos on the horn and clarinet (see *Grove 6* 'London', §V).

In June of 1751 Charle became the proprietor of the New Vauxhall Theatre in Bristol. He managed the concerts there and performed on the horn with his son. However, this business venture was short-lived and unsuccessful (see Hooper 1963: 104–5). The last concert appearance of Charle and his son was on 22 March 1755 at the Assembly Rooms in Edinburgh, where the style of the announcement—'several select Pieces on the clarinet and other instruments' —suggests that the clarinet had become sufficiently important to be the only instrument named (Weston 1971: 27).[15] The clarinet's popularity in Edinburgh continued, and from the 1760s it was played at the Edinburgh Assembly, an aristocratic dancing-club (see Johnson 1972: 48–9). Mr Charle and his family undoubtedly contributed to the clarinet's new-found popularity; he is the only clarinet virtuoso of the early eighteenth century whose lengthy career (over a twenty-two-year period) is documented.

A few newspapers contain reports of other virtuoso clarinettists active before 1760. The *Frankfurter Frag- und Anzeigungs-Nachrichten* for 13 October 1739 advertised: 'Advertisement: Two good clarinettists have arrived at the windmill in All Saints Lane; anyone wishing to hear them perform will be welcome' (Kroll 1968: 47 n. 1).[16] During a performance at the Concert Spirituel in Paris on 25 March 1750, a concerto for the 'clarine' was played by a bassoonist, France de Kermasin.[17] This is the earliest known performance of a clarinet concerto in France. On 30 December 1751 'A Concerto for Clarinette' was performed in London at the New Haymarket theatre, and a 'Concerto for two Clarinettes' was played at the same theatre on 7 January 1752; unfortunately, the names of the clarinettists are not known (*London Stage* 1960–8: iv. 282, 284). The first English clarinettists were Thomas Habgood and Hugh Pearson, who played a 'grand' concerto at the King's theatre on 13 March 1758 (see Highfill *et al.* 1973–: vii. 124; Weston 1971: 121, 192). The diary of Count Carl Zinzendorf reports that on 6 October 1761 the Polish Count Michael Ogínski (1731–1803) played pieces for the clarinet (possibly by Haydn) at the home of Prince Paul Anton Esterházy in Eisenstadt (Landon 1980: 362). Two years later, Ogínski was playing in an orchestra of dilettantes in Moscow, showing an 'astonishing virtuosity' (Stählin 1769: 163–4; Mooser 1951: i. 34 n. 6; Weston 1977: 188).

Another foreign-born musician active in London was the German Carl (or

---

[15] Blandford (1922) states that Charle was in Dublin during 1756 but does not give any details of his activities or a source of information.

[16] 'Advertissement. Zwey gute Clarinettisten sind allhier in der Windmühl auf der Allerheiligen-Gass ankommen; wer solche zu hören beliebet kann sich dasselbst melden.' Quoted in Israël 1876: 29.

[17] *Mercure de France*, Apr. 1750, 183; cited in Pierre 1975: 116, 257, No. 403.

Charles) Weichsel. He played the oboe at the King's Theatre, and was probably the 'Mr Wrexell' who played the clarinet on 28 December 1760 in Arne's *Thomas and Sally* and in his music for an 'Afterpiece: A New Musical Entertainment' (Pohl 1867: i. 64, 71–2, ii. 373).[18] Weichsel may also have played the clarinet during 1762 in Arne's *Artaxerxes* and J. C. Bach's *Orione* (Weston 1977: 267). Although the extant English instruments suggest that Weichsel was playing a classical clarinet, he may have been the player to whom a writer (known only by the initials 'J.P.') referred in *The Harmonicon* of 1830 (pp. 57–8): 'I conjecture, also, that it [the clarinet] is of German invention, for I have heard that a native of that country played on a clarionet with three keys only, many years ago, in this country.'[19]

An interesting pictorial source shows the playing of a baroque clarinet in a setting of a distinctly stylized nature. This is an anonymous Dutch etching of a horn player and a clarinettist, who are portrayed with costumes in the style of the Italian *commedia dell'arte* and have been described by Klerk (1974: 73, No. 163) as 'Musical Harlequins' (see Fig. 5.5).[20] Hoeprich (1984a: 52–3, illus. 4) has recently pointed out the conical profile of this clarinet and its resemblance to the oboe, except for the obvious differences in turning. The association of the clarinet with the horn probably indicates that the etching was made during a time when these instruments were commonly used together—about the mid-eighteenth century. The cheerful descriptive poem describing the clarinet reads:

> With the lovely sound of my bright clarinet
> I cover noise however loud it becomes,
> Even the pleasant sound of the shrill peace-trumpet,
> Must yield in beauty to my clarinet.[21]

A notable characteristic emphasized here is the greater beauty of the tone of the clarinet compared to the peace-trumpet, or natural trumpet.

The foregoing section includes some of the earliest reports of clarinettists in Europe. The efforts of these performers to introduce the instrument to the concert-going public were essential in encouraging the inclusion of the clarinet in court and theatre orchestras.

---

[18] At Covent Garden Weichsel received 5s. a night for playing the oboe and 10s. 6d. for playing the clarinet in *Thomas and Sally*. See *London Stage* 1960–8: iv. 815, 827.

[19] Repr. with commenatary in Rice 1984c.

[20] See Klerk 1976 and Dudok van Heel and Teutscher 1974: 73, No. 163b.

[21] Door 'tliest 'lyk klinken van myn frisse Clarinet. | Verdoof ik het geluid hoe hoog, 'took word verhaven, | En de aagenamen klank der schelle Vré-trompet, | Zy moet haar schoonheld vor myn Clarinet begeven. Trans. Dr Hans Ruyter, The Claremont Graduate School.

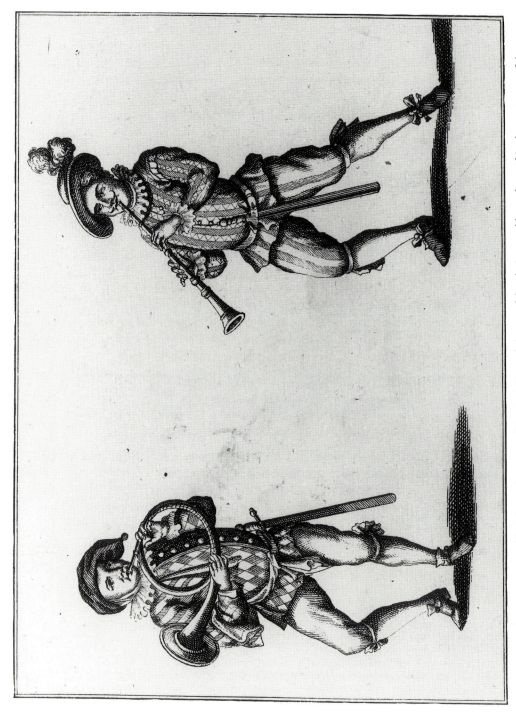

FIG. 5.5. An anonymous mid-eighteenth-century Dutch etching of players of the clarinet and horn dressed in the costumes of the Italian *commedia dell'arte* (*European Musical Instruments* 1976, No. 20 (1.1))

Court Orchestral Clarinettists

The earliest evidence of a court orchestra using the clarinet dates from 1710, when two instruments were ordered from the maker Jacob Denner for the Duke of Gronsfeld (Nickel 1971: 251–2). The next surviving reference is from twenty-three years later: on 17 January 1733, two clarinets were bought for the 'Hof music' in Coblenz, where Johann Peter Spitz played the oboe, clarinet, and viola from 1734 to 1785.[22] Another orchestra owning clarinets was that of the court of Sayn-Wittgenstein at Berleburg. A detailed list of instruments dated 1741 refers to 'In einem Flöten-Casten zwey Paar Clarinetten'.[23]

Weston suggests (1977: 39) that the oboist Carl Barbandt also played the clarinet at the court of Hanover from 1735 to 1752. Subsequently Barbandt lived in London (1753–70), where he was active as a performer on the flute, oboe, and harpsichord and as a composer and teacher (Highfill *et al.* 1973–: i. 279–80). His 'Great Concerto with Clarinets, French Horns and Kettle Drums' was performed on 25 March 1756 (Weston 1977: 39). The nineteenth-century scholar C. F. Pohl (1867: ii. 208 n. 1, 373) listed Barbandt as a clarinettist in London from 1756, and described his playing in a concert on 15 February 1760 as being very expressive. In Hamburg, clarinettists may have been available as early as 1738, since two players of the chalumeau were included in the opera orchestra from this year (Kleefeld 1899–1900: 269, 286; cf. Weston 1977: 60). On the other hand, there does not seem to be any additional evidence of the regular use of the clarinet in Hamburg during the first half of the eighteenth century. The earliest appearance of clarinets in this court orchestra dates from 1795 (see Weston 1977: 60, 147).

The use of the clarinet at the Durlach court in Karlsruhe can be determined by several documents. In the city and address directory of 1771 we find the first mention of a clarinettist:

Flautotraversist:	Johann Reusch
Hautboist:	derselbe
Clarinettist:	derselbe[24]

Reusch or Reisch came to Durlach from Bayreuth in 1730 and was entered in the 1737 register as an oboist and footman. On 23 April 1747 he was promoted out of the livery to the position of court musician. He was entered only as a transverse flautist in the address directory of 1763. However, a manuscript dating from

---

[22] Staatsarchiv Koblenz 1 C5130 fo. 108, cited by Bereths 1964: 44, 48.

[23] Inventarium sämmtlicher Mobiliare, aufgenommen nach Ableben des Grafen Casimir 1741, cited in Domp 1934: 68–9.

[24] From the 'Staats und Addresse Kalender auf das Jahr 1771' quoted by Schiedermair 1912–13: 445.

around 1760, once owned by the composer J. M. Molter, refers to Reusch as either a clarinet or a horn player (Becker 1955: 289): 'Since the band of clarinets and horns was broken up by the retirement of the previous court musician, Jacob Hengel, nevertheless the gap is at present being filled through the particular diligence of the court musician, Reusch, and now since the aforementioned Hengel's salary becomes vacated through his retirement, we ought to . . .'[25]

Although the first mention of a clarinettist in the Durlach register was made in 1771, an ensemble of clarinets and horns existed at least ten years earlier. Since Reusch, who is later listed as a clarinettist, replaced Hengel, we can assume that Hengel played the clarinet in the ensemble (Becker 1955: 289). In another petition, dated 14 August 1769, Reusch specified that he had for some time been 'performing as first flautist, no less than as first player on the clarinet'.[26] Reusch must therefore have played the instrument for some time before taking up this position in 1760, since an inexperienced player would hardly have been capable of playing the first clarinet parts. Hengel was evidently employed by the court for a long period, for he was entered in the salary book as a 'Hofmusicus' as early as 1738. Since both he and Reusch were already employed at the court when the orchestra was enlarged in 1747, it is quite possible that the clarinet was played there during the 1740s and 1750s (cf. Becker 1955: 289–90; *Grove 6* 'Molter, Johann Melchior').[27]

The court orchestra at Cologne included two clarinettists from 1748 onwards: Theodor Klein, originally engaged as a horn player on 3 June 1739, and Joseph Flügel, a viola player engaged on 13 December 1743 (Niemöller 1960: 65–6, 68, 237, 257). They may also have performed on the clarinet at the chapel of St Gereon in Cologne, where two clarinets by an unnamed maker were first purchased for this court orchestra in 1752.[28] In Frankfurt-on-Main on 15 August 1749, a work by the 'Vice Capell-Directore' Heinrich Valentin Beck was performed in which four court virtuosi played the trumpet, clarinet, horn, and flute and recorder.[29] Clarinet players may have been available at this date in Frankfurt but did not appear as regular members of the opera orchestra until 1792.[30]

---

[25] 'Demnach der durch das austreten des gewesenen Hof Musici, Jacob Hengel, zerrissene *Chor de Musique* von Clarinetten und Horn, nunmehro durch Besondern Fleiß des Hof Musici Reuschen anwiederum ergänzet und wir nun auch durch erstgenannten Hengels ausweichen deßen gantze Besoldung ledig werden . . .' [quotation breaks off here.] Quoted in Schiedermair 1912–13: 445; trans. Don Halloran.

[26] 'concertisten und premier Flauto-Stelle, nicht weniger daß premier Blaßen auf dem clarinett'. Schiedermair 1912–13: 445 n. 2.

[27] Becker has suggested a date of *c*.1745 for the composition of Molter's 6 clarinet concertos; see p. 113 above.

[28] Rechn. Mittwochsrentkammer 20. 12. 52, cited by Niemöller 1960: 80 n. 5.

[29] '. . . mit 4 Fürstlichen Virtuosen unter umwechselnden Trombetten, Clarinetten, Waldhorn, Flaut-travers und à bec etc. nur einmahl Musicalisch aufgeführt werden'. Quoted in Israël 1876: 36; see Riemann 1929: 129.

[30] See *Mus. Beobachter* (Frankfurt-on-Main, 1792), cited in Schreiber 1938: 103.

In France, the earliest evidence to indicate that the clarinet was known is shown in a letter written by the Comte de Clermont to the Comte de Billy of Paris on 11 February 1749: 'But let us speak of your menuets. I am currently assembling the virtuosi, the first horn, the second horn, solo violin, viola, violin, clarinet, oboe, *tromba marina*, flageolet, contrabass, fife, timpani, vielle, Jew's harp, recorder, mirliton, chalumeau, bagpipe, musette, castanet, tabor, trombone, organ, barrel-organ, tambourine, harp, harpsichord, and spinet . . .'[31] The first clarinettists to perform in Paris who have been identified (Girdlestone 1969: 294) were Johann Schieffer and Franz Raiffer, who played in the first performance of Rameau's opera *Zoroastre* on 5 December 1749. According to the records of payments of the Opéra, they were among six supplementary musicians who were paid for three rehearsals and twenty-five performances of *Zoroastre* during 1749 and 1750.[32] 'Jean' Schieffer probably played the horn in a performance at the Concert Spirituel in Paris on 9 April 1751, and 'François' Raiffer was listed by this organization as a clarinettist on 25 March 1775 (see Pierre 1975: 260, No. 433, 303, No. 926).

The number of clarinettists who participated in the eighteen performances of *Acante et Céphise* at the Opéra between 19 November 1751 and 7 January 1762 is somewhat uncertain. The following payments are listed in the archives:

Gaspard Procksch pour avoir joué de la Clarinette dans 18. Representations de l'Opera d'Acante et Cephise du 19. November 1761 [*sic*] au 7. Janvier 1762 a raison de 6♯ par chaque Representation . . . . 108.♯
Plus Ledit. a fair Sept Repetition don il . . . . 126.♯
luy en est passé trois suivant l'osayse . . . . 18.♯
Flieger pour idem que dessus . . . . 126.♯
Schencker pour idem que dessus . . . . 126.♯
Louis pour idem que dessus . . . . 126.♯[33]

Each of these musicians received 126 *livres* for eighteen performances and three rehearsals. On the basis of this document, La Laurencie (1911: 16) assumed that Schencker and Louis, as well as Procksch and Flieger, played the clarinet,

---

[31] 'Mais parlons de vos menuets, j'assemble les virtuoses, les Cornos primo, Corno secundo, violino sello, violeta, violino, Clarinetto, aubois, trompette marine, flajolet, Contrebasse, fifre, timbale, viel, guimbarde, flutte douce, flutte à l'oignon, chalumeau, cornemuse, musette, Castagnette, tambourin, trombone, orgue, orgue de Barbarie, timpanon, harpe, clavessin et epinette . . .' Cucuel 1913a: 15.

[32] Etat de Payements qui seront faits à plusieurs sujects cy-après nommez, employez à l'Opèra, par extraordinaire, depuis le 29 aoust 1749, in the Arch. Opéra A. 19. *Emargements*, 1749–51; cited by La Laurencie (1913). Stern (1983: 7–8) was unable to find this record, but suggested that it was lost during the recent transfer (and recataloguing) of the Opéra's documents to the Archives Nationales in Paris.

[33] Etat des Payements à faire à differents Sujets Employés par Extraordinaire dans plusiers Representations de differents Opera, reproduced in Stern 1983, Pl. IV. Cf. an earlier transcription of this document in Rice 1988a: 392.

although the score indicates only two clarinets and two horns.[34] The identification of these players, however, is further clarified by an 'Etat' of 1763, which names the principal musicians of the wealthy amateur La Pouplinière in the performance of *Acante et Céphise*: Procksch and Flieger, clarinet; Schencker, 'Harpe–Cor' (harp and horn); and Louis, 'Contrebasse-Cor' (contrabass and horn) (Cucuel 1913b: 339). Furthermore, Cucuel cites an anonymous eighteenth-century author who described La Pouplinière's orchestra as follows: 'It had the best music in Europe, even before engaging twelve superior musicians, besides two clarinets and two horns of the highest quality . . .'[35] It seems likely that Procksch and Flieger played the clarinet while Louis and Schencker played the horn in *Acante et Céphise*.

There are further reports of the use of clarinets and horns in Paris during the 1750s. For instance, in a letter written in the autumn of 1753, a nephew of La Pouplinière describes a party at his uncle's home, the Château de la Passy: 'All of my uncle's musicians were carefully placed; Stamitz conducting, the horns and clarinets at one end of the gallery, close enough to be heard and they played some airs composed for this most brilliant of parties' (Stern 1983: 3 n. 5).[36] The records of the Concert Spirituel indicate the pairing of clarinet and horn in several subsequent concerts. For example, on 26 and 27 March 1755 'une Symphonie de Stamich [Johann Stamitz] avec clarinets et cors de chasse' was performed (Pierre 1975: 269, Nos. 537–8; Cucuel 1913a: 19).[37] Three days later a performance at the Concert Spirituel included a 'Symphonie avec clarinettes et cors de chasse', probably also by Stamitz (Pierre 1975: 269, No. 541). (Weston 1977: 204, 224, states that both Raiffer and Schieffer played the clarinet under Stamitz's direction in 1753 and 1755.) The concerts for 3 and 4 April 1757 included a 'Symphonie à clarinettes et cors de chasse' (Pierre 1975: 273, Nos. 582–3). During the month of April 1757, there were five concerts which featured clarinets playing alone ('Les clarinettes joue seul'), probably in duets (Pierre 1975: 273, Nos. 587–8, 590, 592–3). After three years, a performance on 30 March 1760 specified clarinets and horns in 'Des symphonie de clarinettes et cors de chasse dont la Tempête suivie du calme' by Ruggi (Pierre 1975: 278, No. 649). The concert on 24 December 1760 included 'Pastorale, Stamich avec cors et clarinettes nouvelle-

---

[34] *Pace* Weston (1977: 199), the entr'acte between acts II and III requires 2 clarinets and 2 horns, not 4 clarinets.

[35] 'Il avait la meilleure musique de l'Europe, ayant à ses gages 12 musiciens des plus excellents, en outre 2 clarinettes et 2 cors admirable . . .' Quoted in Cucuel 1913a: 17–18.

[36] 'Toute la musique de mon oncle était placée; Stamitz à la tête ainsi que les cors et clarinettes étaient à un des bouts de la galerie, assez près pour être entendus et jouaient des airs composés pour la fête la plus brilliante.' See Cucuel 1911: 281.

[37] Bobillier (1900: 249) reported that two clarinettists took part in a performance of a Stamitz symphony in 1754 at the Concert Spirituel, but since this is not verified by its records the date should probably read 1755.

ment arrivés', and that on 1 November 1761 a 'Symphonie avec cors et clarinettes' by Schencker (Pierre 1975: 278, Nos. 658, 668).

At Darmstadt, David Steger, who had been listed in the church records as a chamber musician since 1743, was appointed chamber musician in 1750; in 1757 he was listed as a violin and clarinet player (Noack 1967: 232–3). Another member of this orchestra, Karl Jacob Gozian, played the violin and clarinet from 1754 until his death two years later (Noack 1967: 233). He was replaced on 20 February 1756 by the nineteen-year-old Johann Peter Schüler, who had studied with the court composer Christoph Graupner for two years and who played the clarinet and horn and, by 1766, the musette or bagpipe (Noack 1967: 237).[38] It is noteworthy that two *c'* clarinets were included in a list of instruments dating from 1752 in the Paedagogium at Darmstadt (Noack 1967: 256).

The earliest reference to the clarinet in present-day Czechoslovakia is in the inventory made in 1751 of instruments in the estate of Bernard Nemec at Olomouc (formerly Olmütz). This large collection included four clarinets which were undoubtedly used for several types of music: orchestral, church, dance, and Turkish.[39] The clarinets appear to have gone to the court of Bishop Leopold Egk von Hungersbach in Olmütz, where the instrument is known to have been used from 1758 to 1760. Four clarinets (two in *c'* and two in *a*) are listed in an inventory of his instruments (Sehnal 1972: 296). An extant pay document indicates that Bishop Egk maintained nine regular musicians: a violinist, double bass player, two trumpeters, and a five-member band of clarinets, horns, and bassoon. The clarinettists listed were Anton Fernier (Fournier) and Franz Fogenauer (Pilková 1978: 41; Sehnal 1972: 292–3, 295). A catalogue of the music and instrument collections indicates that the clarinettists also played the English horn: two of these instruments were at the court, and the music collection included eighteen partitas for clarinets, horns, and bassoons and seven for two English horns, horns, and bassoons (Whitwell 1984: 22–3; Sehnal 1972: 298). The musicians must have played clarinets having from three to six keys, which are mentioned by J. K. Rohn in his compendium published in Prague in 1768 (p. 232).

The composer Karl Ditters von Dittersdorf (n.d.: 78) mentioned hearing clarinets in 1754, when they were employed for an outdoor festival at Schlosshof, Austria, near the border of present-day Czechoslovakia. The arrival of the clarinet in the Thurn und Taxis court orchestra of Regensburg was stated by Becker to have occurred in 1755 (1955: 275, *Klarinetten-Konzerte* 1957: p. vii n. 2), but he

---

[38] The 2 clarinet parts of Graupner's cantata 'Lasset eure Bitte im Gebet' (1754) must have been played by Steger and Gozian. See Lawson 1981a: 108.

[39] See Jiří Sehnal, 'Nové příspěvky k dějinám hudby na Moravě', *Časopis Moravského musea* (Vědy společenské, 60; Brno, 1975), 171, as cited in Pilková 1978: 34, 37, 40.

appears to have misread the study which he cites concerning the Regensburg court orchestra, for the earliest listing of the clarinettists Wack and Engelhard Engel appears in a document dated 1765 (Mettenleiter 1866: 270; Titus 1962: 57). Furthermore, according to a later study by Färber (1936: 102, 119–20), who appears to have corrected Mettenleiter, the first year for which the presence of clarinettists at the Thurn und Taxis court can be documented is 1784.

The famous orchestra at the Mannheim court engaged two clarinettists during the course of 1759. Michael Quallenberg and Johannes Hampel appear in the *Almanach Electoral Palatin pour l'Année 1759* but not the manuscript salary list ('Besoldungsliste') dated 28 July 1759 (see Wolf 1981: 343 n. 15; Münster 1983: 39–40, 41 nn. 5, 6). The contemporary writer Jacob von Stählin (1769: ii. 106) recorded the arrival in St Petersburg in 1759 of 'a pair of clever clarinettists', Christopher-Benjamin Lankammer and Compagnon. However, recent research has shown that 'Langhammer', who is mentioned several times as oboist in the *Archives des Théâtres imperiaux*, did not go to St Petersburg until 1763, while Compagnon is not recorded as a member of the orchestra there (see Mooser 1951: i. 55, 203 n. 2). One more example of the orchestral use of what were probably baroque clarinets occurred in Zweibrücken, where three clarinettists were listed as court musicians in 1760: Johann Kertz, Troller (or Broller), and Wilhelm Weisch, sen. (Unverricht 1974: i. 180–1). By 1761 the clarinet and horn were accorded royal recognition in France: they were included in the instrumentation of the royal chapel after its reorganization (Raugel 1957).

In summary, from 1733 to 1760 at least seven court orchestras in Germany made use of the clarinet. By mid-century the instrument was available at the Paris Opéra, in one court orchestra in Bohemia, and in another in Austria (see Table 5.1).

Church and Village Musicians

Frequently, the same musicians who played in a town's court orchestra also played in the local churches. At Eberbach abbey the clarinet must have been played during the second decade of the eighteenth century, since six clarinets were bought for the abbey from Mainz in 1710. (Clarinets were subsequently purchased in 1731, 1735, and 1759; see Gottron 1959: 115–16.) Shortly thereafter, two churches in Nuremberg ordered clarinets from Jacob Denner. Between 1 May 1711 and 30 April 1712, four clarinets were made for the 'Music-Chor' of the Frauenkirche;[40] two years later, the Sebaldkirche also ordered two clarinets.[41]

[40] Landeskirchliches Archiv, Nuremberg, Kirchenrechnung Vereinigtes protestantisches Kirchenvermögen der Stadt Nürnberg 228, Nr. 3, 70; cited in Nickel 1971: 454 n. 1246.

[41] Landeskirchliches Archiv, Nuremberg, Kirchenrechnung 228, Nr. 5, 78; cited in Nickel 1971: 454 n. 1246.

The presence of the clarinet in Italian churches and schools during the first half of the eighteenth century is demonstrated by Vivaldi's use of the instrument in *Juditha Triumphans* (1716) and in three concerti grossi (1720–40), and by Buonanni's description of 1722. At present, however, documentation of its use in cities other than Venice is lacking. According to the lexicographer E. L. Gerber (1812–14: iii/3. 156), Joseph Lacher, Kapellmeister in Kempten and a virtuoso player of the English horn, was taught the oboe and clarinet by his father, a village musician ('Dorfmusikant'), and began to play these instruments at seven years of age in 1746. If Gerber's account is accurate, it documents the popularity of the baroque clarinet among church and village musicians. During this time, the musicians at the abbey of Kremsmünster made use of clarinets; an inventory of their collection of instruments taken in 1747 includes two boxwood clarinets ('2 Buchsbaumerne Clarinett' (see Eitner 1888: 109–10)). The inventory of instruments at the chapel of St Gereon in Cologne in 1749 indicates the use of clarinets in this church also (see Niemöller 1960: 66).

In his autobiography Benjamin Franklin mentioned hearing clarinets while visiting Bethlehem, Pennsylvania, in 1756. He stated: 'I was at their Church, where I was entertain'd with good Musick, the Organ being accompanied with Violins, Hautboys, Flutes, Clarinets, etc.' (Lemay and Zall 1981: 149). However, he wrote this portion of his autobiography between September and October 1788 and was probably relying on a faulty recollection of past events (see Lemay and Zall 1981: p. x). D. M. McCorkle (1956: 600), formerly director of the Moravian Music Foundation, commented that:

Many of Franklin's papers had been destroyed during the Revolution, and he was doubtless writing from memory. It seems safe to assume that he had become familiar with the 'clarinets' in Paris, rather than Bethlehem, and they slipped into this list of woodwinds inadvertently. Certainly, no other evidence has turned up to indicate that the clarinet was known in Bethlehem as early as 1756.

Dr Karl Kroeger, formerly of the Moravian Music Foundation, states in a private communication that later investigations still confirm McCorkle's statement. Indeed, in the music of large Moravian communities in both Bethlehem and Winston-Salem, North Carolina, clarinets are not found among written instrumental parts until after 1800. Table 5.1 lists the appearance of the baroque clarinet from 1710 to 1760 in court and church orchestras as well as in some inventories of instrumental collections by date, country, and city.

TABLE 5.1 *The Clarinet in Court, Church, and Opera Orchestras and Inventory Listings, 1710–60*

Date	Present-day name of country			
	Germany	France	Czechoslovakia	Austria
1710	Nuremberg, Eberbach			
1733	Coblenz			
1735 (?)	Hanover			
1738 (?)	Hamburg			
1741	Berleburg			
1740s	Durlach			
1747	Kremsmünster			
1748	Cologne			
1749	Frankfurt-on-Main (?)	Paris		
1751			Olomouc	
1754	Darmstadt			Schlosshof
1759	Mannheim			
1760	Zweibrücken			

Military Musicians

Two- and three-key clarinets continued to be played in several countries through-out the remainder of the eighteenth century and even during the beginning of the nineteenth century, particularly in military bands. A hand-coloured engraving by James Maurer, published in London in 1753, illustrates a band of eight musicians preceding a grenadier company and comprising two oboes, two clarinets, two horns, and two bassoons.[42] In 1762, the Swiss guards were permitted to establish a band of four bassoons, four hunting-horns, four oboes, and four clarinets (Cucuel 1913a: 21). One year later, a musician who played the clarinet, was sought for a military regiment in Kassel in a newspaper advertisement: 'The Hessian Life-Dragoon-Regiment desires a military musician who can play the oboe, flute, and clarinet and who can furnish good recommendations. Such a person should report to the regiment of Kirchhayn.'[43]

In 1766 the grenadier band ('Grenadiers-Compagnien') of Salzburg consisted of two clarinets, two fifes, and two drums.[44] Two marches for two clarinets and

[42] *A View of [the] Royal Building for his Majesty's Horse & Foot Guards, St. James's Park, London* (London: H. Parker, 1753), reproduced in Hoover 1985: 818, Fig. 436. A detail of the engraving is reproduced in Camus 1980: 82, Fig. 72; a detail of the British Library's engraving of this band is reproduced in Croft-Murray 1980: 152, No. 11, Pl. 110; see also Whitwell 1984: 119 n. 354.

[43] 'Das löb. Hessische Leib-Dragoner-Regiment, verlangt einen Hautboisten, so Hautb. Flutetraversen und Clarnette blasen kan, auch mit guten Attestatis versehen ist; Solcher meldet sich bey schon erwehnten löbl. Regiment zu Kirchhayn.' *Casselische Polizey- und Commercien-Zeitung* (1763), p. 113; quoted in Whitwell 1984: 97 n. 285.

[44] According to a 'Zirkular-Reskript' dated 4 Oct. 1766, quoted in Whitwell 1984: 105. This was reproduced in Hübler's *Sammlung der Militär-, Politischen und Oekonomie Gesetze*, iv (1765–8), pp. 77 f, according to Rameis 1976: 19.

two 'Pfeifer' are extant, presumably written for this band since they are inscribed 'kayserlich-königlichen Exercitium de anno 1765'.[45] Fortunately a description of these two clarinets exists in the Salzburg archives. An 'Essay and Specification of Instruments in the French Pitch required by Military Bandsmen' dated 1769 cites the following: '2 clarinets in D with mouthpieces and B keys as well as joints for tuning them to C' (Birsak 1985: 26).[46] These instruments probably continued to be played because of the conservatism of the bandsmen. Birsak has pointed out that there is in existence in the Salzburg collection (No. 18/2) a three-key clarinet in d' (with an e/b' key for the thumb) by G. Walch, which fits remarkably well the description of 1769 (1985: 27, Photographs 1a–c). According to an inventory of 1776 these two clarinets were still owned by the grenadier band.[47]

Later examples of the use of the baroque clarinet appear in countries outside Germany and Austria. A two- or three-key instrument may also have been used in Swedish military bands beginning in 1762 or 1763 (see Rice 1984a: 19). The Swedish music historian A. A. Hülphers mentioned the clarinet in his treatise of 1773 (p. 87 n. 11) as an instrument 'recently adopted in our Regimental Music'[48] and credited the introduction of the clarinet to a Count Fersen, who 'augmented the field music at the Royal Lifeguards with clarinets . . .' (1773: 103 n. 23).[49] The instruments used by Count Fersen may have been similar to those used by a group of musicians in the infantry described by the organist Johan Miklin in a letter to Hülphers (dated 17 March 1772) as 'consisting of ten persons, namely three oboists, two horns, two bassoons, two clarinets, and one trumpet'.[50] In France the three-key clarinet seems to have been played in the military well into the 1780s. J. B. L. Carré depicted a three-key clarinet (with an e/b' key for the left-hand little finger) together with a recorder, fife, and oboe, in a plate dated 1782 in his treatise on the French military (1783; see Fig. 5.6). He described it as 'resembling a variety of oboe, but different in that the reed is very large and hard, which is why the sound is very silvery and close to the clarino' (p. 373).[51]

---

[45] Entitled 'Mousquetiers Marche' and 'Grenadiers Marche'; reproduced in Brixel, Martin, and Pils 1982: 64–7. Kappey (c.1894: 75–7) printed a nonet (which he dated 1720–30) for 2 oboes, 2 clarinets in d', 2 trumpets in d', 2 horns in d and g, and bassoon. Judging from the instrumentation and the style of the work it must have been written after c.1770 (cf. Titus 1962: 46–7).

[46] Salzburg, Landesarchiv, Akte Landschaft XIII/11, cited in Birsak 1985: 26. This list is reproduced in Birsak and König 1983: 63, *Abb.* 59.

[47] See Oskar Seefeldner, 'Das Salzburger Kriegswesen', Salzburg, MCA, MS IIS 4045, cited in Birsak 1985: 31.

[48] 'aylingen i wår Regements Musik antagne'. Trans. Mrs Kirsten Koblik.

[49] 'har fält-musiken . . . med Clarinetter . . .' Trans. Mrs Kirsten Koblik.

[50] 'uprätter . . . af 10 personer, näml. 3 hautboist., 2 waldth. 2 bassong. 2 clarinett. 1 trompet'. Quoted in Norlind 1937: 44.

[51] 'semble une variété du hautbois, et n'en diffère que par l'anche plus large et plus ferme, pourquoi le son en est plus argentin et plus proche de celui du clairon'.

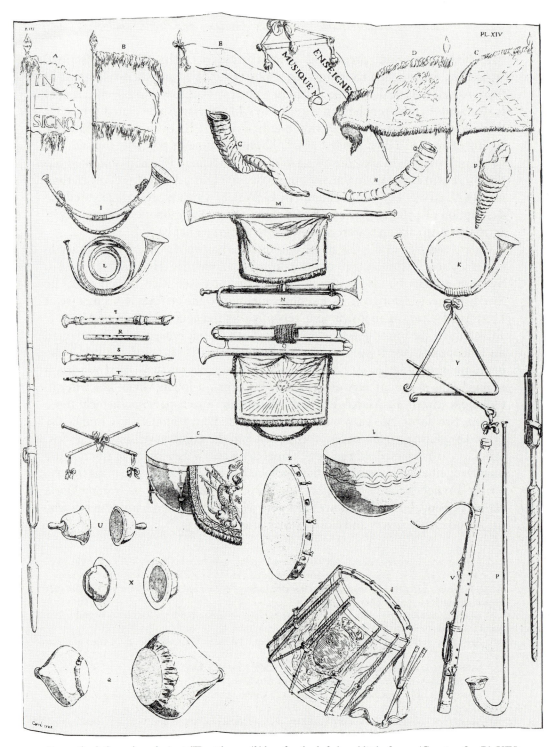

FIG. 5.6. A three-key clarinet (T) with an *e*/*b′* key for the left-hand little finger (Carré 1783, Pl. XIV)

In countries distant from the main centres of musical activity, the baroque clarinet continued to be used. For example, as noted in Chapter 3 (pp. 173–7), a fingering-chart for the three-key clarinet was published in Norway in 1782, and one appeared in a manuscript source in Dublin about 1810. In Holland, Joos Verschuere Reynvaan recorded the ranges of several wind instruments in his *Catechismus der Musijk* (1787, Pl. 15). The range of *f* to *e'''* given for the clarinet suggests that he was referring to a two-key instrument. Furthermore, in his dictionary *Muzijkaal Kunst-Woordenboek* of 1795 (pp. 141, 519), Reynvaan (who also discussed the four- and five-key instruments) called the two-key clarinet a 'piva' and promised a fingering-chart—which never appeared, because the book was never completed.[52]

Conclusion

The baroque clarinet continued to be played throughout Europe during the late eighteenth century and early nineteenth century, particularly in military bands. By the middle of the eighteenth century, the instrument was used in several German court orchestras, at the Paris Opéra, and in one court orchestra in Bohemia and another in Austria. It was slowly supplanted by the classical clarinet, which was introduced by virtuoso players to the great cultural centres of Paris, London, and Berlin and eventually adopted there by the opera and court orchestras.

---

[52] Gerber (1812–14: ii/3, 842–3) claimed that the invasion of Holland during the French Revolution prevented the publication of the 2nd part of this dictionary in its 1795 edn. The MS has not been found and was probably lost by the publisher. See also Broekhuyzen 1848; Fokker 1872–4: 122; and *NNBW* 'Reynvaan, Mr. Joos Verschuere'.

Appendix

A Check-list of Extant Baroque Clarinets

This check-list of two- and three-key clarinets was compiled mainly from catalogues of European instrument museums, my personal observations, and advice generously supplied to me by Dr David Ross, Dr Nicholas Shackleton, Dr Phillip Young, Keith Puddy, Dr André Larson, Brian Ackerman, Jeremy Cooper, and Martin Kirnbauer, woodwind conservator at the Germanisches Nationalmuseum in Nuremberg, and articles by Heyde (1987b) and Ottenbourgs (1989). Where it was obtainable the following information is listed for each instrument: maker and dates, tonality, approximate pitch level in Hz where playable and tested, material of keys, material of body, type of fittings, number of sections, length (L), basic bore size (B), location, and identification number in that collection. Even though I did not personally verify the accuracy of these descriptions, they were thought to be of sufficient value to be presented.

TWO-KEY

1. Boekhout, Thomas Coenraet (1666–1715). In *c'*, brass keys, boxwood stained black, ivory fittings, four sections: mouthpiece-barrel (missing), upper joint, lower joint, stock-bell, L 479 mm., B 14.75 mm.; Brussels, MI, No. 2561.

2. Borkens, Philip (1693–c.1765). In *d'* (*a'* = 415), brass keys, boxwood, unmounted, three sections: mouthpiece-barrel, middle joint, stock-bell, L 545 mm., B 14.35 mm.; The Hague, GM, No. Ea 306–1933.

3. Crone, Gottlieb (1706–68). In *d'* (*a'* = 430), brass keys, boxwood, unmounted, three sections: mouthpiece-barrel, middle joint, stock-bell, L 540 mm., B 12.85 mm.; The Hague, GM, No. Ea 58-X-1952.

4. Denner, Jacob (1681–1735). In *c'* (*a'* = 440), brass keys, boxwood, unmounted, four sections: mouthpiece-barrel, upper joint, lower joint, stock-bell, L 579 mm., B 14.70–14.85 mm.; Berlin, SI, No. 223.

5. ——In *c'* (*a'* = 415), brass keys, boxwood, unmounted, four sections: mouthpiece-barrel, upper joint, lower joint, stock-bell, L 600 mm., B 14.80 mm.; Brussels, MI, No. 912.

6. ——In *d'* (*a'* = 415), brass keys, boxwood, unmounted, three sections: mouthpiece-barrel (contemporary replacement), middle joint, stock-bell, L 543 mm., B 14.5 mm.; Nuremberg, GN, No. MI 149.

7. Deper, M. In *d'*, brass keys, boxwood, unmounted (missing ivory or horn bell-ring), three sections: mouthpiece-barrel (missing), middle joint, stock-bell, L 416 mm.; Linz, OLM, No. Mu 123.

8. IGH. In *d'*, brass keys, boxwood, unmounted, three sections: mouthpiece-barrel, middle joint, stock-bell, L 525 mm., B 12.30mm.; The Hague, GM, No. 50-X-52.

9. Kelmer, G. N. In *c'*, brass keys, boxwood, horn fittings, three sections: mouthpiece-barrel, middle joint, stock-bell, L 552 mm., B 12.6–12.7 mm.; Leipzig, KMU, No. 1469.

10. Oberlender, Johann Wilhelm I (1681–1763). In *d'*, brass keys, boxwood, unmounted, three sections: mouthpiece-barrel (missing), middle joint, stock-bell (missing), original L 540 mm., B 13.70 mm.; Berlin, SI, No. 2870.

11. ——In *c'*, brass keys, boxwood, unmounted, three sections: mouthpiece-barrel, middle joint, stock-bell, L 549 mm., B 13.50 mm.; Leningrad, ITMC, No. 486.

12. Oberlender, Johann Wilhelm II (1712–79). In *c'*, brass keys, boxwood, ivory fittings, three sections: mouthpiece-barrel, middle joint, stock-bell, L 546 mm., B 13.50 mm.; Leipzig, KMU, No. 1470.

13. Rottenburgh, Godefroid-Adrien (1703–68). In *d'*, brass keys, boxwood, unmounted, four sections: mouthpiece-barrel, upper joint, lower joint, stock-bell, L 538 mm., B 13.00 mm.; Brussels, MI, No. 915.

14. ——In *d'*, brass keys, stained boxwood or ebony, unmounted, three sections: mouthpiece-barrel, middle joint, stock-bell, L 539 mm., B 13.75 mm.; Brussels, MI, No. 2571.

15. Scherer, Georg Heinrich (1703–78). In *f'* (*a'* = 415), brass keys, boxwood, ivory fittings, three sections: mouthpiece-barrel, middle joint, stock-bell, L 474 mm., B 13.00 mm.; Eisenach, BH, No. L-4.

16. ——In *f'* (*a'* = 415), brass keys, boxwood, unmounted, three sections: mouthpiece-barrel, middle joint, stock-bell, L 476 mm., B 12.80 mm.; Meiningen, SM, No. MI 19.

17. ——In *d'* (*a'* = 415), silver keys, ivory, unmounted, four sections: mouthpiece-barrel, upper joint, lower joint, stock-bell, L 525 mm., B 14.30 mm.; London, RCM, No. 101.

18. ——In *d'*, silver keys, ivory, unmounted, four sections: mouthpiece-barrel, upper joint, lower joint, stock-bell, L 537 mm., B 13.80 mm.; Paris, MI, No. C.529, E.697.

19. ——In *d'*, silver keys, boxwood, ivory fittings, four sections: mouthpiece-barrel, upper joint, lower joint (with an additional shorter middle joint), stock-bell, L 536 mm., B 13.85 mm.; Onnen-Haren, Verel collection.

20. ——In *d'*, silver keys, boxwood, ivory fittings, four sections: mouthpiece-barrel (not original), middle joint (with an additional lower joint in Verel collection), stock-bell, L 514 mm., B 13.70 mm.; Scarsdale, New York, Rosenbaum collection.

21. Walch, Georg (1690–?). In *eb'*, brass keys, boxwood, unmounted, three sections: mouthpiece-barrel, middle joint, stock-bell, L 488 mm., B 12.35 mm.; Bonn, BH, No. Z 122.

22. ——In *d'* (*a'* = 405–10), brass keys, plum, brass fittings, three sections: mouthpiece-barrel, middle joint, stock-bell, L 530 mm., B 13.15 mm.; Salzburg, MCA, No. 18/1.

23. Wietfeld, Philipp Gottlieb (*c.*1743–93). In *d'*, brass keys, boxwood, ivory fittings, three sections: mouthpiece-barrel (missing), middle joint, stock-bell, L 420 mm., B 12.80 mm.; London, Puddy collection.

24. Willems, Jean Baptiste (*fl.* 1758–1810). In *g'* (*a'* = 435), brass keys, boxwood, unmounted, three sections: mouthpiece-barrel, middle joint, stock-bell, L 412 mm., B 11.70 mm.; Brussels, MI, No. 916.

25. ——In *bb*, brass keys, boxwood, unmounted, four sections: mouthpiece-barrel, upper joint, lower joint, stock-bell, L 658 mm., B 14.15 mm.; Brussels, MI, No. 2573.

26. ——In *f'* (*a'* = 420), brass keys, boxwood, unmounted, three sections: mouthpiece-barrel (missing), middle joint, stock-bell, L 386.9 mm.; Oxford, BC, No. 429.

27. ——In *d'*, brass keys, boxwood, one ivory fitting, four sections: mouthpiece, barrel, middle joint, stock-bell, L 535 mm., B 12.50 mm.; Antwerp, MV, No. 982.9.3.

28. Zencker, Johann Gottfried (1737–74). In *d'* (*a'* = 425–30), brass keys, boxwood, unmounted, three sections: mouthpiece-barrel, middle joint, stock-bell, L 541 mm.; B 12.80 mm.; Nuremberg, GN, No. MIR 424.

29. Unmarked. In *d'*, brass keys, boxwood, unmounted, three sections: mouthpiece-barrel, middle joint, stock-bell, L 517 mm., B 13.10 mm.; The Hague, GM, No. Ea 449-1933.

30. ——In *f'*, brass keys, boxwood, unmounted, four sections: mouthpiece, barrel, middle joint, stock-bell (composite of sections from different instruments), L 440 mm.; Leipzig, KMU, No. 1457.

31. ——In *d'* (*a'* = 415), brass keys, boxwood, unmounted, three sections: mouthpiece-barrel, middle joint, L 543 mm., B 14.50 mm.; London, Rubin collection.

THREE-KEY

1. Denner, Johann Christoph (1655–1707). In *d'* (*a'* = 415), brass keys, thumb *e/b'* key, boxwood, unmounted, three sections: mouthpiece-barrel (missing), middle joint, stock-bell, doubled tone-holes for fingers 3, 4, 6, and 7, L 524 mm., B 14.05–14.45 mm.; Berkeley, UC, No. 19.

2. Fridrich, J. In *c'*, brass keys, thumb *e/b'* key, boxwood, unmounted, three sections: mouthpiece-barrel (missing), middle joint, stock-bell; Prague, HO, No. 666E.

3. GRFUES (Fues, G. R.?). In *bb* or *a*, brass keys, thumb *e/b'* key, boxwood, unmounted, four sections: mouthpiece-barrel, upper joint, lower joint, stock-bell, L 690 mm.; Bochum, SM, No. 50.

4. Kenigsperger, Johann Wolfgang (c.1705–52). In *d'* (marked 'G'), brass keys, thumb *e/b'* key, plum, one horn fitting, three sections: mouthpiece-barrel, middle joint, stock-bell, L 518 mm., B 12.50 mm.; Munich, SM, No. Mu 110.

5. Paur, R. In *c'* (*a'* = 430), brass keys, thumb *e/b'* key, boxwood, unmounted, three sections: mouthpiece-barrel, middle joint, stock-bell, L 611 mm., B 13.45 mm.; Nuremberg, GN, No. MIR 425.

6. Scherer, Georg Heinrich (1703–78). In *d'* (*a'* = 415), silver keys, left-hand little finger *e/b'* key, boxwood, ivory fittings, four sections: mouthpiece, barrel, middle joint, stock-bell, L 569 mm., B 13.30 mm.; Brussels, MI, No. 924.

7. Strehli, I. G. In *c'* (*a'* = 425–7), brass keys, thumb *e/b'* key, boxwood, unmounted, three sections: mouthpiece-barrel, middle joint, stock-bell, L 611 mm., B 12.25–12.65 mm.; Munich, SM, No. 48–40.

8. ISW (I. S. Walch?). In *bb* or *a*, brass keys, thumb *e/b'* key, boxwood, horn fittings, three

sections: mouthpiece-barrel, middle joint, stock-bell, L 692 mm., B 13.75 mm.; Linz, OLM, No. Mu 26.

9. Walch, Georg (1690–?). In *d'* (*a'* = 405–10), brass keys, left-hand little finger (originally thumb) *e/b'* key, pear, unmounted, three sections; mouthpiece-barrel, middle joint, stock-bell, L 571 mm., B 12.30 mm.; Salzburg, MCA, No. 18/2.

10. ——In *c'*, brass keys, thumb *e/b'* key, boxwood, horn fittings, three sections: mouthpiece-barrel, middle joint, stock-bell; Germany, private collection.

11. Unmarked. In *a* (*a'* = 435), brass keys, thumb *e/b'* key, boxwood, unmounted, four sections; mouthpiece-barrel, upper joint, lower joint, stock-bell (composite instrument; only the stock-bell is from a baroque clarinet), L 713 mm., B 14.50 mm.; Brussels, MI, No. 913.

12. ——In *d'*, brass keys, left-hand little finger *e/b'* key, boxwood, unmounted, three sections: mouthpiece-barrel, middle joint, stock-bell, L 555 mm., B 13.30 mm.; Nuremberg, GN, No. MIR 150.

13. ——In *g'* or *ab'*, brass keys, left-hand little finger or thumb *e/b'* key, boxwood, horn fittings, six sections: mouthpiece, barrel, upper joint, lower joint, stock, bell, L 375 mm.; Nuremberg, GN, No. MIR 426.

LIST OF REFERENCES AND
FURTHER READING

MUSIC

Airs à Deux Chalumeaux, Deux Trompettes, deux Haubois, deux Violons, deux Flûtes, deux Clarinelles, ou Cors de Chasse[2] (Amsterdam: E. Roger and M. C. Le Cène, *c*.1717–22).

CALDARA, ANTONIO (1718), Ifigenia in Aulide. Brussels, Conservatoire Royal de Musique de Bruxelles, MS W. 2048.

HANDEL, GEORGE FRIDERIC (1867 edn.), *Solomon*, ed. F. G. Chrysander (Leipzig: Breitkopf & Härtel; repr. edn., Ridgewood, NJ, Gregg Press, 1965).

—— (1952 edn.), *Ouverture (Suite)*, ed. K. Haas (London: Schott & Co.).

Instrumentalkonzerte deutscher Meister, ed. Arnold Schering (*Denkmäler Deutscher Tonkunst*, 29–30; Leipzig; Breitkopf & Härtel, 1906, repr. edn., Wiesbaden: Breitkopf & Härtel, 1958).

Klarinetten-Duette aus der Frühzeit des Instrumentes, ed. Heinz Becker (Wiesbaden: Breitkopf & Härtel, 1954).

Klarinetten-Konzerte des 18. Jahrhunderts, ed. Heinz Becker (*Das Erbe Deutscher Musik*, 41; Wiesbaden: Breitkopf & Härtel, 1957).

KÖLBEL, FERDINAND (*c*.1740–50), 'Trio: Clarinet, Cornu de Schass et Basso'. Darmstadt, Hessische Landes- und Hochschulbibliothek, MS Mus. 1181.

MOLTER, JOHANN MELCHIOR (*c*.1745), Concertos for Clarinet. Karlsruhe, Landesmuseum, MSS 302, 304, 328, 332, 334, 337.

PAGANELLI, GIUSEPPE ANTONIO (1733?), Clarinet Concerto in B flat major. Padua, Archivio Musicale della Cappella Antoniana, No. 1774, lettera D, scaffaleV⁰.

RAMEAU, [JEAN-PHILIPPE] ([1751]), *Acante et Céphise ou La Sympathie* (Paris: author).

—— (1982) edn.), *Les Boréades (1764) tragédie lyrique* (facs. edn. of autograph, Paris: Stil).

RATHGEBER, VALENTIN (1728), *Chelys Sonora Excitans Spiritum Musicorum Digitis, Auribus, Ac Animis Accommodata, et Orbi Data in Bis Duodenis hoc est: XXIV. Concertationibus* (Augsburg: J. J. Lotter).

—— (1968 edn.), *Concerto XV, Op. 6 Es-Dur*, ed. E. Hess (Basle: Kneusslin).

—— (1976 edn.), *Concerto C-Dur, Op. 6, Nr. 19*, ed. E. Nowak (Stuttgart: Carus).

STAMITZ, JOHANN (1953 edn.), *Concerto in B flat major*, ed P. Gradenwitz (New York: MCA Music).

—— (1967 edn.), *Concerto*, ed. W. Lebermann (Mainz: B. Schott's Söhne).

TELEMANN, GEORG PHILIPP (1719), Cantata, 'Jesu, wirst du bald erscheinen'. Frankfurt-on-Main, Stadts-und Universitätsbibliothek, MS FF Mus. 1187, Telemann 456.

—— (1721a), Cantata, 'Christus ist um unsrer Missetat willen'. Frankfurt-on-Main, Stadts- und Universitätsbibliothek, MS FF Mus. 807, Telemann 76.

—— (1721b), Cantata, 'Wer mich liebet, der wird mein Wort halten'. Frankfurt-on-Main, Stadts- und Universitätsbibliothek, MS FF Mus. 1474, Telemann 743.

——(1722), Cantata, 'Ein ungefärbt Gemüte Aufgenommen'. Frankfurt-on-Main, Stadts-und Universitätsbibliothek, MS FF Mus. 953, Telemann 953.

——(1728), 'Serenata, zum Convivio der HH Burgercapitains'. Berlin, Staatsbibliothek Preussischer Kulturbesitz Musikabteilung, Autograph Telemann 28.

VIVALDI, ANTONIO (1947a edn.), *Concerto in do maggiore per 2 oboi, 2 clarinetti, archi et cembalo*, RV 559, ed. A. Ephrikian (Milan: Ricordi).

——(1947b edn.), *Concerto in do maggiore per 2 oboi, 2 clarinetti, archi e cembalo*, RV 560, ed. A. Ephrikian (Milan: Ricordi).

——(1948 edn.), *Juditha Triumphans, Sacrum Militare Oratorium*, fac. edn. (Siena: Accademia Musicale Chigiana); ed. A. Zedda as *Juditha Triumphans* (Milan: Ricordi, [1971]).

——(1949 edn.), *Concerto in do maggiore per 2 flauti, 2 oboi, 2 clarinetti, fagotto, 2 violini, archi e cembalo*, RV 556, ed. A. Ephrikian (Milan: Ricordi).

LITERATURE

The following bibliographical abbreviations are used in this list:

AMZ	*Allgemeine Musikalische Zeitung*
AR	*The American Recorder*
EM	*Early Music*
GSJ	*Galpin Society Journal*
JAMIS	*Journal of the American Musical Instrument Society*
MF	*Die Musikforschung*
ML	*Music & Letters*
MT	*The Musical Times*
SIMG	*Sammelbände der Internationalen Musikgesellschaft*

ABERT, HERMANN (1908), *Niccolo Jommelli als Opernkomponist* (Halle: M. Niemeyer).

ACKERMAN, BRIAN (1989), 'The Development of the Early Clarinet', *The Clarinet* 16/2: 37–40.

ADAM, ADOLPHE (1857), *Souvenirs d'un Musicien* (Paris: M. Levy Frères).

—— (1859), *Derniers Souveniers d'un Musicien* (Paris: M. Levy Frères).

ADLUNG, JACOB (1758), *Anleitung zu der Musikalischen Gelahrtheit* (Erfurt: J. D. Jungnicol, 2 vols; fac. edn., Kassel: Bärenreiter, 1953).

AGRICOLA, MARTIN (1529), *Musica Instrumentalis Deudsch* (Wittenberg: G. Rhaw; repr. edn., Hildesheim: G. Olms, 1969).

Allgemeine Deutsche Biographie, ed. R. W. Liliencron *et al.*, 56 vols. (Leipzig: Duncker & Humblot, 1875–1912).

ALTENBURG, JOHANN ERNST (1795), *Versuch einer Anleitung, zur Heroisch-musikalischen Trompeter- und Pauker-Kunst* (Halle: J. C. Hendel [written *c.*1770]; fac. edn., New York:

Broude, 1966); trans. E. Tarr as *Essay on an Introduction to the Heroic and Musical Trumpeters' and Kettledrummers' Art* (Nashville: Brass Press, 1974).

ALTENBURG, WILHELM (1904), *Die Klarinette: Ihre Entstehung und Entwicklung bis zur Jetztzeit in akustischer, technischer, u. musikalischer Beziehung* (Heilbronn: C. F. Schmidt).

AMMAN, JOST (1589), *Wapen und Stammbuch* (Frankfurt: S. Feyeraben; repr. edn., Munich: Hirth, 1881).

[ANCELET] (1757), *Observations sur la musique, les musiciens, et les instruments* (Amsterdam: Aux depens de la compagnie).

ANDERSCH, JOHANN DANIEL (1829), *Musikalisches Woerterbuch* (Berlin: W. Natorff und Comp.).

Antichi strumenti (1980), *Antichi strumenti della raccolta dei Medici e dei Lorena alla formazione del Museo del Conservatorio di Firenze* (Florence: Giunti-Barbèra).

ANTOLINI, FRANCESCO (1813), *La retta maniera di scrivere per il clarinetto* (Milan: C. Buccinelli).

APEL, WILLI (1972), *Harvard Dictionary of Music*[2] (Cambridge, Mass.: Belknap Press).

ARNOLD, DENIS (1965), 'Instruments and Instrumental Teaching in the Early Italian Conservatories', *GSJ* 18: 72–81.

[AUBIN, NICOLAS] (1716), *Cruel effets* (Amsterdam: E. Roger).

BACKOFEN, JOHANN GEORG HEINRICH (c.1803), *Anweisung zur Klarinette nebst einer kurzen Abhandlung das Basset-Horn* (Leipzig: Breitkopf & Härtel; repr. edn. Celle: Moeck, 1986).

BAERMANN, CARL (1864–75), *Vollständige Clarinett Schule*, 5 vols. (Offenbach: J. André).

BAINES, ANTHONY (1960), 'Provisional Index of Present-Day Makers of Historical Musical Instruments (Non-Keyboard)', *GSJ* 13: 70–87.

—— (1966), *European and American Musical Instruments* (New York: Viking Press).

—— (1967), *Woodwind Instruments and Their History*[3] (London: Faber and Faber).

——(1974), 'Reviews', *GSJ* 27: 151.

BALFOUR, HENRY (1890), 'The Old British "Pibcorn" or "Hornpipe" and its Affinities', *Journal of the Anthropological Institute* 20: 142–54.

BÄR, FRANK (1989), 'Die Sammlung der Musikinstrumente die Fürstlich-Hohenzollern Schloss zu Sigmaringen an der Donau' (MA thesis, University of Tübingen).

BARKER, A., ed. (1984), *Greek Musical Writings* (The Musician and his Art, i; Cambridge: Cambridge University Press).

[BARNICKEL] (1737), *Kurzegefasstes musicalisches Lexicon* (Chemnitz: J. C. and J. D. Stössel).

BASELT, BERND (1963), 'Die Musikaliensammlung der Schwarzburg-Rudolstädtischen Hofkapelle unter Philipp Heinrich Erlebach (1657–1714)', *Traditionen und Aufgaben der Hallischen Musikwissenschaft*, ed. W. Siegmund-Schultze (Halle-Wittenberg: Wissenschaftliche Zeitschrift der Martin-Luther-Universität), pp. 105–27.

——(1978–), *Händel-Handbuch*, ed. W. and M. Eisen, 5 vols., Kassel: Bärenreiter).

BATE, PHILIP (1978), *The Trumpet and Trombone*[2] (New York: W. W. Norton).

BECK, SYDNEY, and ELIZABETH E. ROTH (1965), *Music in Prints* (New York: The New York Public Library).

BECKER, HEINZ (1955), 'Zur Geschichte der Klarinette im 18. Jahrhundert', *MF* 8: 271–92.

——(1966), *Zur Entwicklungsgeschichte der antiken und mittelalterlichen Rohrblatt-instrumenten* (Hamburg: H. Sikorski).

——(1969), 'Das Chalumeau bei Telemann', *Konferenzbericht der 2. Magdeburger Telemann-Festtage* (Magdeburg: Deutsche Kulturband), pp. 68–76.

——(1970), 'Das Chalumeau im 18. Jahrhundert', *Speculum musicae artis: Festgabe für Heinrich Husmann zum 60. Geburtstag* (Munich: H. Fink), pp. 23–46.

BENTZON, ANDREAS FRIDOLIN WEIS (1969), *The Launeddas*, 2 vols. (Copenhagen: Akademisk Forlag).

BERETHS, GUSTAV (1964), *Die Musikpflege am kurtrierischen Hofe zu Koblenz-Ehrenbreitstein* (Mainz: B. Schott's Söhne).

BERG, LORENTS NICOLAI (1782), *Den første Prøve for Begyndere udi Instrumental-Kunsten* (Kristiansand: A. Swane).

'Berichtigungen' (1791), 'Berichtigungen und Zusätze zu den musikalischen Almanachen auf die Jahre 1782. 1783. 1784.', *Musikalische Korrespondenz der teutschen filarmonischen Gesellschaft für das Jahr 1791* 6 (9 Feb.): 41–2.

BERLIN, JOHAN DANIEL (1744), *Musicaliske Elementer* (Trondheim: author).

BERNARDINI, ALFREDO (1989), 'Woodwind Makers in Venice, 1790–1900', *JAMIS* 15: 52–73.

BERNER, ALFRED (1961), 'Nachwort', in Johann Christoph Weigel, *Musicalisches Theatrum* (fac. edn., Kassel: Bärenreiter).

BERNSDORF, EDUARD, ed. (1857), *Neues Universal-Lexikon*, 4 vols. (Dresden: R. Schaefer).

BESSARABOFF, NICHOLAS (1941), *Ancient European Musical Instruments: An Organological Study of the Musical Instruments in the Leslie Lindsey Mason Collection at the Museum of Fine Arts, Boston* (New York: October House).

BIRSAK, KURT (1973a), 'Das Dreiklappen-Chalumeau im Bayerischen National-Museum in München', *MF* 26: 493–7.

——(1973b), *Die Holzblasinstrumente im Salzburger Museum Carolino Augusteum: Verzeichnis und Entwicklungsgeschichtliche Untersuchungen* (Salzburger Museum Carolino Augusteum Jahresschrift, 18; Salzburg: Salzburger Museum Carolino Augusteum).

——(1985), 'Salzburg, Mozart and the Clarinet', trans. G. Schamberg, *The Clarinet* 13/1: 26–31.

——and MANFRED KÖNIG (1983), *Das grosse Salzburger Blasmusik Buch* (Vienna: Brandstätter).

BLANDFORD, W. F. H. (1922), 'The French Horn in England', *MT* 63: 697.

BLASIUS, FRÉDÉRIC (*c.*1796), *Nouvelle méthode de clarinette* (Paris: Porthaux; repr. edn., Geneva: Minkoff, 1972).

BLATT, FRANZ THADDÄUS ([1839]), *Die Kunst des Clarinetblasens / Méthode Compléte de Clarinette* (Paris: Schonenberger).

BOBILLIER, MARIE [pseud.] BRENET, MICHEL (1900), *Les concerts en France sous l'ancien régime* (Paris: Fischbacher).

——(1903), 'Rameau, Gossec et les clarinettes', *Le guide musicale* 49: 183–5, 203–5, 227–8.

BONAVENTURA, ARNALDO (1928), 'Domenico Del Mela e il primo pianoforte verticale', *Bollettino della Società Mugellana studi storici* 4: 9–10; cited in Gai 1969.

BORDERS, JAMES M. (1988), *European and American Wind and Percussion Instruments: Catalogue of the Stearns Collection of Musical Instruments, University of Michigan* (Ann Arbor, Michigan: University of Michigan Press).

[BORJON DE SCELLERY, CHARLES EMMANUEL] (1672), *Traité de la Musette* (Lyons: I. Girin and B. Riviere; repr. edn., Geneva: Minkoff, 1972).

BOYDELL, BARRA (1982), *The Crummhorn and Other Renaissance Windcap Instruments* (Buren: F. Knuf).

——(1988), *A Dublin Musical Calendar 1700–1760* (Dublin: Irish Academic Press).

BOYDEN, DAVID D. (n.d.), *Catalogue of the Collection of Musical Instruments in the Department of Music, University of California, Berkeley* ([Berkeley: University of California]).

BOYER, ABEL (1719), *Dictionnaire Royal François et Anglois* (Amsterdam: P. Humbert, The Hague: Freres van Dole and I. Vaillant).

——(1768), *Dictionnaire Royal François et Anglois* (Lyons: J. M. Bruyset).

BRACHET, AUGUSTE (1878), *An Etymological Dictionary of the French Language* (Oxford: Clarendon Press).

BRANDE, WILLIAM THOMAS, ed. (1842), *A Dictionary of Science, Literature, and Art* (London: Longman, Brown, Green, and Longmans).

BREWSTER, DAVID, ed. (1808–30), *Edinburgh Encyclopædia*, 18 vols. (Edinburgh: W. Blackwood).

BRIXEL, EUGEN, GÜNTHER MARTIN, and GOTTFRIED PILS (1982), *Das ist Oesterreichs Militär Musik: von 'Turkischen Musik' zu den Philharmonischen in Uniform* (Graz: Kaleidoskop).

[BROCKHAUS, FRIEDRICH ARNOLD] (1814–19), *Allgemeine Deutsche Real-Encyclopädie für die Gebildeten Stände (Conversations-Lexikon)*[3], 10 vols. (Leipzig: F. A. Brockhaus).

BROEKHUYZEN, G. H. (1848), 'Joost Verschuere Reynvaan', *Caecilia en die Muziek* 5: 167–8.

BROOK, BARRY S. (1962), *La Symphonie française dans la seconde moitié XVIIIe siècle*, 3 vols. (Paris: Publications de l'Institut de Musicologie de l'Université de Paris).

BROWN, A. PETER (1987), 'Caldara's Trumpet Music for the Imperial Celebrations of Charles VI and Elisabeth Christine', *Antonio Caldara: Essays on his Life and Times*, ed. B. W. Pritchard (Aldershot: Scolar Press), 1–48.

BRÜCKER, FRITZ (1926), *Die Blasinstrumente in der altfranzösische Literatur* (Giessener Beiträge zur romanischen Philologie, 19; Giessen: Selbstverlag des Romanischen Seminars).

BUONANNI [BONANNI], FILIPPO (1722), *Gabinetto Armonico Pieno d'Istromenti Sonori Indicati, e Spiegati* (Rome: G. Placho); 2nd edn. pub. as *Descrizione degl'Istromenti Armonico*, ed. G. Ceruti (Rome: V. Monaldini, 1776).

BURGKMAIR, HANS (1964), *The Triumph of Maxmilian I*, ed. S. Appelbaum (New York: Dover).

BURNEY, CHARLES (1789), *A General History of Music from the Earliest Ages to the Present Period* (London; repr. edn., 2 vols., New York: Dover, 1957).

BUSCH, GABRIEL CHRISTOPH BENJAMIN (1790–8), *Versuch eines Handbuchs der Erfindungen*, 8 vols. (Eisenach: J. G. E. Wittekindt).

—— (1802–22), *Handbuch der Erfindungen*, 12 vols. (Eisenach: J. G. E. Wittekindt).

CAMUS, RAOUL FRANÇOIS (1980), 'Military Music of Colonial Boston', *Music in Colonial Massachusetts 1630–1820*, ed. B. Lambert (Music in Public Places, i; Boston: The Colonial Society of Massachusetts), pp. 75–101.

CARRÉ, JEAN BAPTISTE LOUIS (1795), *Panoplie: ou, Réunion de tout ce qui a trait à la guerre, depuis l'origine de la nation française jusqu'à nos jours*, (Paris: Fuchs [written 1783]).

CARSE, ADAM (1939), *Musical Wind Instruments* (London; repr. edn., New York: Da Capo, 1965).

Catalogue of the Crosby Brown Collection of Musical Instruments of All Nations, 5 vols. (New York: The Metropolitan Museum of Art, 1901–14).

CHAMBAUD, LOUIS (1778), *Nouveau dictionnaire François-Anglois, & Anglois-François* (London: W. Strahan, T. Cadell, & P. Elmsly).

CHARLTON, DAVID (1988), 'Classical Clarinet Technique: Documentary Approaches', *EM* 16: 396–406.

CHATWIN, R. B. (1950), 'Handel and the Clarinet', *GSJ* 3: 3–8.

CLÉDAT, LÉON (1931), *Dictionnaire etymologique de la langue Française* (Paris: Hachette).

COLANGE, L. (1878), *Amies' Universal Encyclopedia: A Compendium of General Information* (Philadelphia: W. T. Amies).

COLLINSON, ROBERT (1966), *Encyclopedias: Their History Throughout the Ages*[2] (New York: Hefner).

The Compleat Tutor for the German Flute (Dublin: J. Delaney, c.1810).

COTGRAVE, RANDLE (1611), *A Dictionarie of the French and English Tongues* (London; repr. edn., Columbia: University of South Carolina Press, 1950).

[COUSSEMAKER, EDMOND H.] (1877), *Catalogue de la Bibliothèque et des Instruments de feu M. Ch. Edm. H. de Coussemaker* (Brussels: F. J. Olivier; repr. edn., Buren: F. Knuf, 1977).

CROFT-MURRAY, EDWARD (1980), 'The Wind-Band in England, 1540–1840', *British Museum Yearbook* 4 (Music and Civilisation): 135–79.

[CROUSAZ, JEAN PIERRE DE] (1715), *Traité du Beau: Où l'on Montre en Quoi Consiste ce qui l'on Nomme ainsi, par des Examples tirez de la Plûpart des Arts & des Sciences* (Amsterdam: F. L'Honoré).

CUCUEL, GEORGES (1911), 'La question des clarinettes dans l'instrumentation du XVIIIe siècle', *Zeitschrift der Internationalen Musikgesellschaft* 12: 280–4.

—— (1913a), *Études sur un orchestre au XVIIIme siècle* (Paris: Fischbacher).

—— (1913b), *La Pouplinière et la musique de chambre au XVIIIe siècle* (Paris: Fischbacher).

DÄHNERT, ULRICH (1973), 'The Newly Restored Silbermann Organ in the Catholic Court Church, Dresden', *Organ Yearbook* 4: 122–4.

The Daily Courant 7624 (24 Mar. 1726), 7929 (14 Mar. 1727); British Library, Burney Papers on Microfilm, 265B.

DAINES, DEIRDRE, ROBIN HEWITT, GERALD VICKERS, and JOHN HANCHETT (1976), 'Some Measurements of Early Wind Instruments', *EM* 4: 461–3.

DART, THURSTON (1951), 'The Earliest Collection of Clarinet Music', *GSJ* 4: 39–41.

——(1953), 'The Mock Trumpet', *GSJ* 6: 35–40.

DAY, CHARLES RUSSELL, ed. (1891), *A Descriptive Catalogue of the Musical Instruments recently exhibited at the Royal Military Exhibition, London, 1890* (London: Eyre & Spottiswoode).

DIAGRAM GROUP, eds. (1976), *Musical Instruments of the World* (New York: Facts on File).

Dictionnaire Universel François et Latin (Nancy: P. Antoine, 1734).

DIDEROT, DENIS, and JEAN LE ROND D'ALEMBERT, eds. (1751–65), *Encyclopédie, ou Dictionnaire Raisonné des Sciences, des Arts et des Métiers par un Société de Gens de Lettres*, 17 vols. (Paris: Briasson, David, Le Breton).

——eds. (1762–72), *Recueil de planches sur les sciences, les arts libéraux et les arts méchaniques, avec leur explication*, 11 vols. (Paris: Briasson, David, Le Breton).

DITTERSDORF, KARL DITTERS VON (n.d.), *Lebensbeschreibung. Seinem Söhne in die Feder diktiert* (Munich: Kösel); trans. A. D. Coleridge as *The Autobiography of Karl von Dittersdorf Dictated to his Son* (London: R. Bentley and Son, 1896; repr. edn., New York: Da Capo, 1970).

Dizionario etimologico italiano, ed. C. Battisti and G. Alessio, 5 vols. (Florence: G. Barbera, 1975).

DOMP, JOACHIM (1934), *Studien zur Geschichte der Musik an Westfälischen Adelshöfen im XVIII. Jahrhundert* (Düsseldorf: H. Krumbiegel).

DOPPELMAYR, JOHANN GABRIEL (1730), *Historische Nachricht von den Nürnbergischen Mathematics und Kunstlern* (Nuremberg: P. C. Monath).

DOWNES, JOHN (1708), *Roscius Anglicanus* (London: H. Playford; repr. edn., Los Angeles: The Augustan Reprint Society, 1969).

DRISCOLL, MARJORIE C., comp. (1921), *The M. H. de Young Memorial Museum* (San Francisco: The Park Commission).

DUDOK VAN HEEL, S. A. C., and MARIEKE TEUTSCHER (1974), 'Beschrijving van de nederlandse instrumenten', *Historische Blaasinstrumenten de Ontwikkeling van de Blaasinstrumenten vanaf 1600* (Kerkrade: Wereldmuziekconcours), pp. 58–60.

DUEZ, NATHANIEL (1694), *Dictionarium Gallico-Germanico-Latinum* (Amsterdam: L. and D. Elzevier).

[EISEL, JOHANN PHILIPP] (1738), *Musicus Autodidaktos, oder Der sich selbst Informirende Musicus* (Erfurt: J. M. Funcken; repr. edn., Leipzig: Zentralantiquariat der DDR, 1976); 2nd edn. pub. as *Der sich selbst Informirende Musicus, oder Gründliche Anweisung zu der Vocal- und Instrumental-Music* (Augsburg: J. J. Lotter, 1762).

[EITNER, ROBERT] (1888), 'Mitteilungen', *Monatshefte für Musik-Geschichte* 20: 12–15, 108–11.

Encyclopaedia Britannica[9], 24 vols. (Edinburgh: A. & C. Black, 1875–88); 11th edn. (Cambridge: University Press, 1910).

EPPELSHEIM, JÜRGEN (1973), 'Das Denner-Chalumeau des Bayerischen National-museums', *MF* 26: 498–500.

——(1983), 'Überlegungen zum Thema "Chalumeau"', *Zu Fragen des Instrumentariums in der ersten Hälfte des 18. Jahrhunderts* (Studien zur Aufführungspraxis und Interpretation von Instrumentalmusik des 18. Jahrhunderts, 19; Blankenburg), pp. 76–99.

——(1986), 'Garsault's "Notionaire" (Paris 1761) als Zeugnis für die Stand des französischen Holzblasinstrumentariums um 1760', *Beiheft zu den Studien zur Aufführungspraxis und Interpretation von Musik des 18. Jahrhunderts (Bericht über das VI. Symposium zu Fragen des Musikinstrumentenbaus—Holzblasinstrumente des 17. und 18. Jahrhunderts, Michaelstein 28./29. November 1985)* (Michaelstein), pp. 56–77.

——(1987), 'Bassetthorn-Studien', *Studia organologica: Festschrift für John Henry van der Meer zu seinem fünfundsechzigsten Geburtstag*, ed. F. Hellwig (Tutzing: H. Schneider), pp. 69–125.

ESTIENNE, ROBERT (1552), *Dictionariolum Puerorium Tribus Linguis Latina Anglica e Gallica* (London: R. Walsium; repr. edn., New York: Da Capo, 1971).

European Musical Instruments on Prints and Drawings on Microfiche. Print Collection of the Music Department of the Haags Gemeentemuseum (Répertoire International d'Icono-graphie Musicale; The Hague, [1976]).

FÄRBER, SIGFRID (1936), *Das Regensburger Fürstlich Thurn und Taxissche Hoftheater und seine Oper 1760–1786* (repr. from *Verhandlung des Historischen Vereins von Oberpfalz und Regensburg* 86).

FAUCHIER-MAGNAN, ADRIEN (1980), *The Small German Courts in the Eighteenth Century*, trans. M. Savill (London: Methuen).

[FELIBIEN, ANDRÉ, SIEUR DES AVAUX] (1706), *Conferences de l'academie royale de peinture et de sculpture* (Amsterdam: E. Roger).

FENAILLE, MAURICE (1904), *Etat général des tapisseries de la manufacture des Gobelins depuis son origine jusqu'à nos jours 1600–1900* (Paris: Hachette et Cie).

FÉTIS, FRANÇOIS JOSEPH (1830), *La Musique Mise a la Portée de Tout la Monde* (Paris: A. Mesnier).

——(1860–5), *Biographie Universelle des musiciens et bibliographie générale de la musique*,[2] 8 vols. (Paris: Didot Fréres).

FISKE, ROGER (1973), *English Theatre Music in the Eighteenth Century* (London: Oxford University Press).

FITZPATRICK, HORACE (1968), 'Jacob Denner's Woodwinds for Göttweig Abbey', *GSJ* 21: 81–7.

FLOOD, W. H. GRATTAN (1913), *A History of Irish Music*[3] (Dublin: Browne and Nolan).

FLORIO, JOHN (1598), *A Worlde of Wordes, or Most copious and exact Dictionarie of the Italian and English* (London: E. Blount; edn., New York: G. Olms, 1972).

——(1611), *Queen Anna's New World of Words or Dictionarie of the Italian and English tongues* (London: M. Bradwood).

FOKKER, G. A. (1872–4), 'Reijnvaan (Mr. Joos Verschuere)', *Bouwsteenen. Tweede Jaar-boek der Vereeniging voor Noord-Nederlands Muziekgeschiedenis*, pp. 119–25.

The Fourth Compleat Book for the Mock Trumpet (London: J. Walsh, J. Hare and P. Randall, *c*.1706–8).

FRAENKEL, GOTTFRIED S. (1968), *Decorative Music Title Pages* (New York: Dover).

FRANCOEUR, [LOUIS-JOSEPH] (1772), *Diapason Général de Tous les Instrumens à Vent* (Paris: Le Marchand; a later printing: Paris: Des Lauriers, *c*.1781, repr. edn., Geneva: Minkoff, 1972).

[FREILLON PONCEIN, JEAN-PIERRE] (1700), *La veritable manière d'apprendre a jouer en perfection du haut-bois, de la flûte et du flageolet* (Paris: J. Collombat).

FRÖHLICH, JOSEPH ([1810–11]), *Vollständige Theoretisch-pracktische Musikschule* (Bonn: Simrock).

FULLER-MAITLAND, J. A., and A. H. MANN (1893), *Catalogue of the Music in the Fitzwilliam Museum, Cambridge* (Cambridge); cited in Chatwin, 1950.

FURÈTIERE, ANTOINE (1727), *Dictionnaire Universel, Contenant generalement tous les mots François* (The Hague: P. Husson, T. Johnson, J. Swart, J. Van Duren, C. Le Vier, and La Veuve Van Dole).

GAI, VINICIO (1969), *Gli strumenti musicali della corte Medicea e il museo del conservatorio 'Luigi Cherubini' di Firenze* (Florence: Licos).

[GALLINI, NATALE] (1953), *Mostra di antichi strumenti musicali della collezione N. Gallini* (Milan: Villa Comunale).

GALPIN, FRANCIS W. (1910), *Old English Instruments of Music* (London: Methuen).

GANDOLFI, RICCARDO (1887), *Appunti intorno al clarinetto compilati ad uso delle scuole del R. Instituto musicale di Firenze* (Florence: Tipografia Galletti e cocci).

GARCIA, MANUEL (1970 edn.), *Traité complet de l'art du chant* (Paris: Brandus et Cie, 1840), trans. B. Garcia as *Hints on Singing* (Canoga Park, Calif.: Summit).

GARSAULT, [FRANÇOIS ALEXANDRE PIERRE DE] (1761), *Notionaire, ou Mémorial Raisonné* (Paris: G. Desprez).

GATHY, A., ed. (1835), *Musikalisches Conversations-Lexicon Encyclopädie der Gesammten Musik-Wissenschaft für Künstler, Kunstfreunde und Gebildete* (Leipzig: Schuberth & Niemeyer).

GAY, JOHN (1733), *Achilles* (London: J. Watts).

GERBER, ERNST LUDWIG (1790–2), *Historisch-Biographisches Lexikon der Tonkünstler* (Leipzig: J. G. I. Breitkopf; repr. edn., Graz: Akademische Druck-und Verlagsanstalt, 1977).

——(1812–14), *Neues Historisch-Biographisches Lexikon der Tonkünstler* (Leipzig: A. Kühnel; repr. edn., Graz: Akademische Druck-und Verlagsanstalt, 1966).

GEVAERT, FRANÇOIS-AUGUSTE (1885), *Nouveau traité d'instrumentation* (Paris: Lemoine & Fils); trans. E. F. E. Suddard as *A New Treatise on Instrumentation* (Paris: Lemoine & Co., n.d.).

GIANELLI, PIETRO (1801), *Dizionario della musica sacra, e profana*, 2 vols. (Venice: A. Santini).

GILLIAM, L. E., and W. LICHTENWANGER, eds. (1961), *The Dayton C. Miller Flute Collection: A Checklist of the Instruments* (Washington DC: Library of Congress).

GIRDLESTONE, CUTHBERT (1969), *Jean-Philippe Rameau, his Life and Work*[2] (New York: Dover).

GÖTHEL, FOLKER, ed. (1972), *Musik in Bayern: II. Ausstellungskatalog Augsburg, Juli bis Oktober 1972* (Tutzing: H. Schneider).

GOTTRON, ADAM (1959), *Mainzer Musikgeschichte von 1500 bis 1800* (Mainz: Auslieferung durch die Stadtbibliothek).

GOTTSCHED, JOHANN CHRISTOPH (1760), *Handlexicon oder Kurzgefasstes Wörterbuch* (Leipzig: C. Fritschischen handlung).

GRADENWITZ, PETER (1936), 'The Beginnings of Clarinet Literature: Notes on a Clarinet Concerto by Joh. Stamitz', *ML* 17: 145–50.

GRÆSVOLD, HANS MAGNE (1976), 'Lorents Nicolai Berg og hans lærbok "Den første prøve for begyndere udi instrumental-kunsten"', *Studia Musicologica Norvegica: Norsk Årsskrift for Musikkforskning* 2: 97–121.

Grand Larousse encyclopédique, 10 vols. (Paris: Librairie Larousse, 1960).

Das große Lexikon der Musik, ed. M. Honegger and G. Massenkeil, 8 vols. (Freiburg: Herder, 1976–80).

GUTMANN, VERONIKA (1982), 'Zur Funktion der Schriften von Mersenne und der Dictionnaires von Richelet und Furètiere in Johann Gottfried Walthers Musicalischem Lexikon—eine Bestandsaufnahme zu instrumentenkundlichen Fachausdrücken', *Basler Jahrbuch für historischen Musikpraxis* 6: 45–59.

HASS, KARL ([*c.*1960]), 'Haydn's English Military Marches', pref. to Joseph Haydn, *Three Military Marches* (London: Musica Rara).

HALFPENNY, ERIC (1952), 'Handel and the Clarinet', in 'Letters to the Editor', *MT* 93: 557.

——(1954), 'Castilon on the Clarinet', *ML* 35: 332–8.

——(1956), 'The French Hautboy: A Technical Survey: Part II', *GSJ* 8: 50–9.

——(1965), 'Early English Clarinets', *GSJ* 18: 42–56.

——(1975), 'The Christ Church Trophies', *GSJ* 28: 81–5.

HAMMERICH, ANGUL (1911), *Das Musikhistorische Museum zu Kopenhagen: Beschreibender Katalog*, trans. E. Bobé (Copenhagen: Breitkopf & Härtel).

HARRISON, FRANK, and JOAN RIMMER (1964a), *European Musical Instruments* (London: Studio Vista).

————eds. (1964b), *Antique Musical Instruments and their Players: 152 Plates from Bonanni's 'Gabinetto armonico'* (New York: Dover).

[HARRISON, LUKE] (1570), *A Dictionarie French and English* (London: H. Bynneman; repr. edn., Menston: Scolar Press, 1970).

HARRISS, ERNEST CHARLES (1969), 'Johann Mattheson's Der vollkommene Capellmeister: A Translation and Commentary', 3 vols. (Ph.D. diss., George Peabody College for Teachers).

HAWKINS, JOHN (1853 edn.), *A General History of the Science and Practice of Music*, 5 vols. (London, 1776, repr. in 3 vols., London: Novello; repr. edn., New York: Dover, 1963).

HAYNES, BRUCE (1978), 'Oboe Fingering Charts, 1695–1816', *GSJ* 31: 68–93.

——(1985), 'Johann Sebastian Bach's Pitch Standards: The Woodwind Perspective', *JAMIS* 11: 55–114.

HELLOUIN, FRÉDÉRIC (1903), *Gossec et la musique française à la fin du XVIIIe siècle* (Paris: Charles).

HEYDE, HERBERT (1970), 'Ein Urahn der Klarinette?' *Deutsches Jahrbuch der Musikwissenschaft*, 15: 121–4.

——(1976), *Historische Musikinstrumente im Bachhaus Eisenach* ([Weimar]: Bachhaus Eisenach).

——(1979), 'Über Rohrblattinstrumente des Musikinstrumentenmuseums der Karl-Marx-Universität Leipzig', *Tibia* 2: 378–83.

——(1987a), 'Blasinstrumente und Bläser der Dresdner Hofkapelle in der Zeit des Fux-Schülers J. D. Zelenka (1710–1745)', *Johann Joseph Fux und die Barocke Bläsertradition*, ed. B. Habla (Kongreßbericht Graz 1985, Alta Musica, 9; Tutzing: H. Schneider), pp. 39–65.

——(1987b), 'Der Holzblasinstrumentenbau in Leipzig in der 2. Hälfte des 18. Jahrhunderts', *Tibia* 12: 481–6.

HICKMANN, HANS (1956), *Musicologie Pharaonique* (Kehl: Hietz).

——(1961), *Musikgeschichte in Bildern: Ägypten* (Leipzig: VEB Deutscher Verlag für Musik).

HIGHFILL, P. H. JUN., K. A. BURNIM, and E. A. LANGHANS, eds. (1973–), *A Biographical Dictionary of Actors, Actresses, Musicians, Dancers, Managers & other Stage Personnel in London, 1600–1800*, 10 vols. (Carbondale: Southern Illinois University Press).

HIRSCHFELD, PETER (1959), *Herrenhäusen und Schlösser in Schleswig-Holstein*[2], ed. O. Vollert (n.p.: Deutscher Kunstverlag).

HOCHSTRASSER, GERHARD (1979), 'Das Problem des Kunstmusik-Chalumeaus (II)', *Glareana: Nachrichten der Gesellschaft der Freunde alter Musikinstrumente* 28/1: 1–24.

HOEPRICH, T. ERIC (1981), 'A Three-Key Clarinet by J. C. Denner', *GSJ* 34: 21–32.

——(1983), 'Finding a Clarinet for the Three Concertos by Vivaldi', *EM* 11: 60–4.

——(1984a), 'Clarinet Reed Position in the 18th Century', *EM* 12: 49–55.

——(1984b), 'The L. C. [*sic*] Denner Clarinet at Berkeley', *GSJ* 37: 114.

——(1985), 'Die Klarinetten Johann Scherers', *Tibia* 10: 435–8.

HOOPER, J. G. (1963), 'A Survey of Music in Bristol with Special Reference to the 18th Century' (MA thesis, University of Bristol).

HOOVER, CYNTHIA ADAMS (1985), 'Epilogue to Secular Music in Early Massachusetts', *Music in Colonial Massachusetts 1630–1820*, ed. B. Lambert (Music in Homes and in Churches, ii; Boston: The Colonial Society of Massachusetts), pp. 715–867.

HORNBOSTEL, ERICH VON, and CURT SACHS (1914), 'Systematik der Instrumentenkunde', *Zeitschrift für Ethnologie* 46: 553–90.

HOTTETERRE, [JACQUES] (*c.*1728), *Principes de la flûte traversiere zu spielen* (Amsterdam: E. Roger; repr. edn., Kassel: Bärenreiter, 1982).

——(1737), *Méthode pour la Musette* (Paris: J. B. C. Ballard; repr. edn., Geneva: Minkoff, 1977).

HUDGEBUTT, JOHN (1679), *A Vade Mecum for the Lovers of Music* (London: N. Thompson).

HUENE, FRIEDRICH VON (1974), 'Makers' Marks from Renaissance and Baroque Woodwinds', *GSJ* 27: 31–47.

HÜLLEMAN, HERBERT (1937), *Die Tätigkeit des Orgelbauers Gottfried Silbermann in Reußenland* (Leipzig: Merseburger & Co.).

HÜLPHERS, ABRAHAM ABRAHAMSSON (1773), *Historisk Afhandling om Music Och Instrumenter* (Westerås: J. L. Horrn; repr. edn., Stockholm: Svenskt musikhistoriskt arkiv, 1969).

ISRAËL, CARL (1876), *Frankfurter Concert-Chronik von 1713–1780* (Frankfurt-on-Main: Selbstverlag des Vereins).

JABLONSKI, JOHANN THEODOR (1767), *Allgemeines Lexicon der Künste und Wissenschaften*[3] (Königsberg: Zeisens Wittwe und Hartungs Erben).

JAHN, FRITZ (n.d.), 'Alte Musikinstrumente im Germanischen Nationalmuseum Nürnberg: beschreibender Katalog' (Nuremberg, n.d.); cited in Nickel 1971: 211, 455 n. 1262.

——(1927–8), 'Das Germanische National museum zu Nürnberg und seine Musik-instrumenten-Sammlung', *Zeitschrift für Musikwissenschaft* 10: 109–11.

JAUBERT, PIERRE (1772–3), *Dictionnaire Raisonné Universel des Arts et Métiers*, new edn., 5 vols. (Paris: P. F. Didot jeune).

JOHANSSON, CARI (1955), *French Music Publishers' Catalogues of the Second Half of the Eighteenth Century*, 2 vols. (Stockholm: Almquist & Wiksells).

JOHNSON, A., and D. MALONE, eds. (1930), *Dictionary of American Biography* (New York: C. Scribner's Sons).

JOHNSON, DAVID (1972), *Music and Society in Lowland Scotland in the Eighteenth Century* (London: Oxford University Press).

JONXIS, J. H. P. (1983), 'Een veiling in de stad Groningen in 1764', *Vereniging van vrieden van het Groninger Museum*, 14, n.p.

KALINA, DAVID LEWIS (1972), 'The Structural Development of the Bass Clarinet' (Ed.D. diss., Columbia University).

KAPPEY, JACOB ADAM (*c.*1894), *Military Music: A History of Wind-Instrumental Bands* (London: Boosey and Co.).

KARP, CARY (1972), 'Baroque Woodwind in the Musikhistoriska Museet, Stockholm', *GSJ* 25: 80–6.

——(1986), 'The Early History of the Clarinet and Chalumeau', *EM* 14: 545–51.

KEESS, STEPHEN EDLER VON (1829), *Darstellung des Fabricks- und Gewerbeswesen in Seinem Gegenwärten Zustande, Vorzüglich in Technischer, Mercantilischer und Statistischer Beziehung*[2] (Vienna: Morschner und Jaspar).

KEILLOR, ELAINE (1975), 'Communications', *Journal of the American Musicological Society* 28: 567.

KIRNBAUER, MARTIN (1987), 'Zwei Klarinetten von Johann Christoph Denner', *Tibia* 12: 451–3.

——(1989), 'Historische Holzblasinstrumente in der Sammlung des Germanischen Nationalmuseums in Nürnberg', *Tibia* 14: 424–9.

KLEEFELD, WILHELM (1899–1900), 'Das Orchester in der Hamburger Oper 1678–1738', *SIMG* 1: 219–89.

KLERK, D. M. (1974), 'Prenten met muziekinstrumenten van de 15e tot de 20e eeuw', *Historische Blaasinstrumenten de Ontwikkeling van de Blaasinstrumenten vanaf 1600* (Kerkrade: Wereldmuziekconcours), pp. 69–77.

KLERK, MAGDA, comp. ([1976]), Index to *European Musical Instruments* 1976 (Répertoire International d'Iconographie Musicale; Zug, Switzerland: Inter Documentation).

KLOSÉ, HYACINTHE (*c.* 1844), *Méthode pour servir à l'enseignement de la clarinette à anneaux mobiles, et de celle à 13 clés* (Paris: Meissonnier).

KOCH, HANS OSKAR (1980), 'Sonderform der Blasinstrumente in der deutschen Musik vom späten 17. bis zur Mitte des 18. Jahrhundert' (Ph.D. diss., Ruprecht-Karl-Universität).

KÖLBEL, HERBERT (1979), 'Ferdinand Kölbel (ca. 1705–1778), der Erfinder des Klappenhorns', *Das Musikinstrument* 28: 806–8.

KOLNEDER, WALTER (1951), 'Die Klarinette als Concertino-Instrument bei Vivaldi', *MF* 4: 185–91.

——(1955a), *Aufführungspraxis bei Vivaldi* (Leipzig: Breitkopf & Härtel).

——(1955b), 'Noch einmal: Vivaldi und die Klarinette', *MF* 8: 209–11.

KRICKEBERG, DIETER (1983), 'On the Social Status of the Spielmann ("Folk Musician") in 17th and 18th Century Germany, Particularly in the Northwest', *The Social Status of the Professional Musician from the Middle Ages to the 19th Century*, ed. W. Salmen, Trans. H. Kaufman and B. Reisner (New York: Pendragon), pp. 97–122.

KROGH, TORBEN (1929), 'Reinhard Keiser in Kopenhagen', *Musikwissenschaftliche Beiträge: Festschrift für Johannes Wolf zu seinem sechzigsten Geburtstage* (Berlin: M. Breslauer), pp. 79–87.

KROLL, OSKAR (1968), *The Clarinet*, rev. and with a repertory by D. Riehm, trans. H. Morris, ed. A. Baines (New York: Taplinger).

KUBITSCHEK, ERNST (1987), 'Block- und Querflöte im Umkreis von Johann Joseph Fux—Versuch einer Übersicht', *Johann Joseph Fux und die Barocke Bläsertradition*, ed. B. Habla (Kongreßbericht Graz 1985, Alta Musica, 9; Tutzing: H. Schneider), pp. 99–119.

KÜNG, ANDREAS (1987), '"SCHLEGEL A BALE". Die erhaltenen Instrumente und ihre Erbauer', *Basler Jahrbuch für Historisches Musikpraxis* 11: 63–88.

LA BORDE JEAN-BENJAMIN DE] (1780). *Essai sur la musique ancienne et moderne*, 4 vols. (Paris: P. D. Pierres).

LA CURNE DE SAINTE-PALAYE, JEAN BAPTISTE DE (1875–82), *Dictionnaire Historique de L'Ancien Langage François*, 10 vols. (Paris: H. Champion).

LA LAURENCIE, LIONEL DE (1911), 'Rameau, son gendre et ses descendants', *Revue musicale mensuelle* 7: 15–16.

——(1913), 'Rameau et les clarinettes', *Revue musicale mensuelle* 9: 27–8.

——ed. (1913–31), *Encyclopédie de la musique et dictionnaire du Conservatoire*, 11 vols. (Paris: Delegrave).

LAMBERT, BARBARA (1985), 'Social Music, Musicians, and their Musical Instruments in and around Colonial Boston', *Music in Colonial Massachusetts 1630–1820*, ed. B. Lambert (Music in Homes and in Churches, ii; Boston: The Colonial Society of Massachusetts), pp. 409–514, 871–1158.

[——and D. SAMUEL QUIGLEY] (1983), *Musical Instruments Collection: Checklist of Instruments on Exhibition* (Boston: Museum of Fine Arts).

LANDON, H. C. ROBBINS (1980), *Haydn: The Early Years 1732–1765* (Bloomington: Indiana University Press).

LANGWILL, LYNDESAY G. (1975), *The Bassoon and Contrabassoon* (London: E. Benn).

——(1980), *An Index of Musical Wind-Instrument Makers*[6] (Edinburgh: author).

LANNING, EDWARD FRANCIS (1969), 'The Clarinet as the Intended Solo Instrument in Johann Melchior Molter's Concerto 34' (DMA diss. University of Missouri at Kansas City).

LAROUSSE, PIERRE (1865–76), *Grand Dictionnaire Universel du XIXe siècle*, 15 vols. (Paris: Administration du Grand Dictionnaire Universel).

LARSEN, JENS PETER (1972), *Handel's Messiah, Origins, Compositions, Sources*[2] (New York: W. W. Norton).

LAVOIX, HENRI (1878), *Histoire de L'instrumentation* (Paris: Didot & Cie; repr. edn., Bologna: Forni, 1972).

LAWSON, COLIN (1974), 'The Early Chalumeau Duets', *GSJ* 27: 125–9.

——(1979), 'The Chalumeau: Independent Voice or Poor Relation?', *EM* 7: 351–4.

——(1980), 'Chalumeau and Clarinet', in 'Observations', *EM* 8: 368.

——(1981a), *The Chalumeau in Eighteenth-Century Music* (Ann Arbor: UMI Research Press).

——(1981b), 'Telemann and the Chalumeau', *EM* 9: 312–19.

——(1983), 'The Baroque Repertoire: Some Observations for the Tercentenary of Johann Christoph Graupner (1683–1760)', *The Clarinet* 11/1: 18–19.

——(1986), 'The Clarinet and Chalumeau Revisited', *EM* 14: 554–5.

LEBERMANN, WALTER (1954), 'Zur Besetzungsfrage der Concerti Grossi von A. Vivaldi' *MF* 7: 337–9.

LEFÈVRE, JEAN-XAVIER ([1802]), *Méthode de Clarinette* (Paris; repr. edn., Geneva: Minkoff, 1974).

LEMAY, J. A. LEO, and P. M. ZALL (1981), *The Autobiography of Benjamin Franklin: A Genetic Text* (Knoxville: University of Tennessee Press).

LEPPERT, RICHARD (1978), *Arcadia at Versailles: Noble Amateur Musicians and their Musettes and Hurdy-gurdies at the French Court (c. 1660–1789), A Visual Study* (Amsterdam: Swets & Zeitlinger).

LESURE, FRANÇOIS (1969), *Bibliographie des éditions musicales publiées par Estienne Roger et Michel-Charles Le Cène (Amsterdam, 1696–1743)* (Paris: Heugel).

LICHTENTHAL, PIETRO (1826), *Dizionario e Bibliografia della Musica*, 4 vols. (Milan: A. Fontana).

LIGTVOET, A. W. (n.d.), *Exotische en oude europese muziekinstrumenten / Exotic and Ancient European Musical Instruments in the Department of Musical History of the Municipal Museum at The Hague* (The Hague: Nijgh & Van Ditmar).

LIPOWSKY, FELIX JOSEPH (1794), *Uebersicht der Deutschen Geschichte* (Munich: J. Lentner).

[LÖBEL, RENATUS GOTTHELF, ed.] (1796), *Conversationslexikon mit vorzüglicher Rücksicht auf die gegenwärtigen Zeiten* (Leipzig: F. A. Leupold).

LOEWENBERG, ALFRED (1978), *Annals of Opera 1597–1940*[3] (Totowa, NJ: Rowman & Littlefield).

The London Stage, 1660–1800, ed. W. van Lennep *et al.*, 5 pts. (Carbondale: Southern Illinois University Press, 1960–8).

LUSCINIUS, OTTMAR (1536), *Musurgia seu Praxis Musicae* (Strasburg: I. Schottum).

MACDONALD, ROBERT JAMES (1968), 'François-Joseph Gossec and French Instrumental Music of the Second Half of the Eighteenth Century', 3 vols. (Ph.D. diss. University of Michigan).

MAHILLON, VICTOR-CHARLES (1892), 'Catalogue des Instruments', *Annuaire du Conservatoire Royale de Musique de Bruxelles* 16: 139–236.

——(1893–1922), *Catalogue descriptif & analytique du musée instrumental du Conservatoire royale de musique de Bruxelles*[2], 5 vols. (Ghent: Librarie générale de A. Hoste).

MAHLING, CHRISTOPH-HELMUT (1983), 'The Origin and Social Status of the Court Orchestral Musician in the 18th and early 19th Century in Germany', *The Social Status of the Professional Musician from the Middle Ages to the 19th Century*, ed. W. Salmen, trans. H. Kaufman and B. Reisner (New York: Pendragon). pp. 221–64.

MAJER, JOSEPH FRIEDRICH BERNHARD CASPAR (1732), *Museum Musicum Theoretico Practicum, das ist Neu-eröffneter Theoretisch-und Practicum Music-Saal* (Schwäbisch Hall: G. M. Majer; repr. edn., Kassel: Bärenreiter, 1954); 2nd edn. pub. as *Neu-eröffneter Theoretisch- und Pracktischer Music-Saal* (Nuremberg: J. J. Cremer, 1741).

MANNICHE, LISE (1975), *Ancient Egyptian Musical Instruments* (Münchner Ägyptologische Studien, 34; Berlin: Deutscher Kunstverlag München).

MARCUSE, SIBYL (1964), *Musical Instrumentals: A Comprehensive Dictionary* (New York: Doubleday & Co.).

——(1975), *A Survey of Musical Instruments* (New York: Harper & Row).

MARPURG, FRIEDRICH WILHELM (1757), *Sammlung einiger Nachrichten von berühmten Orgelwerken in Teutschland* (Buren: C. G. Mayer); repr. in Marpurg, *Historisch-Kritische Beyträge zur Aufnahme der Musik*, 5 vols. (Berlin: G. A. Lange, 1754–78; repr. edn., Hildesheim: G. Olms, 1970).

MASSON, PAUL-MARIE (1930), *L'Opéra de Rameau* (Paris: H. Laurens).

MATTHESON, JOHANN (1713), *Das Neu-Eröffnete Orchestre, oder Universelle und Gründliche Anleitung* (Hamburg: B. Schiller).

——(1739), *Der vollkommene Capellmeister* (Hamburg; repr. edn., Kassel: Bärenreiter, 1954).

——(1740), *Grundlage einer Ehren-Pforte* (Hamburg; repr. edn., Kassel: Bärenreiter, 1969).

McCorkle Donald M. (1956), 'The Moravian Contribution to American Music', *Notes* 13: 597–606.

Meder, Joseph (1932), *Dürer-Katalog: Ein Handbuch über Albrecht Dürer's Stiche, Radierungen, Holzschnitte, deren Züstande, Ausgaben und Wasserzeichen* (Vienna: Gilhofer und Rauschburg).

Mendel, Arthur (1955), 'On the Pitches in Use in Bach's Time, I', *Musical Quarterly* 41: 322–54.

Megerle, Johann Ulrich [Abraham a Sancta Clara] (1709), *Centi-folium Stultorum In Quarto. Oder Hundert Ausbündige Narren* (Vienna: C. Lercher; repr. edn., Dortmund: Harenberg Kommunikation, 1978).

Menke, Werner (1982–3), *Thematisches Verzeichnis der Vokalwerke von Georg Philipp Telemann*, 2 vols. (Frankfurt-on-Main: V. Klostermann).

Mennicke, Carl (1906), *Hasse und die Brüder Graun als Symphoniker* (Leipzig: Breitkopf & Härtel).

Mersenne, Marin (1636), *Harmonie Universelle*, 3 vols. (Paris: S. Cramoisy; repr. edn., Paris: Centre Nationale de La Recherche Scientifique, 1963); trans. R. Chapman as *The Book on Instruments* (The Hague: M. Nijhoff, 1957).

——(1648), *Harmonicorum libri XII* (Paris; repr. edn., Geneva: Minkoff, 1972).

Mettenleiter, Dominicus (1866), *Aus der musikalischen Vergangenheit bayrischer Städte. Musikgeschichte der Stadt Regensburg* (Regensburg: J. G. Bossenecker).

Michel, V. (*c.*1801), *Méthode de Clarinette* (Paris: Cochet).

'Miscellen', *AMZ* 4 (1801–2): 703.

Montagu, Jeremy (1974), *The World of Baroque and Classical Instruments* (New York: Overlook Press).

Mooser, R. Aloys (1951), *Annales de la musique et des musiciens en Russie au XVIIIme siècle*, 3 vols. (Geneva: Mont-Blanc).

Müller, Werner (1982), *Gottfried Silbermann: Persönlichkeit und Werk* (Frankfurt-on-Main: Das Musikinstrument).

Munrow, David (1976), *Instruments of the Middle Ages and Renaissance* (Oxford: Oxford University Press).

Münster, Robert (1983), 'Johann Anton Fils und das Mannheimer Orchester in den Jahren 1754 bis 1760', *Johann Anton Fils (1733–1760). Ein Eichstätter Komponist der Mannheimer Klassik*, ed. H. Holzbauer (Tutzing: H. Schneider), pp. 33–46

Murr, Christoph Gottlieb von (1778), *Beschreibung der Vornehmstem Merkwürdigkeiten* (Nuremberg: J. E. Zeh).

Die Musik in Geschichte und Gegenwart, ed. F. Blume, 16 vols. (Kassel and Basle: Bärenreiter, 1949–79).

Nagy, Michael (1987), 'Holzblasinstrumente der tiefen Lage im Schaffen von Johann Joseph Fux', *Johann Joseph Fux und die Barocke Bläsertradition*, ed. B. Habla (Kongreßbericht Graz 1985, Alta Musica, 9; Tutzing: H. Schneider), pp. 89–98.

The National Cyclopædia of American Biography (New York: J. T. White & Co., 1898).

The New Grove Dictionary of Music and Musicians, ed. S. Sadie, 20 vols. (London: Macmillan Publishers Ltd., 1980).

The New Grove Dictionary of Musical Instruments, ed. S. Sadie, 3 vols. (London: Macmillan Publishers Ltd., 1984).

The New Oxford Companion to Music, ed. D. Arnold, 2 vols. (London: Oxford University Press, 1983).

NICKEL, EKKEHARD (1971), *Die Holzblasinstrumentenbau in der freien Reichsstadt Nürnberg* (Munich: E. Katzbichler).

NICOL, KARL LUDWIG (1981), 'Ein Gang durch die Frühe Geschichte der Klarinette', *Tibia* 6: 423–5.

NICOT, JEAN (1606), *Thresor de la Langue Françoise tant ancienne que moderne* (Paris: D. Doucovr; repr. edn., Menston: Scolar Press, 1970).

NIEMÖLLER, KLAUS WOLFGANG (1960), *Kirchenmusik und reichsstädtische Musikpflege im Köln des 18. Jahrhundert* (Cologne: A. Volk).

Nieuw Nederlandsch Biografisch Woordenboek, ed. P. C. Molhuysen and P. J. Blok, 10 vols. (Leiden: A. W. Sythoff, 1911–37).

NOACK, ELISABETH (1967), *Musikgeschichte Darmstadts vom Mittelalter bis zur Goethezeit* (Mainz: B. Schott's Söhne).

NOINVILLE, DUREY DE, and TRAVENOL (1757), *Histoire du Théâtre de L'Opéra en France, Depuis Son Établissement jusqu'á présent*[2], 2 vols. (Paris: Duchesne).

NORLIND, TOBIAS (1937), 'Abraham Abrahamsson Hülphers och frihetstidens musikliv', *Svensk Tidskrift för Musikforskning* 19: 16–64.

Nouveau Dictionaire du Voyageur (Geneva: Perachon & Cramer, 1732).

OJA, CAROL J. (1978). *The Musical Ensemble ca. 1730–1830: An Exhibition of Photographic Reproductions of Works of Art in all Media, 14 April – 10 May 1978* (New York: City University of New York).

OTTENBOURGS, STEFAAN (1989), 'Die Familie Rottenburgh. Eine der zahlreichen musikalischen Dynastien aus dem barocken Brüssel', *Tibia* 14: 477–89, 577–67.

OWEN, ANGELA MARIA (1967), 'The Chalumeau and its Music', *AR* 8: 7–9.

J. P. (1830), 'On the Clarionet', *The Harmonicon* 8: 57–8.

PAUL, OSCAR (1874), 'Blas- und Schlaginstrumente Bestandtheile', *Amtlicher Bericht über die Wiener Weltausstellung im Jahre 1873*, 2 vols. (Brunswick: F. Vieweg und Sohn), ii. 648–57.

PEATE, IOWERTH C. (1947), 'Welsh Musical Instruments', *Man* 47 (Feb.): 21–2.

PETZOLDT, RICHARD (1974), *Georg Philipp Telemann*, trans. H. Fitzpatrick (New York: Oxford University Press).

PIERRE, CONSTANT (1890), *La Facture Instrumentale à l'Exposition Universelle de 1889* (Paris: Librairie de l'art indépendent).

——(1975), *Histoire du Concert Spirituel 1725–1790* (Société Française de Musicologie, 3rd ser., 3; Paris, Heugel [written 1900]).

PILKOVÁ, ZDENKA (1978), 'Musikzentren in Böhmen: Die größern und kleineren Musikzentren in Böhmen vom Standpunkt des Instrumentariums', *Muzikzentren in der ersten Hälfte des 18. Jahrhunderts und ihre Ausstrahlung* (Studien zur Aufführungspraxis und Interpretation von Instrumentalmusik des 18. Jahrhunderts, 8; Blankenburg), pp. 30–41.

‍

POHL, CARL FERDINAND (1867), *Mozart und Haydn in London*, 2 vols. (Vienna: C. Gerold's Sohn; repr. edn., New York: Da Capo, 1970).

POMAI, FRANÇOIS (1709), *Le Grand Dictionaire Royal* (Frankfurt-on-Main: J. P. Andre).

PRAETORIUS, MICHAEL (1619), *Syntagma Musicum: II. De Organographia* (Wolfenbüttel: E. Holwein; repr. edn., Kassel: Bärenreiter, 1958).

PULVER, JEFFREY (1929), *A Dictionary of Old English Music & Musical Instruments* (New York: E. P. Dutton & Co.).

QUANTZ, JOHANN JOACHIM (1752), *Versuch einer Anweisung die Flöte Traversiere zu Spielen* (Berlin: J. F. Voss; repr. edn., Leipzig: C. F. Kahnt, 1906); trans. E. R. Reilly, as *On Playing the Flute* (New York: Schirmer, 1966).

RAMEIS, EMIL (1976), *Die Österreichische Militärmusik—von ihren Anfängen bis zum Jahre 1918* (Tutzing: H. Schneider).

RAU, ULRICH (1977), 'Die Kammermusik für Klarinette und Streichinstrumente im Zeitalter der Wiener Klassik' (Ph.D. diss., University of the Saarland).

RAUGEL, FÉLIX (1957), 'La Musique à la chapelle du chateau de Versailles sous Louis XIV', *Dix-septième siècle. Bulletin de la société d'étude du XVIIe siècle*, 25; cited in Macdonald 1968: 301 n. 357.

RENDALL, F. GEOFFREY (1971), *The Clarinet: Some Notes upon its History and Construction*[3], rev. and enlarged P. Bate (New York: W. W. Norton).

REYNVAAN, JOOS VERSCHUERE (1787), *Catechismus der Musijk* (Amsterdam: W. Brave).

——(1789–90), *Musijkaal Konst-Woordenboek*, 2 vols. (Middleburg: W. A. Keel and J. De Jongh).

——(1795), *Musijkaal Kunst-Woordenboek* (Amsterdam: W. Brave).

RICE, ALBERT R. (1974), 'The History and Literature of the Chalumeau and Two-Keyed Clarinet', *The Clarinet* 1/4: 11–21.

——(1977), 'Valentin Roeser's Essay on the Clarinet: Background and Commentary' (MA thesis, Claremont Graduate School).

——(1979), 'Garsault on the Clarinet', *GSJ* 32: 99–103.

——(1979–80), 'The Clarinet as Described by Lorents Nicolai Berg', *JAMIS* 5–6: 43–52.

——(1984a), 'Clarinet Fingering Charts, 1732–1816', *GSJ* 37: 16–41.

——(1984b), 'Clarinet Reed Position', *EM* 12: 429, 431.

——(1984c), '"On the Clarionet" from the Harmonicon', *The Clarinet* 11/3: 34–5.

——(1986), 'The Clarinette d'amour and Basset Horn', *GSJ* 39: 97–111.

——(1987), 'A History of the Clarinet to 1820' (Ph.D. diss., The Claremont Graduate School).

——(1988a), 'The Baroque Clarinet in Public Concerts, 1726–1762', *EM* 16: 388–95.

——(1988b), 'More Denner Winds now in Nuremberg', *Newsletter of the American Musical Instrument Society* 17/2: 12–13.

RIEMANN, HUGO (1929) *Musik Lexikon*,[11] ed. A. Einstein (Berlin: M. Hesse).

RIPLEY, GEORGE, and BAYARD TAYLOR (1873), *Cyclopedia of Literature and the Fine Arts* (New York and Chicago: A. S. Barnes and Co.).

ROESER, VALENTIN (1764), *Essai d'instruction à l'usage de ceux qui composent pour la clarinette et le cor* (Paris: Le Menu; a later printing by Mercier, *c.*1794–6; repr. edn., Geneva: Minkoff, 1972).

ROHN, JAN KAREL [JOANNE CAROLO ROHN] (1768), *Nomenclator Artifex, et Mechanicus. To Gest: Gmenowatel U Trogi Řzeči* (Prague: J. Prussowy).

ROSS, DAVID (1979), 'Ridinger's "Youth Playing the Clarinet"', *The Clarinet* 7/1: 34–5.

—— (1983), [cover photo], *The Clarinet* 11/1: 1.

—— (1985), 'A Comprehensive Performance Project in Clarinet Literature with an Organological Study of the Development of the Clarinet in the Eighteenth Century' (DMA thesis, University of Iowa).

ROUSSEAU, EUGENE E. (1962), 'Clarinet Instructional Materials from 1732 to ca. 1825' (Ph.D. diss., North Texas State University).

SACHS, CURT (1910), *Musik und Oper am kurbrandenburgischen Hof* (Berlin: J. Bard).

—— (1913), *Real-Lexicon der Musikinstrumente* (Berlin: M. Hesse; repr. edn., Hildesheim: G. Olms, 1962).

—— (1921), 'Die Litui in Bachs Motette, "O Jesu Christ"', *Bach-Jahrbuch* 18: 96–7.

—— (1922), *Sammlung alter Musikinstrumente bei der Staatlichen Hochschule für Musik zu Berlin: beschreibender Katalog* (Berlin: J. Bard).

—— (1930), *Handbuch der Musikinstrumentenkunde*[2] (Leipzig: Breitkopf & Härtel).

—— (1940), *The History of Musical Instruments* (New York: W. W. Norton).

SAINLIENS, CLAUDE DE (1593), *A Dictionary French and English* (London: T. Woodcock; repr. edn., Menston: Scolar Press, 1970).

'Die Sammlung musikalischer Instrumente im germanischen Museum', *Anzeiger für Kunde der Deutschen Vorzeit*, new ser. 16 (1860): 6–8, 43–6.

SANDS, MOLLIE (1943), 'Music as a Profession in Eighteenth-Century England', *ML* 24: 90–2.

SASSE, KONRAD (ed.) (1961–66), *Katalog zu den Sammlungen des Händel-Hauses in Halle*, 5 vols. (Halle an der Saale: Händel-Haus).

[SAVOYE] (1882), *Collection de M. Savoye: Instruments de Musique Anciens, Rares et Curieux* (Paris: Commissaire-Priseur, Paul Chevallier).

SCHIEDERMAIR, LUDWIG (1912–13), 'Die Oper an den badischen Höfen des 17. u. 18. Jahrhunderts', *SIMG* 14: 199–207, 369–449, 510–50.

SCHMID, KURT (1985), 'Zur Geschichte der Klarinette in der Wienerischen Musik' (thesis, Hochschule für Musik und Darstellende Kunst in Wien).

SCHOELCHER, VICTOR (1857), *The Life of Handel*, trans. J. Lowe (London: Trübner and Co.).

SCHOLES, PERCY, ed. (1970), *The Oxford Companion to Music*[10] (London: Oxford University Press).

SCHREIBER, OTTMAR (1938), *Orchester und Orchesterpraxis in Deutschland zwischen 1700 and 1850* (Berlin: Junker und Dünnhaupt).

SCHRÖDER, HANS (1930), *Verzeichnis der Sammlung alter Musikinstrumente* (Hamburg: Alster-Verlag).

SCHUBART, CHRISTIAN FRIEDRICH DANIEL (1806), *Ideen zu einer Ästhetik der Tonkunst* (Vienna: J. V. Degen [written 1783–5]; repr. edn., Hildesheim: G. Olms, 1969).

SCHULTZ, HELMUT (1929), *Führer durch das Musikwissenschaftliche Instrumenten-Museum der Universität Leipzig* (Leipzig: Breitkopf & Härtel).

SCHWAB, HEINRICH W. (1983), 'The Social Status of the Town Musician', *The Social Status of the Professional Musician from the Middle Ages to the 19th Century*, ed. W. Salmen, trans. H. Kaufman and B. Reisner (New York: Pendragon), pp. 33–59.

SCHWARZ, MAX (1900–1901), 'Johann Christian Bach (1735–1782)', *SIMG* 2: 401–54.

SEEBASS, TILMAN (1973), *Musikdarstellung und Psalterillustration im früheren Mittelalter: Studien ausgehend von einer Ikonolgie der Handschrift Paris Bibliothèque Nationale Fonds Latin 1118*, 2 vols. (Berne: A. Francke).

SEHNAL, JIŘÍ (1972), 'Das Musikinventar des Olmützer Bischofs Leopold Egk aus dem Jahre 1760 als Quelle vorklassischer Instrumentalmusik', *Archiv für Musikwissenschaft* 29: 285–317.

SELFRIDGE-FIELD, ELEANOR (1975), *Venetian Instrumental Music from Gabrieli to Vivaldi* (New York: Praeger).

——(1979), 'Vivaldi's Esoteric Instruments', in 'Correspondence', *EM* 7: 139–40.

——(1987), 'The Viennese Court Orchestra in the Time of Caldara', *Antonio Caldara: Essays on his Life and Times*, ed. B. W. Pritchard (Aldershot: Scolar Press), pp. 115–51.

SELHOF, NICOLAS (1973 edn.), *Catalogue d'une trés belle Bibliothèque de Livres* (The Hague: A. Moetjens, 1759); repr. edn., *Catalogue of the Music Library, Instruments and Other Property of Nicolas Selhof, Sold in the Hague: 1759*, introd. by A. Hyatt King (Amsterdam: F. Knuf).

SHACKLETON, NICHOLAS (1985), 'The "Well Known Clarinet by Lindner"', *GSJ* 38: 137–9.

——(1987), 'The Earliest Basset Horns', *GSJ* 40: 2–23.

SHANLEY, RICHARD A. (1976), 'The Fifth and Sixth Clarinet Concertos by Johann Melchior Molter: A Lecture Recital Together with Additional Recitals' (DMA diss. North Texas State University).

SMILKE, RINEKE (1984), 'De musicq lievende verd bekend gemaekt . . .', *Concerning the Flute*, ed. R. de Reede (Amsterdam: Broekmans & Van Poppel), pp. 115–19.

SMITH, WILLIAM C. (1948), *Bibliography of the Musical Works Published by John Walsh During the Years 1695–1720* (London: Bibliographical Society).

SNOECK, CÉSAR CHARLES (1894), *Catalogue de la collection d'Instruments de musique Anciens ou Curieux* (Ghent: J. Vuylsteke).

——(1903), *Catalogue de la collection d'instruments de musique flamands et néerlandais* (Ghent: I. Vanderpoorten).

SPEER, DANIEL (1697), *Grund-richter kurtz-Leicht- und Nöthiger jetz Wol-Vermehrter Unterricht der Musikalischer Kunst*[2] (Ulm: G. W. Kuhnen).

STÄHLIN, JACOB VON (1769), 'Nachrichten von der Musik in Rußland', in Johann Joseph Haigold [August Ludwig von Schlözer], *Beylagen zum neuveränderten Rußland* (Riga: J. F. Hartknoch), pp. 37–192; repr. in [Johann Adam Hiller], *Musikalische Nachrichten und Anmerkungen auf das Jahr 1770* (Leipzig: Zeitungs-Expedition, 1770; repr. edn., Hildesheim: G. Olms, 1970), pp. 135–9, 143–7, 151–5, 159–65, 167–73, 175–9, 183–217, 221–6, 229–32.

STAINER, JOHN, and W. A. BARRETT ([1889]), *A Dictionary of Musical Terms* (London: Novello, Ewer and Co.).

STANLEY, ALBERT A. (1921), *Catalogue of the Stearns Collection of Musical Instruments*[2] (Ann Arbor: University of Michigan).

STERN, NINA (1983), 'Rameau's Acante et Céphise: The Clarinet in France in the Middle of the Eighteenth Century' (thesis, Schola Cantorum Basiliensis).

——(1984), 'Il clarinetto in Francia nella seconda metà dal Settecento', *Il Flauto Dolce* 10–11 (Jan.–June): 29–31.

——(1985), 'The Clarinet in the Eighteenth Century: Rameau and his Contemporaries', *AR* 26: 71–3.

STOLLBROCK, L. (1892), 'Leben und Wirken des k.k. Hofkapellmeister und Hofkompositors Johann Georg Reutter jun.', *Vierteljahrsschrift für Musikwissenschaft* 8: 161 –203, 289–306.

STREATFIELD, R. A. (1911), 'The Granville Collection of Handel Manuscripts', *The Musical Antiquary* 2: 208–24.

STUBBINS, WILLIAM (1965). *The Art of Clarinetistry*[2] (Ann Arbor: Ann Arbor Publishers).

SÜSS, C., and P. EPSTEIN, eds. (1926), *Katalog der kirchlichen Musikhandschriften des 17. und 18. Jahrhunderts in Frankfurt am Main* (Frankfurt-on-Main); cited in Lawson 1981a: 190 n. 3.

TALBOT, MICHAEL (1978), *Vivaldi* (London: J. M. Dent & Sons).

——(1979), 'Vivaldi's Instrumentation', in 'Correspondence', *EM* 7: 561.

——(1980), 'Vivaldi e lo chalumeau', *Rivista italiana di musicologia* 15: 153–81.

THURSTON, FREDERICK J., and ALAN FRANK (1939), *The Clarinet: A Comprehensive Method for the Boehm Clarinet* (London: Hawkes & Sons).

TILMOUTH, MICHAEL (1961), 'A Calendar of References to Music in Newspapers Published in London and the Provinces (1600–1719)', *RMA Research Chronicle* 1: 1–107.

TITUS, ROBERT AUSTIN (1962), 'The Solo Music for the Clarinet in the Eighteenth Century' (Ph.D. diss., State University of Iowa).

TRICHET, PIERRE (1957 edn.), 'Traité des instruments de musique' (c.1640), pub. as *Traité des Instruments de Musique (vers 1640)*, introd. and notes by F. Lesure (Neuilly-sur-Seine: Société de Musique d'Autrefois).

UNVERRICHT, HUBERT, ed. ([1974]), *Musik und Musiker am Mittelrhein. Ein biographisches, orts- und landesgeschichtliches Nachschlagewerk*, 2 vols. (Mainz: B. Schott's Söhne).

[VAIRASSE, DENIS] (1716), *Histoire des Sevarambes* (Amsterdam: E. Roger).

VAN ACHT, ROB (1988), 'Dutch Wind-Instrument Makers from 1670 to 1820', *GSJ* 41: 83–101.

VANDERHAGEN, AMAND (c.1785), *Méthode Nouvelle et Raisonnée pour la Clarinette* (Paris: Boyer; repr. edn., Geneva: Minkoff, 1972).

VAN DER MEER, JOHN HENRY (1962), 'The Chalumeau Problem', *GSJ* 15: 89–91.

——(1968), 'Denner Revisited', *GSJ* 21: 208.

——(1970), 'Some More Denner Guesses', *GSJ* 23: 117–19.

——(1977), 'Besprechungen von Kurt Birsak: die Holzblasinstrumente im Salzburger Museum Carolino Augusteum', *MF* 30: 248–9.

——(1979), 'Vivaldi's Esoteric Instruments', *EM* 7: 135, 137–8.

——(1982), *Wegweiser durch die Sammlung historischer Musikinstrumente*[3] (Nuremberg: Germanisches Nationalmuseum).

——(1983), 'More About Denner', *GSJ* 36: 127.

——(1987), 'The Typology and History of the Bass Clarinet', *JAMIS* 13: 65–88.

VERTKOV, K. A., G. BLAGODATOV, and E. YOZOVOSKAYA (1975), *Atlas of Musical Instruments of the Peoples Inhabiting the USSR*[2] (Moscow: State Music Publishers).

VIO, GASTONE (1980), 'Precisazioni sui documenti della Pietà in relazione alle "Figlie del cor"', *Vivaldi Veneziano Europeo*, ed. F. Degrada (Florence: L. S. Olschki), pp. 101–22.

VIRDUNG, SEBASTIAN (1511), *Musica getutscht und auszgezogen* (Strasburg: W. Bischoue; repr. edn., Kassel: Bärenreiter, 1931).

WALTHER, JOHANN GOTTFRIED (1955 edn.), 'Praecepta der Musicalischen Composition' (1708), pub. as *Praecepta der musikalischen Composition*, ed. Peter Benary (Leipzig: Breitkopf & Härtel).

——(1732), *Musikalisches Lexicon oder Musikalisches Bibliothek* (Leipzig: W. Deer; repr. edn., Kassel: Bärenreiter, 1953).

WARNER, THOMAS E. (1967), *An Annotated Bibliography of Woodwind Instruction Books, 1600–1830* (Detroit: Information Coordinators).

WATERHOUSE, WILLIAM (1986), 'Joseph Fröhlich on Clarinet Reed Position', *Clarinet and Saxophone* 11/3: 38–9.

WEBER, RAINER (1986), 'Liebesklarinetten im Münchener Musikinstrumentenmuseum', *Die Klarinette* 1: 36–41.

——(1987), 'Baßklarinette oder Bassetthorn von Mayerhofer? Restaurierungsbericht', *Die Klarinette* 2: 28–30.

Webster's New Collegiate Dictionary (Springfield, Mass.: G. and C. Merriam Co., 1973).

WEIGEL, CHRISTOPH (1698), *Abbildung der Gemein-Nutzlichen Haupt-Stände* (Nuremberg).

WEIGEL, JOHANN CHRISTOPH (*c*.1722), *Musicalisches Theatrum* (Nuremberg; fac. edn., ed. A. Berner, Kassel: Bärenreiter, 1961).

WESTON, PAMELA (1971), *Clarinet Virtuosi of the Past* (London: R. Hale).

——(1977), *More Clarinet Virtuosi of the Past* (London: author).

WHITWELL, DAVID (1983), *Wind Band and Wind Ensemble Literature of the Classic Period* (Northridge, Calif.: Winds).

——(1984), *The Wind Band and Wind Ensemble of the Classic Period* (Northridge, Calif.: Winds).

WILLMAN, THOMAS L. ([1826]), *A Complete Instruction Book for the Clarinet* (London: Goulding, d'Almaine & Co.).

WOLF, GEORG FRIEDRICH (1787), *Kurzgefaßtes musikalisches Lexikon* (Halle: J. C. Hendel; 2nd edn., Halle, 1792; 3rd edn., Vienna, 1800).

WOLF, EUGENE K. (1981), *The Symphonies of Johann Stamitz* (The Hague: M. Nijhoff).

Woodwind Instruction Books, 1600–1830: Music 3141, 17 reels of microfilm (Washington, DC: Library of Congress Photo duplication Service, 1978).

The World Book Encyclopedia, 20 vols. (Chicago: Field Enterprises Educational Corp., 1961).

YOUNG, PHILLIP T. (1967), 'Woodwind Instruments by the Denners of Nürnberg', *GSJ* 20: 9–16.

——(1978), 'Inventory of Instruments: J. H. Eichentopf, Poerschmann, Sattler, A. and H. Grenser, Grundmann', *GSJ* 31: 100–34.

——(1980), *The Look of Music: Rare Musical Instruments 1500–1900* (Vancouver: Vancouver Museums and Planetarium Association).

——(1981), 'A Bass Clarinet by the Mayrhofers of Passau', *JAMIS* 6: 36–46.

——(1982a), 'Some Further Instruments by the Denners', *GSJ* 35: 78–85.

——(1982b), *Twenty-Five Hundred Historical Woodwind Instruments: An Inventory of the Major Collections* (New York: Pendragon).

——(1986), 'The Scherers of Butzbach', *GSJ* 39: 112–24.

——(1988), *Loan Exhibition of Historic Double Reed Instruments* (Victoria: University of Victoria).

ZADRO, MICHAEL G. (1975), 'Woods Used for Woodwind Instruments Since the 16th Century', *EM* 3: 134–6, 249–51.

ZEDLER, JOHANN HEINRICH (1731–54), *Grosse Vollständiges Universal–Lexicon aller Wissenschaften und Künste*, 64 vols. (Halle and Leipzig: J. H. Zedler).

ZIMMERMANN, JOSEF ([1967]), *Von Zinken Flöten und Schalmeien: Katalog einer Sammlung historischer Holzblasinstrumente* (Birkesdorf-Düren: A. Bezani).

INDEX